GLOBALIZATION

The constraints of geography are shrinking and the world is becoming a single place. Globalization and the global society are increasingly occupying the centre of sociological debates. It is widely discussed by journalists and a key goal for many businesses, yet has emerged only recently in social science. In this extensively revised and restructured new edition of *Globalization*, Malcolm Waters provides a user-friendly introduction to the main arguments about the process and estimates the direction in which the world is heading.

The book opens with a conceptual framework for understanding globalization as it flows through the regions of economics, politics and culture. The next six chapters are arranged in three groups of two, on economics, on politics and on culture respectively. The first chapter of each pair covers the internationalization period of globalization up to the end of the third quarter of the twentieth century while the second covers the accelerated phase of globalization that succeeds it. Here it covers such topics as planetary environmentalism, the new international division of labour, global tourism and democratization. The last chapter is entirely new, considering and rebutting the main critiques of the globalization thesis that have become current since the first edition was published.

Malcolm Waters is Dean of Arts and Professor of Sociology at the University of Tasmania, Australia.

KEY IDEAS

SERIES EDITOR: PETER HAMILTON, THE OPEN UNIVERSITY, MILTON KEYNES

Designed to complement the successful *Key Sociologists*, this series covers the main concepts, issues, debates, and controversies in sociology and the social sciences. The series aims to provide authoritative essays on central topics of social science, such as community, power, work, sexuality, inequality, benefits and ideology, class, family, etc. Books adopt a strong individual 'line' constituting original essays rather than literary surveys, and for lively and original treatments of their subject matter. The books will be useful to students and teachers of sociology, political science, economics, psychology, philosophy, and geography.

Class
STEPHEN EDGELL

Consumption
ROBERT BOCOCK

Citizenship
KEITH FAULKS

Culture
CHRIS JENKS

Lifestyle
DAVID CHANEY

Mass Media
PIERRE SORLIN

Moral Panics
KENNETH THOMPSON

Postmodernity
BARRY SMART

Racism
ROBERT MILES

Risk
DEBORAH LUPTON

Sexuality
JEFFREY WEEKS

The Symbolic Construction of Community
ANTHONY P. COHEN

GLOBALIZATION

Second edition

Malcolm Waters

LONDON AND NEW YORK

First published 1995
by Routledge
11 New Fetter Lane, London EC4P 4EE

Simultaneously published in the USA and Canada
by Routledge
29 West 35th Street, New York, NY 10001

Reprinted 1996 (twice), 1998 (twice), 2000
Second edition 2001
Reprinted 2001, 2002

Routledge is an imprint of the Taylor & Francis Group

© 1995, 2001 Malcolm Waters

Typeset in Garamond by Keystroke, Jacaranda Lodge, Wolverhampton
Printed and bound in Great Britain by TJ International, Padstow, Cornwall

British Library Cataloguing in Publication Data
A catalogue record for this book is available from the British Library

Library of Congress Cataloguing in Publication Data
Waters, Malcolm, 1946–
    Globalization / Malcolm Waters.–2nd ed.
      p. cm.
    Includes bibliographical references and index.
    1. International economic relations–Social aspects.
    2. International relations–Social aspects.   3. Cultural relations.
    4. International finance–Social aspects.   5. Internationalism.
    6. Globalization.   I. Title

HF1359 .W39 2001
337–dc21

00–055317

ISBN 0–415–23853–6 (hbk)
ISBN 0–415–23854–4 (pbk)

He had bought a large map representing the sea,
  Without the least vestige of land:
And the crew were much pleased when they found it to be
  A map they could all understand.

"What's the good of Mercator's North Poles and Equators,
  Tropics, Zones, and Meridian Lines?"
So the Bellman would cry: and the crew would reply,
  "They are merely conventional signs!

"Other maps are such shapes, with their islands and capes!
  But we've got our brave Captain to thank"
(So the crew would protest) "that he's bought us the best –
  A perfect and absolute blank!"

                    Lewis Carroll, *The Hunting of the Snark*

CONTENTS

FIGURES

PREFACE TO THE FIRST EDITION

Although conceivably surpassed by Tierra del Fuego or Outer Mongolia, Tasmania's geographical location makes it just about the perfect place from which to assess the extent of globalization. If one can sit here at the spatial edge of human society, looking northward across the vast desert continent of Australia and southward towards emptiness and desolation, knowing that one is thousands of kilometres from the 'global cities' of Tokyo, Frankfurt or LA, and still feel that one is part of the world, then globalization truly is an impressive process. Tasmanians know that they live on one planet because other people's aerosol sprays have caused a carcinogenic hole in the ozone layer over their heads, because their relatively high rate of unemployment is due to a slump in the international commodities markets, because their children are exposed to such edifying role models as *Robocop* and *The Simpsons*, because their university is infested by the managerialist cultures of strategic planning, staff appraisal and quality control, just like everyone else's, because British TV-star scientists may drop in for a week to save their environment for them, and because their gay community may at long last be able to experience freedom of sexual expression because it has appealed to the human rights conventions of the United Nations. It has become a commonplace to argue that globalization and localization are Janus-faced aspects of the same process but in this little local society of less than half a million souls that truth comes home more fully than in most.

I would like to be able to say that this book took many grinding years to write and that it needed the support of armies of friends and colleagues. Actually, it was one of those fortunate projects that took on a life of its own so that the book almost wrote itself in a relatively short time. Nevertheless, some important thanks are due. Chris Rojek must have been 'thinking globally' when he passed through Hobart and commissioned the project. Bryan Turner, a sociologist with a truly international reputation who happens to work just on the other side of Bass Strait, encouraged it from the outset. Rowena Stewart and Christina Parnell made the sort of skilful administrative contribution for which I have to thank them far too often. Scott Birchall and Robert Hall made sure that my attempt at political science was not entirely off the planet. My thanks also must go to my family: to my wife, Judith Homeshaw, an 'ex-pom' political scientist who cheerfully responds to my jibes at her discipline with her own withering criticisms of mine; and to our children, Penny (currently on a Rotary International student exchange in Germany) and Tom (an adept at soccer, marketed here as 'the world game'), for keeping me up to date on developments in global popular culture, whether I want to be or not.

Malcolm Waters
Hobart, Tasmania

PREFACE TO THE SECOND EDITION

It is a testament to the impact of globalization that books about it should sell well enough to move rapidly into new editions.

As well as the normal updating, this edition involves a more fundamental reorganization. Some readers found that, in the first edition, the isolation of theoretical and conceptual issues at the front of the volume made them both indigestible and detached from the substantive issues covered elsewhere. Accordingly these issues are considered throughout the new edition in direct relation to the substantive issues that they address. I have also taken the opportunity to move the phasic model of globalization that appeared almost as an afterthought in the conclusion to the first edition to the front of the new volume where it stands as an organizing framework for the substantive chapters.

The substantive chapters themselves are arranged in three groups of two, on economics, politics and culture, respectively. The first chapter of each pair covers the internationalization period of globalization up to the end of the third quarter of the twentieth century while the second covers the accelerated phase of globalization that succeeds it. The last chapter is entirely new, considering and rebutting the main critiques of the globalization thesis that have become current since the first edition was published.

I did most of the work while a visiting scholar at the University of Texas, Austin. The support of Professors Robert

Cushing and John Higley was crucial and the warm hospitality shown by Frances Cushing of the Edward A. Clark Center for Australian Studies perhaps even more so. I must also recognise the support and forbearance of my own University in taking the unusual step of providing study leave to a Dean.

Malcolm Waters
Hobart, Tasmania

Abbreviations

AGIL	Adaptation/goal-attainment/integration/latent pattern-maintenance and tension management
APEC	Asia-Pacific Economic Council
ASEAN	Association of South-East Asian Nations
BINGO	Business international non-government organization
BT	British Telecom
CENTO	Central Treaty Organization
CFC	Chloro-fluoro carbons
CNN	Cable News Network
CPE	Centrally planned economy
DME	Democratic market economy
EC	European Community
ECSC	European Coal and Steel Community
EEC	European Economic Communities
EU	European Union
FAO	Food and Agriculture Organization of the United Nations
FDI	Foreign direct investment
G7	Group of seven leading industrial economies
GATT	General Agreement on Tariffs and Trade
GDP	Gross domestic product
IATA	International Air Transport Authority
IGO	International government organization

ILO	International Labour Organization
IMF	International Monetary Fund
INGO	International non-government organization
IPU	International Postal Union
IR	International Relations (academic discipline of)
ISA	International Sociological Association
ITU	International Telecommunications Union
JIT	Just-in-time production system
LDC	Less-developed country
MAD	Mutually assured destruction
MDC	More-developed country
MNC	Multi-national corporation
MNE	Multi-national enterprise
NAFTA	North American Free Trade Area
NATO	North Atlantic Treaty Organization
NIC	Newly industrializing country
NIDL	New international division of labour
NIEO	New International Economic Order
OECD	Organization for Economic Co-operation and Development
OED	*Oxford English Dictionary*
OPEC	Organization of Petroleum Exporting Countries
QCC	Quality control circle
SDR	Special drawing right
SEATO	South-East Asia Treaty Organization
TNC	Trans-national corporation
UN	United Nations Organization
UNCTAD	United Nations Council for Trade and Development
UNESCO	United Nations Educational, Scientific and Cultural Organization
UNICEF	United Nations International Children's Emergency Fund
UNRRA	United Nations Relief and Rehabilitation Administration

WHO	World Health Organization
WTO	World Trade Organization
WWF	World Wildlife Fund

1

A WORLD OF DIFFERENCE

Think global. Act local.
Theodore Levitt

Social change is now proceeding so rapidly that if a social scientist had proposed as recently as 15 years ago to write a book about globalization they would have had to overcome a wall of stony and bemused incomprehension. But now, just as postmodernism was *the* concept of the 1980s, globalization may be *the* concept, the key idea by which we understand the transition of human society into the third millennium. Curiously 'globalization' is far less controversial than 'postmodernism' (see Smart 1993). With the exception of the 'civilization analysts' who we shall mention elsewhere in this book most social scientists seem to accept that such a process is under way. Such controversies as there are appear to surround the issue of whether old Marxist or functionalist theories can be adapted to explain globalization or whether we need to construct novel arguments. This may be because theories of social change have almost always implied the universalization of the processes that they explain. The concept has therefore found instant appeal across a range of intellectual interests. It remains for social science to connect the concept with its own vital theoretical traditions. This short book seeks to contribute to this task.

Although the word 'global' is over 400 years old (*OED* 1989, *s.v.* global) the common usage of such words as 'globalization', 'globalize' and 'globalizing' did not begin until about 1960.[1] *The Economist* (4/4/59) reported 'Italy's "globalised quota" for imports of cars has increased' and in 1961 *Webster* became the first major dictionary to offer definitions of globalism and globalization. In 1962 the *Spectator* (5/10/62) recognized that: 'Globalisation is, indeed, a staggering concept' (*OED* 1989, *s.v.* globalism, globalization, globalize, globalized).

The concept certainly staggered or stumbled into academic circles. Robertson (1992: 8) informs us that it was not recognized as academically significant until the early or possibly the mid-1980s but thereafter its use has become, well, globalized. Although he says that its pattern of diffusion is virtually impossible to trace, it is beyond reasonable doubt that he is himself centrally responsible for its currency. The many items he has published on the topic include what is possibly the first sociological article to include the word in its title (1985), although he had used the concept of 'globality' somewhat earlier (1983). Overall, the number of publications which use the word 'global' in their titles has now probably reached five figures but the processual term 'globalization' was still relatively rare at the beginning of the 1990s. In February 1994 the catalogue of the Library of Congress contained only 34 publications with the term or one of its derivatives in the title. By February 2000 this number had risen to 284. None of these was published before 1987.

The definitions of globalization given in general dictionaries are often couched in such unhelpful terms as 'to render global' or 'the act of globalizing'. Even if we delete the tautology as in 'to render world-wide' or 'the act of diffusion throughout the world' this is misleading because it implies intentionality. Many aspects of globalization are indeed intentional and reflexive, including both the increasing level of business planning for global marketing and action by the environmentalist movement to save the planet. However, many globalizing forces are impersonal and beyond the control and intentions of any individual or group of individuals. The development of Islamic fundamentalism as a response to the effects of Western modernization, or variations in the price of wheat are examples of just such effects.

The key figure in the formalization and specification of the concept of globalization is, then, Roland Robertson. His own biography might itself be seen as an instance of a link between what might be called trans-nationalization and global consciousness. He began his career in Britain where his initial studies sought to link the functionalist concept of modernization into an international context. At that time, like just about every other sociologist, he focused on the nation-state-society as the unit of analysis, but he identified the nation-state as an actor in an international arena. By the 1970s Robertson had moved to the USA where initially he pursued studies in the sociology of religion. However, his interpretation of religious developments was also essentially planetary in its orientation. Rejecting the prevailing commitment to secularization as the central social process, he became interested in developments in Islamic fundamentalism that indicated a link between religion and politics on a world scale. He was also interested in Weber's argument that Protestantism tended exactly to focus the consciousness on the material, as opposed to the spiritual world. He was thus able to return to his earlier interest in international society and his first general papers on globalization began to appear in the mid-1980s. By now the globe and its culture, rather than the nation-state, had become the primary concern. He had begun to untie the straightjacket of the concept of national society which had left social science out of touch with the big changes going on in the world and in which he had himself felt uncomfortable from the beginning of his career:

> In an autobiographical sense my own perspective on this matter is undoubtedly to this day colored by the fact that one of my earliest, serious intellectual choices revolved around the

question of whether I should study sociology or international relations as an undergraduate.

(1992: 4)

Robertson's definition of globalization runs as follows:

Globalization as a concept refers both to the compression of the world and the intensification of consciousness of the world as a whole . . . both concrete global interdependence and consciousness of the global whole.

(1992: 8)

The first part of the definition, global compression, resembles the arguments of theories of dependency and of world-systems. It refers to an increasing level of interdependence between national systems by way of trade, military alliance and domination, and 'cultural imperialism'. Wallerstein (1974) tells us that the globe has been undergoing social compression since the beginning of the sixteenth century but Robertson argues that its history is in fact much longer. However, the more important component of the definition is the idea of an intensification of global consciousness which is a relatively new phenomenon.

There are some clear links between Robertson's definition and Giddens' earlier one.

Globalisation can . . . be defined as the intensification of world-wide social relations which link distant localities in such a way that local happenings are shaped by events occurring many miles away and vice versa. This is a dialectical process because such local happenings may move in an obverse direction from the very distanciated relations that shape them. Local transformation is as much a part of globalisation as the lateral extension of social connections across time and space.

(Giddens 1990: 64, italics deleted)

This definition usefully introduces explicit notions of time and space into the argument. It emphasises locality and thus territoriality and by this means stresses that the process of globalization is not merely or even mainly about such grand, centre-stage activities as corporate mega-mergers and world political forums but about the autonomization of local lifeworlds. Globalization, then, implies localization, a concept that is connected with Giddens' other notions of relativization and reflexivity. The latter imply that the residents of a local area will increasingly come to want to make conscious decisions about which values and amenities they want to stress in their communities and that these decisions will increasingly be referenced against global scapes. Localization implies a reflexive reconstruction of community in the face of the dehumanizing implications of rationalizing and commodifying.

The position taken in this book on the meaning of globalization is broadly consistent with the work of Robertson and of Giddens. In seeking to offer a comprehensive definition perhaps the best approach might be to try to specify where the process of globalization might end, what a fully globalized world will look like. In a globalized world there will be a single society and culture occupying the planet. This society and culture will probably not be harmoniously integrated although it might conceivably be. Rather it will probably tend towards high levels of differentiation, multi-centricity and chaos. There will be no central organizing government and no tight set of cultural preferences and prescriptions. In so far as culture is unified it will be extremely abstract, expressing tolerance for diversity and individual choice. Importantly territoriality will disappear as an organizing principle for social and cultural life; it will be a society without borders and spatial boundaries. In a globalized world we will be unable to predict social practices and preferences on the basis of geographical location. Equally we can expect relationships between people in disparate locations to be formed as easily as relationships between people in proximate ones.[2] We can therefore define globalization as: *A social process in which the constraints of geography on economic, political, social and cultural arrangements recede, in which people become increasingly aware that they are receding and in which people act accordingly.*

The concept of globalization is an obvious target for ideological suspicion because, like modernization, a predecessor and related concept, it appears to justify the spread of Western culture and of capitalist society by suggesting that there are forces operating beyond human control that are transforming the world. This book makes no attempt to disguise the fact that the current phase of globalization is precisely associated with these developments. Globalization is the direct consequence of the expansion of European culture across the planet via settlement, colonization and cultural replication. It is also bound up intrinsically with the pattern of capitalist development as it has ramified through political and cultural arenas. However, it does not imply that every corner of the planet must become Westernized and capitalist but rather that every set of social arrangements must establish its position in relation to the capitalist West – to use Robertson's term, it must relativize itself. It must be said that in increasing sectors of the world this relativization process involves a positive preference for Western and capitalist possibilities, but rejection and denial of Western capitalism is equally possible. But globalization is also highly Europeanized in another sense. The deterritorialization of social and especially of political arrangements has proceeded most rapidly in the Western part of that continent – borders are becoming disemphasized and varieties of supra- and infra-nationalism are proliferating. This means that the model of globalization that is being globalized is itself a European model, i.e., developments within the EU are widely touted as the example for global deterritorialization (e.g. see Lash and Urry 1994: 281–3; see Mann 1993 for counter-arguments).

One of the theoretical debates about globalization surrounds when it began. Three possibilities can be specified:

- that globalization has been in process since the dawn of history, that it has increased in its effects since that time, but that there has been a sudden and recent acceleration;
- that globalization is cotemporal with modernization and the development of capitalism, and that there has been a recent acceleration; or

- that globalization is a recent phenomenon associated with other social processes called postindustrialization, postmodernization or the disorganization of capitalism.

The position taken in this book is that some measure of globalization has always occurred but that until about the middle of the second millennium it was non-linear in its development. It proceeded through the fits and starts of various ancient imperial expansions, pillaging and trading oceanic explorations, and the spread of religious ideas. However, the European Middle Ages, in particular, were a period of inward-looking territorialism that focused on locality, a slump in the globalization process. The linear extension of globalization that we are currently experiencing began in the fifteenth and sixteenth centuries, the 'early modern' period. Technically, and if one assumes that globalization is at least partly a reflexive process, globalization could not begin until that time because it was only the Copernican revolution that could convince humanity that it inhabited a globe. More importantly, until then the inhabitants of Eurasia-Africa, the Americas and Australia lived in virtually complete ignorance of each other's existence. So the globalization process that is of most interest here is that associated with modernization.

GLOBALIZING SOLVENTS: THE CLASSICAL ACCOUNTS

Curiously, globalization, or a concept very much like it, put in an early appearance in the development of social science (Robertson 1992: 15–18; Turner 1990: 344–8). Saint-Simon noticed that industrialization was inducing commonalities of practice across the disparate cultures of Europe. Seeking to hasten the process he argued for a utopian internationalism that included a pan-European government and a new and universalizing humanistic philosophy. These ideas were promoted through a publication presciently called the *Globe*. Saint-Simon's ideas found their way through Comte to Durkheim, although the First World War led him to emphasize national rituals and patriotism. However, Durkheim's genuine legacy to globalization is his theories of differentiation and culture. To the extent that the institutions of societies become more specialized, commitment to such institutions as the state must be weakened because they are more narrow in their compass. In parallel, the national culture must progressively become more weak and abstract in order to encompass intra-societal diversity. All of this implies that industrialization tends to weaken collective commitments and to open the way for dismantling the boundaries between societies.

A similar comment might be made about Weber's contribution, except that he was even more bound up than was Durkheim in his own national politics. Just as Durkheim identified structural specialization ('differentiation'), Weber identified rationalization as the globalizing solvent. He was fundamentally concerned with the success of rationalization, with its spread from the seed-bed origins of Calvinistic Protestantism to infest all Western cultures and to set up an 'iron cage' for all moderns. Rationalization implies that all cultures will become characterized by: 'the depersonalization of social relationships, the refinement of techniques of calculation, the enhancement of the importance of specialized knowledge, and the extension of technically rational control over both natural and social processes' (Brubaker 1984: 2). Although Weber did not recognise it, this implies a homogenization of cultures as well as that reduced commitment to such values as patriotism and duty of which he was acutely aware. But even this globalizing effect was restricted to Western Europe. Weber saw no prospect of the spread of rationalized cultural preferences to, say, India or China, which he regarded as inevitably mired in religious traditionalism.

Of all classical theorists, the one most explicitly committed to a globalizing theory of modernization is Marx. Globalization caused an enormous increase in the power of the capitalist class because it opened up new markets for it. Indeed, the discovery of America and the opening of navigation routes to Asia established a 'world-market' for modern industry (1977: 222–3).

The bourgeoisie rushed into this opportunity with alacrity: 'The need of a constantly expanding market for its products, chases the bourgeoisie over the whole surface of the globe. It must nestle everywhere, settle everywhere, establish connections everywhere' (1977: 224). But this development is cultural as well as economic, Marx argues, because it gives a cosmopolitan character not only to production but to consumption:

[National industries] are dislodged by new industries . . . that no longer work up indigenous raw material, but raw material drawn from the remotest zones; industries whose products are consumed, not only at home, but in every quarter of the globe. In place of the old wants, satisfied by the productions of the country, we find new wants, requiring for their satisfaction the products of distant lands and climes. In place of the old local and national seclusion and self-sufficiency, we have intercourse in every direction, universal interdependence of nations. And as in material, so also in intellectual production. The intellectual creations of individual nations become common property. National one-sidedness and narrow-mindedness become more and more impossible, and from the numerous national and local literatures, there arises a world literature.

(1977: 224–5)

Nor is this process restricted to Western Europe. The bourgeoisie draws even 'barbarian' nations into its 'civilization' using the 'heavy artillery' of cheap commodities to batter down 'all Chinese walls'. The bourgeoisie is, for Marx, recreating the world in its own image.

However, notice that territorial boundaries remain. Marx refers to the interdependence of nations and recognizes the continuing existence of the nation-state. There is a seed of destruction, however, even for this. In establishing itself as a world capitalist class the bourgeoisie also causes the world proletariat to coalesce in opposition. The rise to power of the proletariat will, he argues, destroy all bourgeois institutions including the nation-state:

National differences and antagonisms between peoples are daily more and more vanishing, owing to the development of the bourgeoisie, to freedom of commerce, to the world-market, to uniformity in the mode of production and in the conditions of life corresponding thereto.

The supremacy of the proletariat will cause them to vanish still faster. United action, of the leading civilized countries at least, is one of the first conditions for the emancipation of the proletariat.

In proportion as the exploitation of one individual by another is put an end to, the exploitation of one nation by another will also be put an end to. In proportion as the antagonism between classes within the nation vanishes, the hostility of one nation to another will come to an end.

(1977: 235–6)

Although Marx's utopian vision of globalization might be regarded as as romantic and unrealistic as Saint-Simon's, the discussion of the link between capitalist production and a global consumer culture has remained highly influential.

DIMENSIONS OF GLOBALIZATION

One of the features of theories of social change that developed in the hundred or so years after 1870 was their uni-dimensionality. All social phenomena were held to be determined by events occurring within a single region of human life: for Marx or his epigone, Althusser, the critical region was structures of material production; for Mead or Schütz it was subjective meaning; and for Parsons it was culture. Not surprisingly then, during that period most theories of the reduction of the constraints of geography were also uni-dimensional, but they did collectively succeed in identifying what the several critical dimensions might be.

If we leave aside the romanticized internationalist aspirations of Saint-Simon and Comte, among the theorists reviewed above the one who first commits himself to a theory of globalization is Marx. In so doing he identifies an economic dimension of the process. Marx's view that the political-territorial boundaries of the nation-state remain intact and will only disappear under a future proletarian supremacy is supported by many twentieth-century theories of change, including not only Marxisant dependency theory (e.g. Amin 1980; Frank 1971) and world-system theory (Wallerstein 1974, 1980) but also functionalist modernization theory (Levy 1966; Parsons 1977) and convergence theory (Kerr et al. 1973). In each of these examples a logic of the economy (e.g. capitalist accumulation, adaptive upgrading, technological imperatives) drives globalization, but only as far as the deterritorialization of the economic system.

Among these instances globalization theory only appears genuinely to be prefigured by the work of Wallerstein (1974, 1980), whose conceptualization of world-systems appears to argue for an economic determination of the process. However, three aspects of world-systems theory are incompatible with the globalization processes now being witnessed. First, Wallerstein's conception of the world is entirely phenomenological and not geographical. The Roman Empire is an instance of a world-system because it constituted a bounded set of societies and other units within which individuals lived and conceptualized their lives, and not because it encompassed or needed to encompass the planet – 'they are in common parlance "worlds"' (1974: 348). Second, within Wallerstein's modern world-system that might be the vehicle for globalization, nation-states play a key structural role in stabilizing the system. Under current conditions the integrity of the nation-state is being called into question. Third, Wallerstein insists that any world-system can contain a multiplicity of separate cultures. Current conditions again suggest an amalgamation or at least a relativization of cultures that his conceptualization cannot encompass. Wallerstein's recent work (1990) argues that the incorporation of the entire globe within the capitalist world-system does give rise to some commonality of culture, although he does continue to insist on the saliency of the state and so stands against globalization theory proper.

The discovery that globalization has a political dimension first surfaced in the work of Burton (1972), Keohane and Nye (1973) and Rosenau (1980). Each of these political scientists noticed that political action was decreasingly confined to the sphere of the nation-state and that an elaborated web of trans-national connections was emerging alongside it. In general, contemporary political scientists continue to insist on this duality in the globalization process – the state is argued to retain sovereignty even while losing some of its effectivity. Dualism can be inspected in two recent influential accounts. Rosenau's later work (1990) theorizes the existence of two 'worlds' on the planet, a state-centric and a multi-centric world, the interaction between which creates turbulence. Equally, the political economist Gilpin, stresses that the expansion of the global market is 'driven largely by its own internal dynamic' but affirms simultaneously that it is 'profoundly affected' by the operations of states (1987: 65). An important exception is Held's argument for the emergence of a system of global governance in which the powers of the state are severely curtailed (1991).

The central focus of structural-functionalist and Marxist theories of change on material issues led to a neglect of culture as a dimension of globalization. However, culture was the central focus of what perhaps was the most successful popular proposal about the process, McLuhan's important and iconic formulation of the 'global village' (Carpenter and McLuhan 1970: xi; McLuhan 1964). McLuhan was possibly the first to notice that the 'industrial' media, transportation and money are being displaced by electronic media that can restore the collective culture of tribalism but on an expansive global scale.

If these three dimensions can be combined we can show that, even prior to 1985, social theory had systematically addressed globalization in a manner that is consistent with contemporary formulations. Speaking broadly, the following common proposal can be constructed out of these diverse arguments:

1 The emergence of capitalism represents a major globalizing dynamic. Capitalism is such an effective form of production that it confers enormous power on those in control of it. This power can be used to subvert, control or by-pass religious, political, military or other power resources.

2 Capitalism encompasses two major processes that tend to increase the level of societal inclusion. First, it is driven by a logic of accumulation that depends on progressively increasing the scale of production. Second, it is driven by a logic of commodification or marketization that drives it towards an increasing scale of consumption.

3 Capitalism also cloaks itself in the mantle of modernization. It offers the prospect not only of general and individual increases in the level of material welfare but of liberation from the constraints of tradition. This renders modernization unavoidable and capitalism compelling.

4 Modernization is more than an ideology, however. Its differentiating trends release a series of activities, especially production and political activities, from local and traditional contexts allowing them to be recombined nationally and trans-nationally.

5 A key emergent modern structure is the nation-state. It becomes the principal vehicle for the establishment of collective social goals and their attainment. Originally focused on security and on internal order and dispute resolution, these goals have progressively become widened to include the management of both collective and individual material conditions, within the registers of the national economy and the welfare system.

6 The attainment of national goals obliged states to establish relations with other states and there emerged a system of international relations. The key processes of the nineteenth-century pattern of international relations were war, alliance, diplomacy and colonialism. During the twentieth century these expanded to include trade, fiscal management and cultural relations.

7 However, international relations are no longer the only links between societies. A stable system of international relations allowed the development of 'trans-national practices', inter-societal linkages primarily focused on economic exchanges but also extending to tastes, fashions and ideas.

8 Electronic communications and rapid transportation are critical technologies for the development of these trans-national practices. Their 'instant' character raises the possibility of a general cultural shift in a globalized direction.

MULTI-DIMENSIONAL THEORY

Explicit theorizing about globalization began in about 1985. Although such figures as Beck (1992), Harvey (1989), Lash and Urry (1994) and Rosenau (1990) have made important contributions, the key proposals have come from Robertson (1992) and Giddens (1990, 1991). The significant features of each of their proposals are first that they are multi-causal or multi-dimensional in their approach, and second, that they emphasise subjectivity and culture as central factors in the current acceleration of globalization processes.

For Robertson, globalization involves the relativization of individual and national reference points to general and supra-national ones. It therefore involves the establishment of cultural, social and phenomenological linkages between four elements (1992: 25–31): the individual self, the national society, the international system of societies, and humanity in general. For Giddens, by contrast, globalization is intrinsically bound up with modernization. Modernization establishes three critical processes: time–space distanciation, disembedding and reflexivity, each of which implies universalizing tendencies that render social relations ever more inclusive. Complex relationships develop between local activities and interaction across distances.

The common theoretical elements of this new paradigm of globalization are the following:

1 Globalization is at least contemporary with modernization and has therefore been proceeding since the sixteenth century. It involves processes of economic systematization, international relations between states and an emerging global culture or consciousness. The process has accelerated through time and is currently in the most rapid phase of its development.

2 Globalization involves the systematic interrelationship of all the individual social ties that are established on the planet. In a fully globalized context, no given relationship or set of relationships can remain isolated or bounded. Each is linked to all the others and is systematically affected by them. This is especially true in a territorial sense, i.e., geographical boundaries in particular are unsustainable in the face of globalization. Globalization increases the inclusiveness and the unification of human society.

3 Globalization involves a phenomenology of contraction. Although commentators often speak of the shrinking of the planet or the annihilation of distance, this is a phenomenological rather than a literal truth, that is, the world appears to shrink but (pretty obviously) does not materially do so. The particular phenomenological registers that alter the scalar appearance of the world are time and space. Because space tends to be measured in time,[3] to the extent that the time between geographical points shortens so space appears to shrink. In so far as the connection between physically distant points is instantaneous, space 'disappears' altogether.[4] A more recent phenomenon is that of localizations of time. Globalization implies the phenomenological elimination of space and the generalization of time.

4 The phenomenology of globalization is reflexive. The inhabitants of the planet self-consciously orient themselves to the world as a whole – firms explore global markets, counter-cultures move from an 'alternative community' to a 'social movement' action configuration, and governments try to keep each other honest in terms of human rights and dash

to commit military assistance to the maintenance of world order.

5 Globalization involves a collapse of universalism and particularism. The earlier phase of gradual globalization was characterized by a differentiation between arenas in which general and rational standards could apply and others in which the particularities of relationships and the qualities of individual persons were paramount. This differentiation is registered in the well-known sociological distinctions between life-chances and lifestyles, gesellschaft and gemeinschaft, public and private spheres, work and home, and system and lifeworld. The separation was largely accomplished by boundaries in time and space but because accelerated globalization annihilates time and space the distinctions can no longer apply. Each person in any relationship is simultaneously an individual and a member of the human species – they can simultaneously say 'I am myself' and 'I have rights' (cf., Beck 1992).

6 Globalization involves a Janus-faced mix of risk and trust. In previous eras one trusted the immediate, the knowable, the present and the material. To go beyond these was to run the risk of injury or exploitation. Under globalization individuals extend trust to unknown persons, to impersonal forces and norms (the 'market' or 'human rights') and to patterns of symbolic exchange that appear to be beyond the control of any concrete individual or group of individuals. In so doing they place themselves in the hands of the entire set of their fellow human beings. The fiduciary commitment of all the participants is necessary for the well-being of each individual member. A fiduciary panic (e.g. the 'Asian meltdown' financial collapse of 1998, the human rights catastrophe in Kosovo in the Balkans in 1999) creates the risk of global systemic collapse.

AN EXPLANATORY THEOREM

We can now move towards providing an explanation of these transformations. We can begin by suggesting that globalization should be traced through three regions of social life that have come to be recognised as fundamental in many theoretical analyses:

- The economy: social arrangements for the production, exchange, distribution and consumption of land, capital, goods and labour services.
- The polity: social arrangements for the concentration and application of power that can establish control over populations, territories and other assets, especially in so far as it is manifested as the organized exchange of coercion and surveillance (military, police, bureaucracy etc.); such institutionalized transformations of these practices as authority, regulation, administration and diplomacy; and such resources as electoral support, political donations, capacities for redistribution, citizenship rights, taxation support, lobbying, and obedience.
- Culture: social arrangements for the production, exchange and expression of symbols (signs) that represent facts, affects, meanings, beliefs, commitments, preferences, tastes and values.

Following Weber (1978: 928–40) and Bell (1979: 3–30), we can take these three arenas to be structurally autonomous. The argument here, therefore, stands opposed both to the Marxist position that the economy is constitutive of polity and culture and to the Parsonsian position that culture determines the other two arenas. However, it also makes the assumption that the relative effectivity of the arenas can vary across history and geography. A more effective set of arrangements in one arena can penetrate and modify arrangements in the others.

A concrete example can illustrate the point. For most of the twentieth century Russia and its adjacent territories and populations were controlled by the highly organized Soviet state, an effective polity. Here the state organized culture, allowing only certain forms of artistic expression and religious commitment, and it also organized the economy in a command system of state factories, farms, banks and shops. Here then we can speak of a culture and an economy as having been politicized. In other contexts we might be able to speak of the culturalization of an economy and polity in which they are reconstructed as systems of signs and images rather than of material issues and interests, or of an economic domination of polity and culture. The latter is best represented in the now discredited Althusserian claim about structural determination of politics and ideology (Althusser 1977). We can also conceive of joint domination of two of the arenas over the other, as in Habermas' theory of internal colonization in which the steering systems of the economy and the polity invade the cultural arena of the lifeworld by means of monetarization and juridification (1987).

We can now start to link these themes into an argument about globalization.

The claims of the theory of globalization centre on the relationship between social and cultural organization and territoriality. The proposal that drives the present theoretical argument is that this link is established by the types of exchange that predominate in social relationships at any particular historical moment. Three different types of exchange are possible:

- material exchanges including trade, tenancy, wage-labour, fee-for-service and capital accumulation;
- power exchanges by such means as party membership, election, the exercise of command and leadership, coercion and social control, the enactment of legislation, the redistribution of surplus, and engagement in international relations; and
- symbolic exchanges (exchanges of signs) by means of oral communication, publication, performance, teaching, oratory, ritual, display, entertainment, provision of information or advice, propaganda, advertisement, public demonstration,

research, data accumulation and transfer, the exchange and transfer of tokens, exhibition and spectacle.

Each of these types of exchange organizes social relations in space in a particular fashion. Specifically we can propose that:

- Material exchanges tend to tie social arrangements to localized spaces. This is mainly because the production of commodities involves local concentrations of labour, skill, capital, raw materials, and components. While trade can link distant localities, commodities can be costly to transport, which mitigates against long-distance trade unless there are significant cost advantages – indeed, barter trade over great distances is extremely difficult. Equally wage-labour, especially manual wage-labour, frequently involves face-to-face supervision and service delivery is also most often face-to-face. Material exchanges are therefore fundamentally rooted in localized markets, factories, offices and shops. Long-distance trade is carried out by specialist intermediaries (merchants, sailors, financiers etc.) who stand outside the central relationships of the economy. In so far as trade takes place across space it will involve chains of commodity exchanges in which each link typically is localized and interpersonal.
- Power exchanges tend to tie social arrangements to extended territories. Indeed, they are specifically directed towards controlling the population that occupies a territory and harnessing its resources in the direction of territorial integrity or expansion. Political exchanges therefore culminate in the establishment of territorial boundaries that are coterminous with nation-state-societies. The exchanges between nation-states, known as International Relations (i.e. war, diplomacy, alliances and imperialism), tend to confirm their territorial sovereignty.
- Symbolic exchanges release social arrangements from spatial referents. Symbols can be proliferated rapidly and in any locality. It is much more difficult to monopolize the resources

(human ingenuity) required to produce signs than it is to monopolize the resources (capital) involved in producing material objects or those involved in the exercise of power (coercion) and therefore much more difficult to concentrate them in space. Moreover, they are easily transportable and communicable. Importantly, because symbols frequently seek to appeal to human fundamentals they can often claim universal significance.

In summary then, the theorem that underpins the new theoretical paradigm of globalization is that: *material exchanges localize; political exchanges internationalize; and symbolic exchanges globalize.*

We need to make a point here which is subtle and complex but which is extremely important. The apparent correspondence between the three arenas of social life – economy, politics and culture – and the three types of exchange – material, power and symbolic – should not mislead us into thinking that each type of exchange is restricted to a single arena. For example, firms, resolutely located in the economy obviously include many material exchanges but they also involve power exchanges between managers and workers and symbolic exchanges about such matters as work norms, dress, sets of rules and so on. Similarly, governments enter into (material) employment relationships and legislate national symbols, and opera companies negotiate government subsidies (power) and occupy buildings (material). However, there is a general tendency for material exchanges to originate in the economy, for power exchanges to originate in the polity and for symbolic exchanges to originate in culture.

Globalization will be more advanced to the extent that:

1 There is, in the economy, a shift in the proportions of material and power exchanges towards the latter. [In more substantive language, the bigger and more elaborate firms become, the more likely they are to expand their activities across the planet.]

2 There is, in the economy and polity, an increase in the proportion of exchanges that are symbolic rather than oriented to material or power issues. [The more such exchanges consist of free-flowing information rather than goods and services or authority, the more possible it is to make exchanges over long distances.]

3 There is a general expansion of the political arena at the expense of the economy. [Each local production unit will become part of a territorially wider system.]

4 There is a general expansion of the cultural arena at the expense of the economy and the polity. [The more that people are engaged in exchanging information, values and artistic expression with each other, especially where these are mass mediated, the more likely it is that these exchanges will occur over long distances.]

This is why both McLuhan and Giddens stress the introduction of monetary tokens as a starting point for globalization – monetary tokens symbolize commodities, in effect, dematerializing them. We can also expect that if globalization is highly advanced it will be more highly developed in the cultural than in the other two arenas.

GLOBALIZING DEVELOPMENTS

We can now proceed to link the theorem to the historical development of globalization. This summary of that development will inevitably make sweeping and occasionally offensive claims, brushing aside the particularities of individual corners of the planet and the raggedness of social transformations in an effort to make generalized, perhaps overgeneralized, sense out of daunting complexity. The effort does not seek to deny the rich tapestry of human experience, but if, as is widely recognized, globalization is indeed taking hold then it must by definition affect human behaviour wherever it transpires.

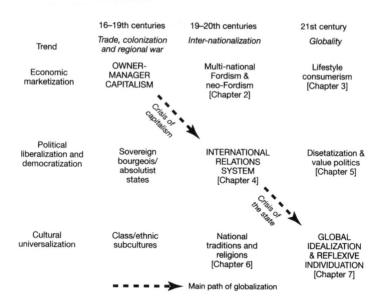

Figure 1.1 The path of globalization through time

Figure 1.1 summarizes the argument. The three arenas through which globalizing processes take effect, the economy, the polity and culture, are listed in the left column. The relevant long-run general process in each region that supports globalization is as follows:

- economies trend towards marketization, that is, freedom from command, constraint and status and class monopolization;
- polities trend towards liberalization and democratization, the deconcentration of power; and
- culture trends towards universalization, the abstraction of values and standards to a very high level of generality that will permit extreme levels of cultural differentiation.

These processes are carried forward through history by changes in the relative efficacy of the three arenas. Historical time is indicated by the column headings. This is largely a Western

European periodization, since Western European societies and their derivatives and mimics are the source and the leading edge of globalization. In the 'early modern' period between the sixteenth and nineteenth centuries the critical development was the emergence of capitalism. It was focused on a set of material exchanges that proved highly effective in disrupting the traditionalistic ties of medieval society and it also penetrated and dominated politics and culture. Because such exchanges empowered a new capitalist class, it seriously weakened monarchies, either constitutionalizing them or rendering them ineffective, or it took over the state, reconstituting it as bourgeois and liberal. Equally, cultures were divided and pervaded by ideology. The most important global links were those of trade, exploration and military adventure but, although they constituted a beginning they were relatively ineffective in establishing global integration.

At about the middle or end of the nineteenth century the family form of industrial capitalism hit a crisis. Workers started to refuse endless exploitation and misery, markets were failing to expand and accumulation possibilities were threatened. Working-class action was often political in character and their struggles infused the polity with a new effectivity, moderate in many societies but extreme in the socialist and fascist states. The state took a steering role relative to economy and culture. The economy was corporatized, governed within a power relationship between managers, unions and state officials. Culture was harnessed to the service of the state by the development of national traditions and the subordination of ethnic minorities. The main globalizing trend was the internationalizing of state action under the development of such phenomena as alliances, diplomacy, world wars, hegemons and superpowers. Capitalism, as economic practice and culture, was carried to many parts of the globe under hegemonic sponsorship where it often collided with fascist and state-socialist ideological rivals.

At the end of the twentieth century there occurred a widely recognized crisis in which states appeared unable to make economies grow, unable to meet the claims of their citizens, unable to offer transparency and value for money in the exercise of power, and unable to ensure a certain future for their populations. These populations have become more unwilling to surrender individual autonomy to superordinate organizations and have legitimated that claim by reference to universalized standards. This has involved an invocation of new political symbols and therefore a revitalization of cultural effectivity. The symbolic appeals centre on human rights, the planetary environment, liberal democratization, consumption rights, religious traditionalism, ethnic diversification, and cosmopolitanism, each of which institutionalizes globalizing practices and phenomenologies. Cultural action is now disrupting states, especially where they are most highly organized, and party politics is being disrupted by universalizing and diffuse social movements. Territorial boundaries are thus becoming more difficult to maintain. Meanwhile the economy is becoming dominated by lifestyle choices, both in terms of the displacement of production by consumption as the central economic activity and in terms of the diversification of possible occupational experiences. The economy is becoming symbolically mediated and reflexive, which detaches it from locality.

Lastly, the cultural arena is itself becoming more activated and energetic. A principal development has been the collapse of cultural divisions between what might be called high and popular culture. High culture is the property of elites and tends to focus on the core values of the nation-state-society. The collapse of elite into popular culture, discussed in theories of postmodernity, combined with the mediatization or technological transmission of popular products opens up national cultural boundaries and renders them penetrable. Cultural products become more fluid and can be perceived as flows of preference, taste and information that can sweep the globe in unpredictable and uncontrolled ways. Even the most casual inspection of such preference issues as environmental concerns, Pokemon games, investment in high-tech shares, skirt lengths, roller blading and the Aids panic can confirm this development. These accelerated and increasingly effective cultural flows indicate an oncoming culmination of the globalization process.

The next six chapers of this book are organized in terms of these phasic developments. Chapter 2 focuses on the emergence of an international economy and Chapter 3 on globalizing developments that are impacting upon it. Chapters 4 and 5 do a similar job on politics, while Chapters 6 and 7 equally analyse the international and globalizing phases of cultural developments.

NOTES

1 Without becoming too pedantic this word has at least three meanings: spherical, total/universal, and world-wide. It is the third of these that is relevant here.

2 There are obviously certain kinship relationships which are immune to globalizing effects. However, geographically distant spousal relationships are already becoming more common.

3 We tend to think, for example, of London and New York as being 'closer' by Concorde than by 747. Astrophysics has long since gone all the way on this one, measuring distances between stars in 'light years'.

4 This might be illustrated by the phenomenological disjunctions that are now appearing between real time and computed time, between physical space and cyberspace, and between reality and virtual reality. In a sense the computer simulations of time, space and reality that curve around the physical counterpart might be held phenomenologically to be 'more real'.

2

TRADING PLACES: THE INTERNATIONAL ECONOMY

The working men have no country.

Karl Marx

Anticipating more systematic theories of globalization, the historians contributing to the *Times Atlas of World History* (Barraclough 1978) decided that, by the middle of the twentieth century, a period of European dominance had ended and the world had entered 'the age of global civilisation'. Interestingly, the editor reasoned that this development was economic rather than political or even cultural. Global civilization was not staked out between the emerging American and Russian superpowers, nor was the world being civilized by common understandings about human rights and the environment, or even decivilized by Big Macs and hip-hop. Rather the central events were the formation of the European Economic Community (now EU), the rise of Japan as an industrial power and an emerging and testy confrontation between rich and poor nations. However, the key features of this world economy, the *Atlas* argues, had been 'knitted together' between 1870 and 1914. These were threefold

(Barraclough 1978: 256–7). The first was the development of transportation and communication networks that physically linked together different parts of the planet, especially by railways, shipping and the telegraph. The second was the rapid growth of trade with its accompanying pattern of dependency, especially between the relatively industrialized countries of Western Europe and the rest. The third was a huge flow of capital mainly in the form of direct investment by European firms in non-industrialized areas.

These developments, which form the substance of this chapter, achieved full fruition by about the middle of the twentieth century. By that time, some forms of communication (e.g. the telephone and fax) had become instantaneous although still relatively costly; it had become possible, again at some cost, for any individual to move from any inhabited part of the planet to any other within 30 hours or so; trade in goods approached about a quarter of global production, and approached half of GDP in many non-industrialized countries; and foreign direct investment by multi-national corporations dominated non-industrialized economies. However, it is important to stress that these developments began in the second half of the nineteenth century.

It is small wonder then that Marx developed an early theory of capitalist internationalization at about this time. Marx writes of the way in which the capitalist seeks to transsect national boundaries extending transportation and communication into the furthest reaches of the planet, restlessly seeking to expand markets throughout the world and to appropriate ever greater tranches of labour power. Capitalism is clearly the vehicle of economic internationalization because its peculiar spectrum of institutions – financial markets, commodities, contractualized labour, alienable property – are highly mobile and fluid, facilitating economic exchanges over great distances. For this reason, many theories of globalization take their lead from Marx in stressing its economic foundations. For these authors, as capitalism expands across the globe it internationalizes the associated pattern of social relations known as class. For some authors (e.g. Frank 1971; Wallerstein 1974, 1980) the international class system consists of struggles between states as the working class in core countries becomes 'embourgeoised' and as a third-world proletariat develops in the periphery. Others (e.g. Sklair 1991: 8) reify a global capitalist class that effectively runs the planet on its own behalf.

The following sections outline the various means by which global economic relationships are accomplished: trade, investment, production, financial exchanges, labour migration, international economic co-operation and organizational practices. These will provide the evidence on whether claims about the development of an international class structure can be sustained.

INDUSTRIALIZATION AND MODERNIZATION

In the introduction to this book we note that Durkheim had argued that the general direction of change in society is one of structural differentiation. In the middle of the twentieth century, structural-functionalist sociologists expanded and modified Durkheim's argument to encompass the globalizing effects of differentiation. In thematic terms their thesis ran as follows. Industrialization involves a primary social separation between capitalization and collective production on one hand, and domestic production and reproduction on the other. To the extent that a society can make this separation, its material wealth and therefore its political success relative to other societies will increase. Once the option of industrialization is available, political and economic leaders will tend to choose and pursue it. Therefore, industrialization spreads from its seed-bed out into societal contexts in which it is not indigenous and the world becomes more industrialized.

Industrialization carries with it more general societal ramifications. It introduces the pattern of differentiation to other areas of social life as these areas articulate increasingly with the industrial core: families specialize in biological reproduction and in consumption, schools teach differentiated skills to the labour force, specialized units of government provide economic infrastructure, the mass media sell appropriate symbolizations, churches promulgate supporting values, and so on. These structural changes induce value shifts in the direction of individualization, universalism, secularity and rationalization. This general complex of transformations is called 'modernization'. As industrialization spreads across the globe, it carries modernization with it, transforming societies in a unitary direction. Imitating societies may even adopt modern institutions, such as universities or airlines, before effectively industrializing.[1]

Parsons (1964, 1966) takes the lead in arguing that this social change has a specific evolutionary direction and a logic or dynamic which drives it in this direction. The logic or dynamic is adaptation: 'the capacity of a living system to cope with its environment' (1964: 340). Modernization proceeds in the direction of adaptive upgrading:

> If differentiation is to yield a balanced, more evolved system, each newly differentiated sub-structure . . . must have increased adaptive capacity for performing its primary function, as compared with the performance of that function in the previous, more diffuse structure. Thus economic production is typically more efficient in factories than in households.
>
> (1966: 22)

The institutional path which adaptive upgrading forces on any society can be traced through a series of 'evolutionary universals' (Parsons 1964), a concept based on the idea of natural selection in organisms. They are defined as: 'any organizational development sufficiently important to further evolution that, rather than emerging only once, it is likely to be "hit upon" by various systems operating under different conditions' (1964: 329). Parsons identifies four base universals found in all, even the most undifferentiated of societies: technology, kinship, language and religion. Then there are two universals associated with evolution to an intermediate stage exemplified by ancient empires and feudalism.

These are status stratification and explicit cultural legitimation (written preservation of tradition). A further four universals are associated with the emergence of modern societies: bureaucratic organization, money and markets, a universalistic legal system, and democratic association (both governmental and private). The key breakthrough from intermediate to modern society is an industrial production system based on individualized employment contracts and occupational specialization. This in turn sets up tensions of co-ordination and control and of commitment which induce the emergence of markets, bureaucracy and democracy.[2]

A much more explicit link between modernization and the inter-societal system is developed by Parsons' student, Levy. Levy effectively reduces modernization to industrialization by defining it in the following way: 'A society will be considered more or less modernized to the extent that its members use inanimate sources of power and/or use tools to multiply the effects of their efforts' (1966: 11). Levy's argument, although frequently unrecognized within contemporary sociology, is significant within the conceptualization of globalization because he is able to show that latecomer modernization is essentially reflexive[3] and that this reflexivity establishes a systemic pattern of interrelationships between societies. For Levy the members of every society on the planet are faced with two questions: whether the modernization of non-modernized societies can be achieved in a stable (i.e. non-violent) fashion; and whether highly modernized societies can maintain their high rate of modernization. Taken together, these issues set up what might be called a 'globalizing problematic', a common issue that confronts all inhabitants of the planet: 'If those instabilities exist, they will spread with massive effects for all other individuals on the planet given the levels of interdependence already characteristic of the members of the different societies of the world' (1966: 790). For Levy then, modernization is not only a common feature of social structure but a central problem-focus that phenomenologically unites the members of all societies.

CONVERGENCE

The most influential theory of internationalizing impacts of industrialization comes not from any sociologist but from a group of Californian labour market theorists (Kerr et al. 1973). Kerr, Dunlop, Harbison and Myers propose that industrialization causes societies to become more alike. While they insist that industrial societies in the internationalization phase are not identical or even similar, they do claim that such societies are enmeshed in a process of convergence, moving towards a point where they are identical. They support this claim with two arguments. First, they suggest that industrial societies are more similar to each other than to any non-industrial society. Second, although the industrialization process may be generated in different ways in different societies, industrial societies will over time become increasingly similar to one another. The driving force for this convergence is the 'logic of industrialism' – as societies progressively seek the most effective technology of production their social systems will also progressively adapt to that technology. Technological development will more closely determine some social relations than others, particularly the economic arenas of employment and consumption. However, technology will necessarily affect most areas of social life.

Kerr et al. outline the key features of this societal convergence. Individual skills become highly specialized so that the labour force becomes highly differentiated into occupations. As science and technology advance, the occupational system will change, inducing high rates of occupational mobility. This process will be underpinned by very high levels of educational provision and credentialization. Equally, industrial technology demands large-scale social organization in order to support mass production and mass marketing. Industrial societies will therefore be organized spatially into cities; governments will expand to provide a socialized infrastructure for industry. And organizations will generally be large in scale, hierarchical and bureaucratic. Industrial societies will also develop a distinctive value-consensus focused on materialism, commitment to work, pluralism, individual achievement, and progress for its own sake. They conclude that: 'The industrial society is world-wide' because 'The science and technology on which it is based speak in a universal language' (1973: 54).

However, by the beginning of the third quarter of the twentieth century it was clear that such materialistic or techno-logical arguments could not substantively be supported. There was an increasing recognition that culture could not be reduced to economic or class relationships. Indeed, by this time most occupational activity was not directed to the production of material commodities and did not employ machine technology. However, there was one last attempt to: 're-write the last chapter of [Durkheim's] *The Division of Labour* with a happy ending', as Archer (1990: 101) puts it. This is Bell's (1976) forecast of the emergence of 'post-industrial' society but this time the focus was on service production rather than the production of goods. In caricature, Bell specifies the post-industrial society as a game between people rather than a game between people and things. Its central characteristics are as follows:

- The number of people engaged in occupations producing services predominates over the number engaged in producing raw materials or manufactured goods; these occupations are predominantly professional and technical in character.
- The class structure changes in the direction of a system of statuses; the predominant status consists of members of professional and technical occupations and the locus of power shifts from the economic to the political sphere.
- Theoretical knowledge predominates over practical knowledge and becomes the main source of innovation and policy formulation.
- Technological development comes within the ambit of human control and planning; technological goals can be set and activities co-ordinated to accomplish them; invention is no longer an individualized activity governed by chance.

- The most important technology is no longer physical but intellectual, so that human decisions previously based on intuitions and judgements can now be based on rational calculations within formulae.

However, the fundamentals of the argument are not too different from the convergence thesis. Kerr et al. argue that technologies for the production of goods create similarities between societies; Bell argues that emerging intellectual technologies for the production of services create that convergence. In Bell the emerging society is governed by a single axial principle (the use of theoretical knowledge to produce services) and it is specified as the only possible principle of future social organization. Therefore, all the societies on the planet march resolutely forward to a singular postindustrial future.

Bell's only explicit statement on globalization is contained in a short article (1987) that aims to forecast the future of the USA and the world in the years to 2013. Here he foreshadows some of the arguments reviewed in the subsequent chapters of this book. For example he forecasts the elimination of geography as a 'controlling variable'. Markets can increasingly consist of electronically integrated networks and indeed employees will need less to be concentrated in a single place of work. The international economy will therefore be tied together in real time rather than in space. He also forecasts the disappearance of the nation-state. The evidence for this is the increasing internal fragmentation of states along national lines (1987: 13–24). They are fragmenting, he argues, because nation-states are inadequate to problems of global economic growth, third-world modernization and environmental degradation, and are equally unresponsive and distant relative to the diversity of local needs and aspirations. However, it needs to be stressed that Bell's is not a fully fledged globalization thesis because it offers statements neither on the emergence of a phenomenology or culture of globalism nor on the systemic character of global social structure. Indeed, it is altogether pessimistic about the fragmentation of inter-state politics and the disruptive threats of population growth.

WORLD CAPITALISM

The view that societies proceed along a continuum of modernization dominated social scientific thought on global development in the 30 or so years after the Second World War. The predominant pardigm, and one that was appropriate for this international economy, was that of 'development'. The idea of development, especially of societies experiencing low levels of industrialization, was the focus in the middle years of the twentieth century, not only for social scientists but for politicians and journalists. An appropriate metaphor for this view is that of countries as a series of mountain climbers clawing their way up 'Mount Progress'.[4] The strongest are near the top while others lag behind hampered by smallness of stature, poor equipment or lack of training. They meet blockages on their paths and cannot easily withstand natural calamities visited on them by landslide and climatic inclemency that occasionally throw them further down the mountain. The climbers near the top will often throw down ropes to haul the others up. Frequently the ropes are not strong enough because the good climbers never throw down their best ropes and are always selective about which of those lower down will receive help. However, most of the stragglers believe that by following in the footsteps of the lead climber they will all get to the summit in the end. There are those who select an alternative route and refuse help from the lead climber but they are not doing nearly as well. When everyone gets to the summit they will join hands in mutual congratulation because they are all in the same place.

There has always been a problem in describing countries with differing positions in this developmental ascent. In the 1960s there were 'developed' and 'underdeveloped' countries; in the 1970s the 'first world' and the 'third world', with the 'second world', the state-socialist societies, poised awkwardly between them; in the 1980s we spoke of 'more developed' and 'less developed' countries (MDCs and LDCs); and today of industrialized and newly industrializing countries (NICs). All of these indicate bipolarity in development terms, but, more seriously, they imply that the origins of lower levels of development reside in the internal structure of a society. More recently, consideration of late industrialization has turned to the view that late and low industrializers are confirmed in that position by the relationships between themselves and the early industrializers. In so far as inter-societal stratification is confirmed by such relationships we can affirm the existence of a single international system.

The origin of this argument about inter-societal stratification can be found in the work of the Bolshevik revolutionary, Lenin (1939). In his analysis of imperialism as the last or highest stage of capitalism Lenin argues that an international system of exploitation develops out of the social relations of capitalist production. The path of capitalist development which gives rise to this formation leads in the following direction. The earliest phase of capitalism is highly competitive as emerging capitalists seek to maximize profit at the expense of others. However, as some become more successful, unevenness between the performances of firms in the capitalist market leads to the monopolization of its sectors as companies are forced out or absorbed by their more successful competitors. Monopolization allows price control, which grows capital rapidly and allows it to be stored in a highly fluid and mobile form in banks, rather than being reinvested. A finance-capital oligarchy emerges out of an institutional amalgamation between bank capital and industrial capital. This provides the mechanism for an extension of capitalist exploitation beyond national boundaries by means of capital exports. International capitalist monopolies form, dividing the world between themselves both economically and, through the agency of the colonial state, territorially.

We can now concentrate on two sympathetic refinements of Lenin's thesis. If we take the argument to its extreme, capital exports will eventually result in high if uneven levels of development in all parts of the world. However, this widespread level of development plainly did not occur. Monopoly-capitalist imperialism has indeed survived with considerable stability for about a century, but the reason, argues Frank (1971) (see also Cockroft, Frank and Johnson 1972), is that monopolistic firms only give the appearance of being capital exporters when they are in fact net capital importers. They import profits made in colonies which provide for internal capital accumulation. Capital exports to economic colonies are only 'seed money' investments, principally directed to the exploitation of labour for the production of food and raw materials. Colonial commodities can be imported to the centre at low prices while manufactured goods can be exported at high prices with the difference providing a surplus which returns to the investor and thus makes capital grow. As a consequence, underdevelopment is perpetuated as a pattern of dependency between the colonialist and the colonized.

The most influential sociological argument for considering the world as a single economic system comes from Wallerstein (1974, 1980; also Hopkins and Wallerstein 1980, 1982). His primary unit of analysis is the world-system, a unit which has a capacity to develop independently of the social processes and relationships which are internal to its component societies or states. There are three possible types of world-system:

- World-empires, in which a multiplicity of cultures are unified under the domination of a single government; there have been many instances of world-empires, e.g. ancient Egypt, ancient Rome, ancient China, Moghul India, feudal Russia, Ottoman Turkey.
- World-economies, in which a multiplicity of political states, each typically focusing on a single culture ('nation-states'), are integrated by a common economic system; there has been only one stable instance of a world-economy, the *modern world-system*, integrated by a single capitalist economy (which includes state-socialist societies).
- World-socialism, in which both the nation-state and capitalism disappear in favour of a single, unified political-economic

system which integrates a multiplicity of cultures; there is no instance of world-socialism and it remains a utopian construct.

It is the second of these, the modern world-system, that corresponds with the notion of an inter-nationalized economy.

Wallerstein concentrates on the emergence and evolution of the modern European world-system which he traces from its late medieval origins to the present day. He describes the emergent phenomenon in the following way:

> In the late fifteenth and early sixteenth century, there came into existence what we may call a European world-economy. It was not an empire yet but it was as spacious as an empire and shared some features with it. . . . It is a 'world' system, not because it encompasses the whole world, but because it is larger than any juridically-defined political unit. And it is a 'world-*economy*' because the basic linkage between the parts of the system is economic, although this was reinforced to some extent by cultural links and eventually . . . by political arrangements and even confederal structures.
>
> (1974: 15; original italics)

A critical feature of Wallerstein's argument that differentiates it from the dependency theory of Frank and Amin is that the focal point of pressure in the world-economy is the state structure. The state helps to stabilize capitalism by absorbing its costs and managing the social problems which it creates. The modern world-system is stratified into three types of state, depending on the interaction between them as the primary source of stability:

- *Core states* have a strong governmental structure integrated with a national culture, and are developed, rich, and dominating within the system; late-twentieth-century examples include the EU, Japan and the USA.
- *Peripheral areas* have weak indigenous states and invaded cultures, and are poor and therefore economically dependent

on the core states; late-twentieth-century examples include the 'newly industrializing countries' of the 'South' i.e. in Asia, Africa and Latin America.

- *Semiperipheral areas* include countries with moderately strong governmental structures, single-commodity or low-technology economies and that are somewhat dependent on core states; they may be earlier core states in decline or they may be emerging from the periphery; late-twentieth-century examples include oil producers, former socialist states in Eastern Europe, and the 'young dragon' societies of South-East Asia.

There is a division of labour between states in each of these regions: 'tasks requiring higher levels of skill and greater capitalization are reserved for higher-ranking areas' (Wallerstein 1974: 350). However, the position of the semiperipheral areas is of special theoretical importance because their existence prevents polarization and conflict between the core and the periphery.

Capitalism functions in relation to long-term cyclical rhythms, the central one of which is the regular boom/bust pattern of expansion and contraction of the whole economy (Wallerstein 1990: 36). In a spectacular piece of anthropomorphism, Wallerstein identifies one of the responses to this cyclical pattern:

> [T]he capitalist world-economy has seen the need to expand the geographic boundaries of the system as a whole, creating thereby new loci of production to participate in its axial division of labour. Over 400 years, these successive expansions have transformed the capitalist world-economy from a system located primarily in Europe to one that covers the entire globe.
>
> (1990: 36)

To be fair, Wallerstein does indicate that the consciousness of this need resides in the minds of the political, economic and military rulers of the world-system who deliberately employ multiple pressures to overcome resistance in areas being subjected to the process of 'incorporation'. One of the techniques they use is to 'sell' Western domination as the universalizing process of modernization which increases its palatability.

Although some have hailed Wallerstein's theory as a precursor of more genuine globalization theory (e.g. Giddens 1990: 68–70), his argument is fundamentally at odds with such formulations. It only genuinely applies to the period of internationalization that culminated at about the middle of the twentieth century. For Wallerstein the mechanisms of geosystemic integration are exclusively economic – they are constituted as trading and exploitative relationships between relatively sovereign states and relatively independent cultures. By contrast, genuine globalization theories involve a global unification of cultural orientations which 'turns on' and breaks down the barriers between national polities and local economies. More importantly, the existence of a world-system or systems does not itself imply global unification. Wallerstein's worlds are phenomenological not material. Several world-systems can coexist on the planet. The world-system argument can only truly inform us about globalization if it can give an account both of the incorporation of all states into a capitalist world-system and of the integration of polities and cultures by virtue of that expansion. The former is given in Wallerstein's recent statements on the cyclical nature of capitalist development; the possibility of political and cultural integration appears for the moment only to reside in his utopian formulation of world-socialism.

Although bearing a family resemblance to Wallerstein and Frank, Sklair's argument (1991) is an injunction to social scientists to pay more attention to trans-national relationships that emerge under globalization and is therefore more explicitly a theory of it. The resemblance to Wallerstein lies in the argument that the global system of trans-national practices is largely structured by capitalism. Trans-national practices operate on three levels, analytically distinguished, the economic, the political and the cultural-ideological, each dominated by a major institution that heads the drive towards globalization. Respectively then, the main locus of trans-national economic practices is the trans-national corporation; of political practices, the trans-national capitalist class; and of cultural-ideological practices, the culture of consumerism. Sklair is equivocal about the balance of effectivity between trans-national practices and nation-states. The nation-state is 'the spatial reference point' for them, the arena within which they intersect, but another, perhaps more significant reference point is: 'the global capitalist system, based on a variegated global capitalist class, which unquestionably dictates economic transnational practices, and is the most important single force in the struggle to dominate political and cultural-ideological transnational practices' (1991: 7).

However, Sklair returns even the 'global' capitalist class to the internal workings of a national social system, albeit that of a hegemon: 'there is only one country, the United States, whose agents, organizations and classes are hegemonic in all three spheres' (1991: 7). In an argument reminiscent of Gilpin then (see Chapter 5), it is hegemonic states that promote capitalism as the global system: Britain in the nineteenth century and the USA in the twentieth. Unlike Gilpin, however, Sklair attributes altruism to neither hegemon, holding them individually responsible for global inequalities constructed in their own interests.

WORLD TRADE

The original and continuing fundamental of economic internationalization is trade. Trade can link together geographically distant producers and consumers, often establishing a relationship of identification as well as interdependence between them. The British taste for tea, for example, could not have been cultivated in that damp little island had it not been able to export its cheap textiles to Southern Asia, albeit to sell them in captive colonial markets, along with common law, cricket and railways. Despite the collapse of colonialism, the cultural ties remain. Equally, under current circumstances, wearing Armani fashions or grilling food on a hibachi barbecue (itself a polyglot phrase) provides an opportunity for commonality of lifestyle across the globe. Indeed, the trans-national relationships that are established by means of trade can undermine or at least circumvent inter-state relations.

Overall, in the period of industrialization, world trade, understood as the exchange of commodities and services between nation-states, has expanded very rapidly. One indicator is the positive ratio of growth rates in trade to growth rates in production throughout the nineteenth century and the second half of the twentieth. Only during the global conflict and associated economic depression that marked the first half of the twentieth century did that ratio turn negative. Even then global trade continued to grow except in the 20 years following the Great Depression of the 1930s (Gordon 1988: 43). There were two main phases of trade growth: the mid- to late nineteenth century when British military and economic hegemony allowed it to set up protected markets in its colonies and 'free trade' in manufactured goods outside them; and the 30 or so years after the Second World War when the USA was so economically and militarily dominant that it too could impose a freer trade regime, secure in the knowledge that its own manufactured exports would succeed and that it could extend special forms of trade access to its friends, those 'most favoured nations'.

As Marx noticed, the great expansion of world trade began in the final quarter of the nineteenth century. Between 1800 and 1913 international trade grew, as a proportion of world product, from 3 to 33 per cent, tripling between 1870 and 1913 (Barraclough 1978: 256). The pattern was mainly imperialistic in character. It involved the transfer of primary products from the non-industrialized world (which for most of the century mainly comprised the settler colonies of the Americas, Southern Africa and Australasia rather than the conquest colonies of Africa and Asia, India being the notable exception) in exchange for European manufactures. In 1914 only 11 per cent of world trade took place between primary producers themselves but trade between industrialized countries was growing as fast as 'imperialist' trade. Britain led the pack, being the largest trading nation in mid-century but by 1900 the European states and the USA were catching up (see Figure 2.1[5]). Nevertheless, in the period up to the Great Depression world trade was dominated and organized by four nation-states, Britain, France, Germany and the USA.

The inter-war period saw a return to protectionism as national governments strived to restore their shattered economies by curtailing imports and subsidizing exports. However, the emergence of the USA as the post-Second World War political, military and economic hegemon gave it an opportunity to establish a trade system that suited its interests. In so far as much of the rest of the industrialized world had been exhausted or devastated by war, the USA was well placed to take advantage of a liberalized trade regime. The main vehicle was the General Agreement on Tariffs and Trade (GATT; now the World Trade Organization or WTO), an organization established by 23 countries in 1947.

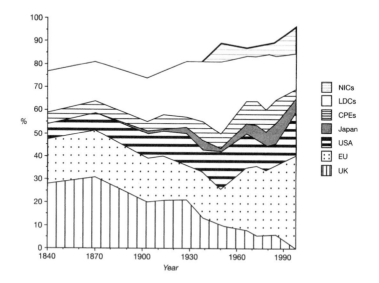

Figure 2.1 Geographical distribution of international trade, 1840–1998
Sources: Gordon 1988: 46–7; World Trade Organization

GATT has since globalized to include over 100 members. GATT's two-pronged strategy has been to encourage members to restrict protection to tariff duties only (as opposed to quotas, subsidies etc.) and then to seek consensus on tariff reduction. With American encouragement, at least until about 1980, it was very successful, going through seven rounds of tariff reduction. American tariffs on industrial goods were reduced from an average of 60 per cent in 1934 to 4.3 per cent in 1987, at which point Japanese industrial tariffs averaged 2.9 per cent and the EU averaged 4.7 per cent (Walters and Blake 1992: 16).

World trade grew by 6.6 per cent per annum between 1948 and 1966 and by 9.2 per cent per annum between 1966 and 1973. The critical geographical shift during this period was the relative decline of the British share of world trade, the increased trading effectiveness of the EEC (now EU) and the emergence of Japan as a trading power. Taken together the share of world trade taken by less-developed countries (LDCs) and newly industrializing countries (NICs) improved in the 1950s and has since remained stable at 25 to 30 per cent. This has generally increased the level of global economic interdependence.

Social scientists have become accustomed to interpreting global trade relations in terms of asymmetrical dependency, for which Wallerstein (1974, 1980) offers one of the strongest arguments. However, the declining concentration of world trade in Europe and the USA, and the increasing extent to which trade accounted for most national GDPs, moved dependency relationships in the direction of greater symmetry during the post-war period. There was, for example, a dramatic increase in the proportion of trade in manufactured goods and most of that trade took place between industrialized countries. The proportion of the manufactured exports going from industrialized countries to other industrialized countries increased from about 30 per cent in 1935 to 64 per cent in 1983 (Gordon 1988: 47).

THE INTERNATIONAL DIVISION OF LABOUR

World trade implies a division of labour between societies. Classical arguments about the division of labour consider it as an intra-societal process operating in two dimensions, the social and the technical. The social division of labour concerns the degree of specialization of jobs or occupations, the technical the degree of specialization of tasks within occupations. One of the more revelatory discoveries offered by social science in the twentieth century is that colonialism and imperialism produce an international division of labour of the social kind. Core or metropolitan societies do capital-intensive, high value-adding production while peripheral societies do labour-intensive, low value-adding production. This division of labour produces a relationship of domination and mutual dependency which is self-reproducing. Thus, the customary vision of a partly globalized world is that it is fractured by a binary division variously characterized as developed/underdeveloped, modern/traditional, core/periphery, industrialized/industrializing, more developed/less developed, first world/third world, North/South or simply rich/poor.

The sources of this division are the trade and investment patterns discussed in other sections of this chapter. By the middle of the twentieth century these patterns had produced an ever-widening gap between rich and poor. On an income per head basis the rich:poor ratio was about 2:1 in 1800, by 1945 it was 20:1, by 1975 it was 40:1, and by 1990 it was 64:1. In 1975, GDP per capita in the USA was $6,500, but there were 17 countries with a total population of 200 million living on less than $100 per year per head. Poverty is accompanied by pathological rates of literacy, life expectancy, infant mortality, nutrition, morbidity and population growth (Barraclough 1978: 294; Thomas 1997: 456).

A particular form of neomercantilist strategy has been practised by LDCs engaged in primary production. This is the formation of producer cartels that aim to restrict production and to maintain or enhance prices. The most successful example and the model for other attempts is the Organization of Petroleum Exporting Countries (OPEC) formed in 1960 to prevent a price reduction forced by the oligopsonizing MNE cartel known as the 'seven sisters'. OPEC really became active in the 1970s, a period of sharply increased demand and concentration of supply, imposing for example a fourfold increase in the price of oil in the first 'oil shock' of 1973. That shock was clearly a global experience affecting the mightiest industrial nation and the humblest LDC with equal severity. OPEC's General Secretary, Sheikh Ahmed Zaki Yamani, became a recognized and respected, and occasionally feared, figure throughout the world. However, in the 1980s OPEC's influence waned as alternative sources of supply were found and conservation measures took effect. Similar cartels sought to control the supply and price of copper, bauxite, tin, bananas, coffee, cocoa, rubber, iron ore, phosphates and mercury. Among these only the non-ferrous metals cartels were at all successful.

So, despite the best efforts of producer cartels, the gap between rich and poor societies widened. But effects on LDC economies were not entirely negative. While it can partly be accounted for by a low base, economic growth in the LDCs outstripped that in the MDCs. Between 1950 and 1980, LDC growth averaged 4.9 per cent per year, while that in MDCs averaged 3.5 per cent (Thomas 1997: 454). LDC growth was unevenly distributed, the highest rates being experienced in Asia, followed by central and South America, with the lowest rates being experienced in Africa (Thomas 1997: 455). In the period 1960–89, 19 African countries experienced absolute declines in their GDP. In part, this might be accounted for by a 'march through the sectors' industrial restructuring which rendered some countries less competitive than others. So, between 1960 and 1980, agriculture declined from 32 per cent of GDP to 16 per cent, and manufacturing industry increased from 21 to 34 per cent (Thomas 1997: 454). The sectoral structure of LDC economies was beginning to approximate that of MDCs, with many having nominally moved directly into a postindustrial configuration.

MULTI-NATIONAL ENTERPRISES

The main focus for many hopes and fears about economic globalization is the MNE or TNC. For critics of capitalism they are the vehicles by which intolerable and inhuman practices of exploitation are spread across the globe, and for its friends they are the virtuous sources of investment, technology transfer and upgrading of the labour force. Until recently it was also possible to offer the more moderate critique of MNEs that they had grown so large and powerful that they undermined the legitimate and often democratically established sovereign authority of the nation-state, but in the current context of the delegitimation of the state the debate has become polarized.

Among critics, MNEs tend only to be defined theoretically rather than operationally – Sklair (1991), for example, gives no definition of a TNC. By contrast, Dunning, who is more friend than enemy, defines an MNE as: 'an enterprise that engages in FDI [foreign direct investment] and organizes the production of goods or services in more than one country' (1993: 6).[6] However, Dunning stresses that this definition cannot capture the extent to which trans-national activities can vary in their scope and intensiveness. They vary their multi-national engagement according to: the number of subsidiaries; the number of countries; the proportion of activities accounted for by foreign activities; the degree to which ownership and management are internationalized; the extent to which central administrative and research activities are internationalized; and the balance of advantages and disadvantages to the countries in which they operate. A classical example of a 'villainous' MNE might be General Motors, but only about a third of its assets and a third of its sales are outside the USA (and most of these are in first-world Canada, Europe and Australia). Perhaps a more appropriate example of a 'true' multi-national might be the Swiss-Swedish engineering group, Asea Brown Boveri, or the Dutch electronics firm, Philips, each of which have over 85 per cent of their sales outside their country of origin (data from Emmott 1993: 6).

We can now consider the general extent of MNE activity in the international economy. Dunning (1993: 14–15) estimates that in 1988 there were about 20,000 MNEs with foreign assets amounting to US$1.1 trillion (equivalent to 8 per cent of gross world product) and total assets of over US$4 trillion. They accounted for: 25–30 per cent of combined GDP in all market economies; 75 per cent of international commodity trade; and 80 per cent of international exchanges of technology and managerial skills. The largest 300 MNEs account for 70 per cent of total FDI and 25 per cent of the world's capital (Dunning 1993: 15; Emmott 1993: 6). In 1987, TNCs employed about one-third of the 90 million manufacturing workers in the world (Gill and Law 1988: 191–2). Overall, FDI increased fourfold between 1970 and 1990 but most of this increase occurred during the late 1980s (Emmott 1993: 8). Over 90 per cent of FDI is sourced in ten developed countries, and about two-thirds originated in only four (US, UK, Japan, Germany). However, MNEs are themselves becoming internationalized, in so far as these rates have declined over the past 20 years.

There is a significant increase in the number of MNEs originating in the developing societies, the oil producing countries, and the Asian dragons (NICs). For example, the Asian share of FDI rose from 3.6 per cent in 1973 to 9.3 per cent in 1988 (Dunning 1993: 21). The destinations of FDI largely match the sources, and indeed 'there appears to be a growing symmetry between outward and inward foreign capital stake in the case of most [individual] countries' (Dunning 1993: 24). One feature of this was a rapid increase of Japanese FDI into the USA in the 1980s. This must give at least some pause for thought to critics who insist that MNEs are the trojan horse for first-world economic domination of the third world. Nevertheless, the USA is still the predominant country of origin of TNCs with 45 per cent of FDI in 1978 (Gill and Law 1988: 196).

The combined effects of these trends allow Dunning (1993: 40) to identify a series of what he describes as 'true global industries', those that are dominated by large corporations of diverse national origins, producing and marketing in all of the world's largest economies. The most important example is the petrochemical industry but others, in descending order of importance, include cars, consumer electronics, tyres, pharmaceuticals, tobacco, soft drinks, fast food, financial consultancies and luxury hotels. We can add to this list emerging multi-national alliances (which normally involve much lower levels of FDI but high levels of managerial co-ordination) in airlines, telecommunications, and banking and insurance (see the next chapter for details).

As in the case of many of the components of globalization, the development of MNEs is a long-term process with a recent acceleration rather than a sudden and qualitative shift. This development is traced through several phases by Dunning (1993: 96–136; see also Gilpin 1987: 238–45):

- *Mercantile capitalism and colonialism (1500–1800)*: exploitation of natural resources and agriculture in colonized regions by state-sponsored, chartered companies (e.g. Dutch East India, Hudson's Bay, Massachusetts Bay, Muscovy, and Van Diemen's Land Companies).
- *Entrepreneurial and financial capitalism (1800–75)*: embryonic development of control of supplier and consumer markets by acquisition; infrastructural investment by finance houses in transportation and construction.
- *International capitalism (1875–1945)*: rapid expansion of resource-based and market-seeking investments; growth of American-based international cartels.
- *Multi-national capitalism (1945–60)*: American domination of FDI; expanded economic imperialism; expansion in scale of individual MNEs.
- *Globalizing capitalism (1960–90)*: shift from resource-based and market-seeking investment to spatial optimization of production and profit opportunities; growth of European and Japanese sourced FDI; increased FDI in the European ex-state socialist societies; expansion of inter-firm alliances and joint ventures; increased offshore outsourcing of components.

PRODUCTION SYSTEMS

In the years just after the turn of the century many American industrial organizations went through a famous transformation. The Ford Motor Company of the USA invented the moving assembly line and thus established an ideological paradigm for economic organizations that recently has come to be called Fordism. Fordism advocates the mass production of standardized items for mass markets made affluent by high incomes. It aims to reduce the cost per item by intensive mechanization and by economies of scale in the utilization of capital equipment. Fordism became the idealized system of production not only in the capitalist West but in the socialist East.[7] In so far as Fordism was exported by MNEs and in so far as it was mimicked, it became a major feature of the global economy in the period just after the Second World War. However, Fordism owed its success not to its capacity to produce and market goods on a wide scale but to its social and political consequences. It was an extraordinarily effective means both of controlling the labour process and of satisfying workers' aspirations at a material level. In the terms of a well-known formulation it turned proletarians into instrumental workers.

But Fordism is not a complete paradigm. In particular it leaves untouched the vast issue of who makes decisions and by what processes. In many instances this issue was resolved in terms of a parallel paradigm of work called Taylorism (after the engineer F.W. Taylor who invented it) that specified a radical differentiation between the functions of management and labour. However, Taylorism did not achieve the global impact that Fordism did, partly because it was challenged by a humanistic though equally manipulative paradigm called 'human relations'. Industrial organizations could therefore vary across societies according both to the pattern of state action in regulating, co-ordinating, subsidizing and socializing the economy, and to cultural prescriptions of appropriate economic behaviour (see Lash and Urry 1987). So, for example: in the USA large companies were run by ex-engineers making highly rationalized technical decisions in relation to technology and markets; in Germany firms were organized and influenced jointly by state managers and finance houses; in France, large firms were centralized, state-managed bureaucracies; in Britain there was a concentration on the maintenance of the managerial status group, at the possible expense of relative industrial effectiveness; and in Scandinavia there was a deliberate effort to dedifferentiate managers and workers.

FINANCIAL MANAGEMENT

Among the dimensions of economic life being considered in this and the next chapters possibly the most globalized are the markets for raising loans and capital. These markets have a long history of internationalization. Many point to the 'black Monday' stock market crash of October 1987 as convincing evidence of a globalized effect. Indeed, that fall in share prices globalized very rapidly. However, the planetary effects of the 'Wall Street crash' of 1929 were far more serious, if less rapid in their dispersal.

Gilpin (1987: 308–14) identifies three eras in the development of international financial markets:

- *1870–1914*: Britain was the major capital exporter and international finance therefore centred on the City of London. Here foreign holdings increased fivefold in the period. The 'City' managed the world financial system.
- *1920–39*: The First World War forced many European governments, including the British, to liquidate overseas investments. Simultaneously the USA was becoming a powerful economic player. Until 1929 the USA provided liquid funds to the financial system but curtailed foreign lending in that year. Thereafter markets remained illiquid until the Second World War.
- *1947–85*: New York became the international financial centre, that is, the clearing house, the banker for foreign reserves, the main capital market and the lender-of-last-resort. American

financial management was accomplished via the World Bank and the International Monetary Fund (IMF), and governmental international aid rose to equal prominence with private capital as a source of finance.

Nominally the global financial system was thus internationalized and subjected to collective fiscal management. In the post-Second World War period, the key treaty was the so-called Bretton Woods Agreement of 1944 that established the IMF. The IMF's brief was to maintain stability in rates of currency exchange by providing temporary loans to carry states through periodic balance-of-payments deficits without massive structural readjustment. For some 25 years the IMF thus effectively returned American balance-of-payments surpluses to countries in deficit, although in chronic instances it did demand readjustment, and in many cases states simply went ahead and devalued. An important stabilizing factor was the linking of the value of the dollar to a specific price of gold.

Although highly internationalized neither the pre-war nor the post-war system was fully globalized because each depended on centralized management and underwriting by a single state. The London system had failed to function in the 1930s when no government was prepared to underwrite it and a similar crisis occurred in the early 1970s. The key source of the crisis was the relative decline of American industrial and trading power (discussed earlier). Several factors contributed to the American decline – the rise of regional trading blocs, the emergence of Japan and the NICs, and the OPEC oil shock. The USA became a debtor rather than a creditor nation and began to finance its debt by pumping dollars into the market at just about the same time as the OPEC nations were doing the same with their dollar-denominated surpluses. Many of these liquid funds found a home in the LDCs which ran up uncontrollable levels of debt. More importantly, a market for American dollars, known as the Eurodollar or Eurocurrency market, developed beyond the managerial reach of New York. This globalized 'stateless' money increased in volume from US$50 billion in 1973 to US$2 trillion in 1987, almost the same as the amount circulating in the USA itself (Harvey 1989: 163).

MIGRANT LABOUR

If, among factor exchange systems, financial markets are the most globalized, labour markets are the least so. No other area of economic life remains so much under the thrall of states and so resistant to globalizing effects. This is possibly because governments remain accountable to electorates in terms of the delivery of individual economic welfare and the admission of migrants appears to threaten employment prospects and to dilute the value of public services. And while government prohibition is the major constraint on labour mobility it is not the only one. Members of the EU have the right to live and work anywhere within the Union, for example, but internal migration has been minimal despite internal variations in living standards (Emmott 1993: 6). It would appear that only quite severe economic or political disadvantage can overcome the local constraints of kin, language, domestic investments and cultural familiarity.

In fact, the earliest stages of global expansion saw the highest levels of labour mobility. In its initial phase much of this mobility was incontrovertibly forced. Between 1500 and 1850 slave traders moved 9.5 million people from Africa to the Americas, including 4 million to the Caribbean, 3.5 million to Brazil and another 400,000 to the Southern USA. The forced convict settlement of Australia and America, although almost as harsh, affected much lower numbers (McEvedy and Jones 1978: 277). Until 1800 'free' white settler colonization was relatively slight – up to that year less than a million Europeans had crossed the Atlantic. The nineteenth century saw the 'Great Migration'. Between 1845 and 1914 41 million people migrated to the Americas, mainly from Europe and mainly to the USA (McEvedy and Jones 1978: 279). After the First World War the USA placed restrictions on the number of immigrants but it continues to absorb relatively large numbers. It was still receiving 600,000 per year in the late 1980s (Emmott 1993: 7).

American immigration restrictions in the twentieth century diverted much European migration to the former British settler colonies of Australia, Canada, New Zealand and South Africa, Australasia having received a total of 5.5 million migrants (McEvedy and Jones 1978: 325). A huge proportion of these migrants moved on the basis of purely economic motivations. However, this mass migration pattern no longer applies. Following the economic crises that began in around 1970 most of the societies that previously had been 'open' placed numerical and qualification restrictions on immigration.

Since the Second World War the main patterns of international migration have been as follows (see Cohen 1987):

- continued European and Asian settler migration to North America, Australasia and Southern Africa;
- post-Vietnam war refugee migration;
- Latin-American migration to the USA mainly from Cuba, Mexico and Puerto Rico;
- return migration from ex-colonies to the European 'mother countries', especially to Britain (from black Africa, South Asia and the West Indies), France (from North Africa), the Netherlands (from Indonesia) and Portugal (from Africa);
- *Gastarbeiter* 'temporary' migration from Southern Europe (mainly Turkey and ex-Yugoslavia) into the booming economies of Northern Europe (especially Western Germany and Switzerland);
- 'temporary' migration of Asians to the oil-exporting countries of the Middle East and to Japan;
- Jewish migration to Israel, especially from Russia and Eastern Europe;
- East European migration to Western Europe and the USA (Western Germany, for example, has been receiving 440,000 immigrants per year for five years [Emmot 1993: 7]).

These developments are patchy and by no means represent a globalized picture. In a genuinely globalized market movements of labour and patterns of settlement would be entirely unrestricted by states. However, there are some inklings of evidence that, even here the powers of nation-states may be waning. If they are numerous enough, individual decisions can overwhelm the regulative practices of even the most draconian preventative measures. Several events bear witness to this: the mass 'illegal' migration of Mexicans into the USA; successful migrations by Indo-Chinese 'boat people'; the collapse of the barbed-wire frontier between Eastern and Western Europe; the student migration from China following the Tianamen Square massacre in 1989; and the determination of European *Gastarbeiter* to achieve full citizenship rights even in the face of violent racial assaults. As global consciousness increases so too will the pressures in favour of a single labour and settlement market.

TRANS-NATIONAL CLASSES

Traditional views of class focus on the nation-state-society-economy as the object of class action. In Marxist analyses classes struggle for the control and eventual abolition of the state. Indeed, as we saw in Chapter 1, Marx envisioned true globalization as the outcome of proletarian revolutionary success. Similarly in Weberian analyses, classes struggle at the state level about the distribution of rewards in society. If one accepts the veracity of class analysis then classes must be specified as nationalized collective actors. We must therefore now ask whether classes can continue to exist under two sets of conditions that might be seen as having a decomposing effect on them. The first is the decline of the state, discussed in Chapter 5, that removes the prize, the object of the struggle. The second is the marketization and globalization of the international economy that may be depriving classes of an arena in which to struggle. In a global economic market that has no centre there might be no place in which classes can confront one another.

The strongest claim that the class struggle has simply moved up a notch from the national to the international level is made by such authors as van der Pijl (1989). Van der Pijl argues that as globalization proceeds the capitalist class transforms itself in an international direction in three moments:

- it develops an international class consciousness – this occurs relatively early within, for example, Grotius' concepts of international law and Kant's postulation of the need for a world state;
- it develops a controlling state-like structure at the international level – this can be witnessed in the League of Nations and the United Nations which, armoured by American power, made the world safe for capitalism; and
- it socializes labour in order to demarcate an international economic space – this is accomplished by the internationalization of trade, investment and production that divides the world into exploiting and exploited states.

These provide the conditions for the development of an informal international capitalist class that consists of a network of big companies linked together by interlocking directorates and cross-shareholdings. These, plus such organizations as the UN, allow this class to manage an international division of labour in such a way as to allow the bourgeoisie to maintain its position in the core societies by exporting poverty.

The analysis of globalization processes presented throughout this book would tend to deny the possibility of the internationalization of class, at least in so far as it is represented in such vulgar formulations as this. The following arguments apply: there cannot be a ruling class without a state, and the UN scarcely qualifies as a world state; internal social divisions of labour are tending to dedifferentiate so that the functions of conceptualization and execution are tending to be reintegrated; firms are downscaling so that core large firms will decreasingly be able to dominate the system; markets are becoming tokenized and decentred so that they are becoming increasingly difficult to control; and the key means of production are no longer physical plant and machines but human expertise, symbolized information and aesthetic products, each of which is ephemeral, non-accumulable and uncontrollable. This does not mean that the global economy is without its powerful individual movers and shakers. It is impossible to deny the impact of a Rupert Murdoch or George Soros.[8] However, they are powerful precisely because of their individual talents and not because they are the members of a class.

This is not to suggest, however, that economic stratification has disappeared from the face of the earth. Rather, that stratification pattern is now focused on possibilities for consumption rather than production relations. The emerging pattern is indeed an international one, in which members of rich societies, even if they are unemployed, tend to enjoy significantly better consumption possibilities than employees in developing societies. This has been apparent for some time, but a significant feature of the current acceleration is the way in which the two worlds are beginning to mingle in global cities. Lash and Urry (1994) identify a new configuration that juxtaposes an affluent post-industrial service class or middle mass in high-paying relatively autonomous occupations with a disadvantaged *Gastarbeiter* class or underclass that supports its consumption within routine underpaid and insecure labour situations. Under globalization, migration has brought the third world back to the global cities, where its exploitation becomes ever more apparent.

MAIN CHARACTERISTICS OF AN INTER-NATIONAL ECONOMY

A primary characteristic of an inter-nationalized economy is that it is industrialized. Its firms are large in scale, they are mechanized, they specialize in what they produce and they focus on material products. Firms typically are based in single nation-states with which they identify, but they often operate across borders. They trade their raw materials and products inter-nationally, directly invest their capital in foreign societies, and provide economic inducements to labour migration between nation-state-societies. The predominant organizational form is the multi-national corporation, which broadly operates by seeking serially to dominate one national market after another, beginning with its home market. MNCs may achieve this either by setting up foreign subsidiaries or by taking over local firms.

The nation-state-society becomes the most important focus not only for identity and sovereignty but for economic manage-ment. Such management extends not only to fiscal stability and the regulation of inter-firm relations but also to the reproduction of the labour force through the provision of education, health and welfare and the provision of economic infrastructure. The focus on the nation-state-society as the main territorial and spatial focus means that an inter-nationalized economy cannot be regarded as a fully globalized economy. But in extinguishing the global, the nation-state also extinguishes the local. Minority cultures and identities, individual tastes and commitments, small local firms operating in niches, family enterprises and minority religions are subsumed in the state-centred nation.

The key point of debate about the inter-nationalized economy that emerged during the twentieth century is the extent to which it was systemic, that is the extent to which change in one part of the system could have ramifications throughout the world. The answer is given by Wallerstein and others. An inter-nationalized economy is systemic to the extent that it is dominated by a political-economic hegemon. Possibly the first and best example of this phenomenon is the way in which the American stock market crash of 1929 triggered an economic depression that was felt equally seriously throughout Europe and its former colonies. Equally, in the 1950s and 1960s American prosperity extended to Europe and Japan. In neither case did these developments have serious impacts on societies not dominated by the USA, includ-ing Russia, China and India, which remained isolated by their own sovereignty. Sovereignty allowed them to protect internal markets for domestic products, restrict currency exchange and thereby resist inflation and maintain both employment and low wage levels by fiat.

NOTES

1   While many modernization theorists insist on a logic of choice, several accept that modernization spreads through the impositions of political or economic imperialism.

2   For a more comprehensive but nevertheless short account of Parsons' theory of evolution see Waters (1994: 305–7)

3   The term 'reflexive' is derived from ethnomethodology, a theoretical scheme developed by Garfinkel (1967). A reflexive act is one in which the individual projects a future goal state, analyses the steps that will need to be taken to achieve that goal, and then acts out the steps.

4   I first heard this metaphor used by Ronald Dore in Moncton N.B. Canada in 1975.

5   In this diagram and throughout this chapter the following abbreviations apply: CPEs = centrally planned economies (usually the former USSR, People's Republic of China, former post-war socialist states of Eastern Europe), in later contexts, e.g. WTO data, these are called 'transitional economies'; DMEs = democratic market economies (usually North America, Japan, Western Europe, Australasia); EU = European Union (including its predecessors EC (European Communities), EEC (European Economic Community; data often exclude the UK), ECSC (European Coal and Steel Community) (data prior to 1960 are often for (W) Germany and France only); LDCs = less-developed countries (usually any country not in any other group); NICs = newly industrializing countries (usually the Asian dragons plus Brazil, Chile and Mexico)

6   This is less inclusive than the UN definition: 'all enterprises which control assets – factories, mines, sales offices, and the like – in two or more countries' (1973: 5).

7   Fordism was indeed paradigmatic and idealized rather than generalized. It never accounted for more than 10 per cent of manufacturing labour, even in the USA (Crook et al. 1992: 172).

8   Although Soros has been mentioned widely in academic circles as an example of a capitalist who can move governments he did so

because he speculated against their currencies and not because he ruled or controlled them. Soros cannot be regarded as a traditional industrial capitalist located in a class struggle with a proletariat. He is simply a market speculator on a grand scale.

3

OPEN SPACES: THE GLOBALIZING ECONOMY

The WTO kills people. Kill the WTO!

People's Global Action

By the end of the third quarter of the twentieth century an internationalized economy had been established: between 1950 and 1975 world trade had increased about tenfold while gross world product had increased only about threefold; world production was dominated by 50 or so trans-national corporations mainly based in the USA, Europe and Japan; national economic policy-making took place in the context of meetings between the political leaders of the economically dominant powers and was regulated through their joint institutions; and some LDCs in Asia and Latin America were moving into the ranks of the NICs and even MDCs.

However, the predominant focus for economic activity and the decisions that attended it remained the nation-state-society. While these developments can arguably be counted as part of the process of globalization, they cannot be argued to have brought the world into a globalized condition. In a completely globalized economy, space would provide no barrier to trade so that, on average, the ratio of external to internal trade of any given territory would correspond to the ratio of gross world product to gross domestic product. Firms would have no specific territorial location or national identity and the locus of decisions and allocation of resources within such firms would be fluid and flexible, determined by market advantage rather than by tradition. Such territorially based political units as nation-states would have severely diminished or negligible economic sovereignty. That sovereignty would be unlikely to be aggregated within global institutions but rather would be dispersed and disaggregated to a myriad of marketized individual decisions. Lastly, distinctions between LDCs and MDCs would disappear, as structures of wealth and poverty become detached from territory. Exploitation and disadvantage would be without political organization.

Clearly none of this has yet come to pass. Trade matters, for example, are still subject to the political actions of mercantilist blocs, and the acronyms TNC and LDC are by no means redundant. However, during the last quarter of the twentieth century a significant shift has occurred in economic affairs that confirms that the planet is entering a final globalization phase. In part this involves the elimination of space from economic transactions, an issue which threads its way through many of the theoretical accounts of the change that is under way. It is with these that we begin.

NEW ECONOMIES OF TIME AND SPACE

By way of a first example, Giddens theorizes globalization in terms of his four dimensions of modernity (capitalism, surveillance, military order and industrialism) (1990: 70–8). First, the world economy is increasingly constituted as a capitalist world-system, in Wallerstein's terms. The world economy is dominated by trans-national corporations that operate independently of political arrangements and indeed can achieve economic domination over them. These corporations set up global linkages and systems of exchange so that the globe is increasingly constituted as a single market for commodities, labour and capital. Globalization is then for Giddens a multi-causal and multi-stranded process that is full of contingency and uncertainty. Globalization appears to be inexorable but because the imperatives that propel the world forward on the juggernaut of modernization are contained within four, relatively insulated arenas, particular outcomes are unpredictable. Globalization: 'is a process of uneven development that fragments as it coordinates' (1990: 175).

This development is driven by certain dynamic processes. In a McLuhanist formulation, the primary process is the *distanciation* or *separation of time from space* (Giddens 1990:17–21, 1991: 16–17). In premodern contexts both time and space were fundamentally linked to a person's immediate location. The temporal rhythms of everyday life were determined by local diurnal and seasonal cycles. Equally, space was confined to what one immediately could perceive and was measured in relation to one's home location, even if one travelled. In the eighteenth century the invention and diffusion of the mechanical clock had the effect of universalizing time, prising it away from particular localities and allowing its social reorganization into a global system of zones. Equally, space, as expressed in global maps, became a universal social dimension whose reality is independent of any individual social location. The liberation of time and space is an entirely modernizing development because it allows the stable organization of human activity across vast temporal and spatial distances – it is a prerequisite for globalization.

Time–space distanciation is also a prerequisite for the modernizing process that Giddens calls *disembedding*: 'the "lifting out" of social relations from local contexts of interaction and their restructuring across time and space' (1990: 21). Giddens identifies two types of disembedding mechanism: symbolic tokens and expert systems. The former include such universal media of exchange as money, which is the only such medium to which Giddens devotes much analysis. Money can transfer value from context to context and can thus make social relations possible across great expanses of time and space. Expert systems consist of repositories of technical knowledge that can be deployed across a wide range of actual contexts, either socially or spatially differentiated. An expert system gives guarantees about what to expect across all of these contexts.

The reason for this extensive treatment of Giddens' theory of modernization is that, *contra* Robertson (see Chapter 7), he views globalization as its direct consequence. Each of the main dynamics of modernization implies universalizing tendencies which render social relations ever more inclusive. They make possible global networks of relationships, e.g. the system of international relations or the modern world-system of capitalism, but they are also, for Giddens, more fundamental in extending the temporal and spatial distance of social relationships. Time–space distanciation and disembedding mean that complex relationships develop between local activities and interaction across distances. Security of employment for an Australian sheep shearer, for example, might be affected by trends in Japanese fashions, the 'Millennium' round of WTO negotiations, the cost of synthetic fibres which is in turn determined by the price of oil which might in turn be determined by American military intervention in the Persian Gulf, and the extent to which the Australian government accepts prevailing global ideologies of marketization and privatization.

Lash and Urry's application of concepts of time–space distanciation and reflexivity (1994), while influenced by Giddens, arrives at a distinctly different conclusion about the nation-state. Their analysis takes off from earlier work about the decomposition of what they call 'organized capitalism' (1987). Under organized (twentieth-century) capitalism flows of finance, commodities, means of production and labour are tightly arranged in time and space by large business corporations and states. Disorganized capitalism involves an expansion of these flows in the international arena and an increase in their velocity. Speed and the reduction of time invade culture, it becomes 'postmodernized', focused on instant consumption and flexibility in the application of labour. However, objects are not the only items that become highly mobile in a postmodern world: individual persons or subjects also become mobile by means of migration, instrumental travel and tourism. And as objects become more mobile they progressively dematerialize and are reproduced as symbols ('signs').

Two sorts of sign are possible: cognitive signs, symbols that represent information; and aesthetic signs, symbols that represent consumption. Their proliferation, in turn, promotes two kinds of reflexivity. First, it promotes a pattern of what they call 'reflexive accumulation', the individualized self-monitoring of production. Second, it promotes an aesthetic or expressive reflexivity in which individuals constantly reference self-presentation in relation to a normatized set of possible meanings given in the increasing flow of symbols – people monitor their own images and deliberately alter them. The contemporary global order, Lash and Urry argue, is therefore: 'a structure of flows, a de-centred set of economies of signs in space'. In so far as these flows of symbols are undermining nation-state-societies we can identify a process of globalization.

Giddens is notable within the current upsurge of interest in general social change for his insistence that current transformations constitute a continuation of rather than a break with modernity. The key figure arguing for a radical shift in the direction of a postmodern epoch is the geographer, David Harvey (1989). His argument draws on concepts of time and space similar to those used by Giddens. Like Giddens, Harvey begins with an analysis of premodern conceptions of space and time (1989: 239–59), although the issue of space is here held to be primary. In the feudal context space was conceived within the terms of a relatively autonomous community that involved a fused social structure of economic, political and religious rights and obligations. Equally, temporal organization was determined by community rhythms. Space outside the community was only dimly perceived, time even more so. These localized conceptions of space and time were only reconstructed during the Renaissance period, as European voyages of discovery established the limits of space. The planet was discovered to be discontinuous with the cosmos and could therefore be mapped and objectivated and, in art, perspectivized. The mechanical watch equally reconstituted time as a linear and universal process.

Here, Harvey's analysis departs from Giddens. Giddens has time *differentiating* from space. More convincingly, Harvey argues that the objectification and universalization of concepts of space and time allowed time to *annihilate* space. He calls this process time–space compression, a development in which time can be reorganized in such a way as to reduce the constraints of space, and vice versa. Time–space compression involves a shortening of time and a 'shrinking' of space – progressively, the time taken to do things reduces and this in turn reduces the experiential distance between different points in space. We might argue that if people in Tokyo can experience the same thing at the same time as others in Helsinki, say, a business transaction or a media event, then they in effect live in the same place; space has been annihilated by time compression. Harvey (1989: 241) illustrates the process in a diagram which shows four maps of the world over time, each smaller than the previous with size determined by the speed of transportation. The world of the 1960s is about one-fiftieth the size of the world of the sixteenth century precisely because jet aircraft can travel at about 50 times the speed of a sailing ship.

The process of time–space compression is not gradual and continuous but occurs in short and intense bursts during which the world changes rapidly and uncertainty increases. In a Marxisant analysis, Harvey attributes these bursts to crises of overaccumulation in the capitalist system. One such burst occurred in the second half of the nineteenth century and is associated with the cultural movement known as modernism (1989: 260–83). The crisis occurred as a result of a collapse of credit in 1847–8 due to overspeculation in railroad construction (i.e. an attempt to control space) and was resolved by the establishment of unified European capital and credit markets organized by a pan-European class of financial capitalists. Time was compressed as capital flowed more rapidly through this reorganized system and this provided the springboard for the further conquest of space by investment in railroads, canals, shipping, pipelines and telegraphy. Towards the turn of the century space shrank further with inventions in ground transport (the bicycle and automobile), aviation (improved balloons, the aircraft) and communication (wireless telegraphy, radio, TV, mass printing, photography, cinema). Europe established colonial hegemony over the planetary surface. Henry Ford reorganized the space of production into an assembly line, thus reducing the time (and cost) of production, and thereby allowing a further reorganization of space in mass production terms. Industrialized mass production and rapid transportation fuelled the first global war of 1914–18 and this in turn allowed a reorganization of territorial space under the Versailles agreements. By 1920 global systems of finance capital and of international relations had been established and mass production had become the predominant pattern of industrial organization.

In about 1970, argues Harvey (1989: 159–72), a further burst of time–space compression began. It began with an over-accumulation crisis in the system of mass production. Fordist mass production had become so successful and efficient that workers began to be laid off, thus effectively reducing demand for products, at the same time as output was expanding rapidly. Consumer markets were saturated to such an extent that governments were unable to correct the imbalances and were also unable to meet the commitments entailed in their welfare programmes. Their only response was to print money and thereby to set in train a wave of uncontrollable inflation. The crisis shook the system to such an extent that it actually began to tackle the rigidities entailed in the mass production process. This involved a dismantling of the corporatist compromises between management and workers and the management of consumer markets to accept standardized products. A regime of 'flexible accumulation' emerged in which flexibly contracted workers flexibly use their multiple skills and computerized machinery to dovetail products to rapidly shifting tastes. As in the nineteenth century, some of the earliest and most profound effects were felt in the structures of financial markets. They have experienced the typical globalizing trends of long-range international links on one hand and decentralization and dispersal on the other. There is no longer a finance capitalist class that runs the system. The system is chaotic, continuous, fluid and of enormous scope. It has also become much more powerful, subordinating the actions of both national governments and trans-national corporations to market constraints. National fiscal policy, for example, is subjected to constant reflexive checks via floating currency exchange rates. The outcome is truly globalizing:

> The formation of a global stock market, of global commodity (even debt) futures markets, of currency and interest rate swaps, together with an accelerated geographical mobility of funds, meant, for the first time, the formation of a single world market for money and credit supply.
>
> The structure of this global financial system is now so complicated that it surpasses most people's understanding. The boundaries between distinctive functions like banking, brokerage, financial services, housing finance, consumer credit, and the like have become increasingly porous at the same time as new markets in commodity, stock, currency, or debt futures, have sprung up, discounting future into present time in baffling ways. Computerization and electronic communications have pressed home the significance of instantaneous international co-ordination of financial flows.
>
> (Harvey 1989: 161)

Flexible accumulation itself represents a particular form of time compression. It was principally directed at reductions in turnover time, the period between the acquisition of components and the delivery of products, by the development of outsourcing, 'just-in-time' inventory systems and small batch production.

Harvey's version of the importance of time and space is preferable to that of Giddens because Giddens' term 'distanciation' leaves the impression that time and space are becoming stretched. This is not, of course, the meaning that he intends, which is rather that social relationships are becoming stretched across great distances. Even this is misleading, however – new communications technologies are ensuring that trans-global social relationships, say between kin or colleagues, are becoming more intense and robust rather than stretched and attenuated. Harvey's notion of compression of social relationships so that spatial distance becomes unimportant fits the proposal of a globalizing trend far more closely. What is unsatisfactory in Harvey is his determination to cling to historical, or in his own terms, historical-geographical materialism as an explanatory logic. The link between flexible accumulation and globalization is tenuous at best, even if it could be confirmed that flexible accumulation has been successfully institutionalized. Harvey leaps from the incipient practices of JIT inventories and contractualization to global capital flows and mass-mediated images. It is surely possible that the advantages which instant electronic communication offers to the latter developments would have been decisive even if there had been no accumulation crisis.

TRADE

We can now assess some of the substantive developments implied by the analyses of Giddens and Harvey. By most reckonings, in the 1970s and 1980s the rate of acceleration in world trade slowed. The USA could no longer count on manufacturing advantages against Japanese and European expansion and turned protectionist. Indeed, the USA met Japanese and European neomercantilism expressed as non-tariff trade barriers and production and export subsidies with similar measures of its own. During the 1980s world trade was organized as a series of competing trade blocs (e.g. ASEAN, EU, NAFTA) that sought to remove trade barriers between members but were protectionist relative to the rest. Consequently the 'Uruguay Round' of GATT negotiations, concluded in 1993, and focusing on agriculture, services and non-tariff barriers, was the most protracted and difficult of all. Nevertheless, trade has continued to grow, albeit at a slower rate.

This neomercantilist pattern might suggest that globalization in the area of trade has slowed. However, it must be remembered that the globalization proposal does not imply an absence of global conflict. In these terms, the formation and expansion of NAFTA, for example, might be seen as a globalizing strategy precisely because it is intentionally directed to accomplishing economic security in an increasingly competitive global arena. It indicates that even as large and powerful an economy as that of the USA can no longer rely on its domestic market for economic security. This is borne out by data on the expansion of world trade. While that expansion slowed somewhat in the 1970s it re-accelerated in the 1980s and 1990s so that between 1950 and 2000 trade had increased twentyfold while world product increased only sixfold. In that year trade accounted for 26 per cent of global output, still well below the criterion for absolute globalism outlined in the introduction to this chapter but well along the road to globalization (*The Economist* 27/11–3/12/99).

In fairness though, it must be admitted that much of this expanded trading activity is intra-trading-bloc activity. The 1980s and 1990s saw the globalization of the idea of the trading bloc as a means to the expansion of national trade. Initially such blocs were established as free trade areas (i.e. having reduced trade barriers between members) and customs unions (i.e. having common regulation of trade with non-members) but they have progressively expanded their activities to include the harmonization of economic policies, labour laws, environmental regulation, competition policy, taxation policy and even towards currency union. These developments are most advanced in the paradigm case of the ever-expanding European Union which even extends its ambit to such non-economic issues as citizenship, eduation, and foreign affairs and defence. The main copycat and competitor blocs, the North American Free Trade Area (Canada, Mexico and the USA), formed in 1989, Mercosur (Argentina, Brazil, Paraguay and Uruguay) formed in 1995, and the Asian Free Trade Area (based on ASEAN) formed in 1992, are much less well developed. The formation of such blocs raises the question of whether trade between, say, the Netherlands and Belgium, which are formally sovereign but are de facto components of a single federated mega-state, ought to be counted as international trade.

Certainly, the formation of such trading blocs has led many to claim that international economic activity is moving into a neomercantilist phase in which it is dominated by three geographically organized centres, Europe, North America and Pacific Asia, whose representative trading blocs exclude the others from internal markets and compete aggressively for third markets. Such a view would not be lost on the WTO. As is noted above, each progressive round of trade liberalization has been more difficult to achieve. This is partly because each progressive round will cut closer to the bone of national interests but it is also because such interests have been pooled within blocs. The Uruguay Round proved to be a complex and difficult negotiation but the Millennium Round which began in 1999 did not even manage to survive into the new millennium at least partly because the Europeans were not prepared to allow significant liberalization on agriculture (with Asian support) or cultural services, and the Americans were unwilling to liberalize competition policy.

The expansion of world trade has not been lost on companies catering to mass consumer markets. The American fast food operator McDonald's, for example, faces huge competition in a home market that is expanding by less than 5 per cent a year and in which it already has 90,000 outlets. The only possibility for increased profitability is globalization. This it is doing – two-thirds of the outlets it opens each year are now outside the USA where only two-thirds of all its restaurants are now located. It is also engaged in transferring its management culture to regional centres, e.g. to Hong Kong for expansion into China (*The Economist* 13/11/93: 69–70).

THE NEW INTERNATIONAL DIVISION OF LABOUR

Three recent globalizing effects have altered the clarity of the traditional division between LDCs and MDCs: first, some LDCs have developed very rapidly to become NICs; second, new forms of multi-national enterprise (MNE) imply a dispersion of production tasks across the globe and part of this process involves the relocation of some types of manufacturing production to LDCs; and, third, some LDCs have managed to cartelize and thus to improve returns from primary production. Taken together they indicate that the global division of labour is now proceeding on a technical as well as a social level, and so we consider each of these developments in turn.

The liberal trade environment provided by the American hegemon after 1950 allowed certain LDCs to take advantage of neomercantilist policies in order to shift their position in the international division of labour. The Asian NICs (Hong Kong, Singapore, South Korea, Taiwan and latterly Malaysia and Thailand) have generally used export-oriented measures while the Latin American NICs (Brazil, Chile and Mexico) prefer import-substitution measures. Specific policy initiatives include tax incentives to investors, duty-free importation of components and capital goods, wage suppression, and depressed currency values (Walters and Blake 1992: 190). So rapidly have the Asian dragons developed that they have overtaken many DMEs (developed market economies) on the usual indicator of wealth, GDP per capita. Moreover, they produce sophisticated consumption items and components, often at the leading edge of technology, as well as traditional labour-intensive items such as clothing.

The consequences of these developments can be viewed in Figure 3.1. The key development is the decline of British industrial dominance from the nineteenth century onwards. The USA expanded its share of world production in the twentieth century

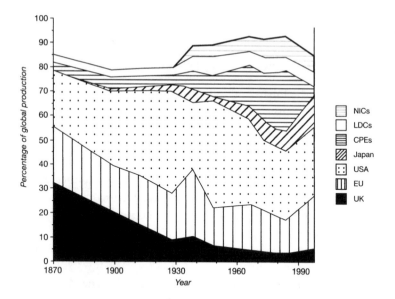

Figure 3.1 Geographical distribution of industrial production, 1870–1998
Sources: Gordon 1988: 32; World Bank

but since about 1960 its share has shrunk to nineteenth-century levels, to 27 per cent by 1994 (Dicken 1998: 28). In all then, the share of industrial production in Europe and the USA has contracted considerably since the Second World War in the face of expansion in Japan, the centrally planned economies (CPEs), the LDCs and the NICs, although the dismantling of the CPEs after 1989 led to a rapid decline in industrial production in those areas. Between 1960 and 1994 the Japanese share of global industrial production grew from 5 to 21 per cent (Dicken 1998: 28). At least some of this shift must be attributable to the establishment of the New International Economic Order (NIEO) in 1974 under the sponsorship of UNCTAD (the UN Commission for Trade and Development) under which industrialized states gave preference to manufactured exports from LDCs.

Dicken's analysis (1998) reveals the impact of these developments on several key global industries, as follows:

- The textile and clothing industries had originally developed during the nineteenth century in Western Europe, especially Britain. Human labour is the main factor of production in these industries and the key source of cost pressure. As a society develops, labour costs tend to rise, and firms tend to relocate to low-labour cost areas. The big shift in production in the last half of the twentieth century has been to Asia, especially to China, which now has about seven and a half million textile and clothing workers, and India, which has about 1.6 million. The industries of North America and Western Europe are tending to focus on high-value-added products such as designer clothing.

- The automobile industry is often treated iconically both in relation to the modernization of production and to its globalization. It is particularly susceptible to globalization because it assembles a large number of diverse components into a finished product. On one hand, the manufacture of these components can be dispersed across space, and on the other, assembly systems are relatively easy to relocate. As in the case of textiles, the industry originated in North America and Western Europe. A key shift in production has been the expansion of the Japanese industry. In 1960 it produced 165,000 vehicles but by 1995 it produced 7.6 million or 21 per cent of the global total. In fact its share in the late 1980s had been much higher, but during the 1990s production began to expand rapidly elsewhere in Asia, especially the Republic of Korea, and in Latin America, especially Brazil. Share of car production declined significantly in the USA and Western Europe. The prospect now lies open for production expansion in such centres as China, India and Eastern Europe.

- By contrast, the electronics industry is a much more recent development. The capital-intensive semiconductor industry is highly concentrated in the USA and Japan. By contrast, the more labour-intensive consumer electronics industry is more globally dispersed. The latter has, along with textiles and automobiles, become characteristic of industrial development in

NICs. Production levels in China, Korea, Hong Kong, Singapore, Malaysia, Brazil and Mexico now outstrip production levels in any European country and most of these are greater than in the USA.

- Although theoretically services are highly mobile because they involve both tokens and expertise, the actual extent of globalization of the service industries is highly variable. Personal services remain highly localized. By contrast such industries as information technology, banking, insurance and advertising are moving into an internationalization phase either by means of subcontracting or by means of alliances and mergers that allow the establishment of branches. Perhaps the only genuinely globalized service industry is that which manages international flows of capital and credit. This industry is becoming increasingly dispersed as the dominance of traditional financial centres declines.

- However, some industries have remained resistant to globalization, especially where they are capital-intensive, monopolistic and resistant to outsourcing. For example, the chemical, oil refining and aircraft manufacturing industries are dominated by the EU and USA. For different reasons the construction industry remains primarily domestic because it is tied to localities. It is dominated by the EU, whose share has increased to over half and the USA whose share has declined to about a quarter; Korea is the only major non-OECD contributor (OECD 1992).

Speaking broadly, there are two possible interpretations for these events (Gordon 1988). The first, promoted by the OECD and similar organizations, argues that production has indeed been undergoing globalization. A fully globalized production system would see in any locality the emergence of a balance of production in terms of capital intensivity and sectoral distribution except those conferred by natural and geographical advantages. Fröbel, Heinrich and Kreye's alternative argument is in favour of a 'new international division of labour' in which: 'commodity production is being split into fragments which can be assigned to whichever part of the world can provide the most profitable combination of capital and labour' (1980: 14). This new international division of labour is technical in character and it therefore can be the vehicle for a genuine globalization of production. The emergence of high levels of structural unemployment that it produces in the DMEs might be the first evidence of equalization in the international system of stratification.

These arguments might arise because they are too concentrated on divisions of labour in the production of material commodities. However, a key feature of the contemporary period is the dematerialization of commodity production (Lash and Urry 1994) especially in the most economically advanced parts of the world that have managed to export the most labour-intensive aspects of goods production. These are experiencing the extreme effects of two processes. The first is postindustrialization (Bell 1976) in which a majority of the labour force is now engaged in the production of commodified services rather than material commodities. One group of workers thus engaged constitutes Bell's new and dominant professional and technical class, another is an urban underclass producing menial services in a context of uncertain employment. The second is the hypercommodification and industrialization of culture, what Lash and Urry call the exchange of signs for finance or what might be called an exchange of money for meanings. There is nothing particularly new about this development except that it has expanded enormously. For the moment, as the section on mass media in Chapter 7 argues, large organizations proliferate cultural products in a dazzling collage of symbolized meanings.

Postindustrialization and the industrialization of culture imply the production of more mobile and easily tradable products. Services are most often exported by mobilizing individuals as in the visit from head office, the international conference, the overseas expert or the 'foreign' student. However, they can also increasingly be exported by electronic transmission, which is especially the case for financial services. Aesthetic commodities can be exported more directly especially in so far as broadcasting technology becomes more widely available. Generally speaking, globalization will increase to the extent that world production is devoted to these non-material commodities precisely because they are so mobile.

ALLIANCES OF CAPITAL

The extent to which the latest phase represents a globalizing shift or acceleration is indicated by Gilpin, who himself resists the notion that recent developments are anything more than neomercantilism:

> These developments foretell the end of the old multinationalism. The day is passed when corporations of the United States and a few other developed countries could operate freely in and even dominate the host economies and when foreign direct investment meant the ownership and control of wholly owned subsidiaries. Instead, a great variety of negotiated arrangements have been put in place: cross-licensing of technology among corporations of different nationalities, joint ventures, orderly marketing agreements, secondary sourcing, off-shore production of components, and crosscutting equity ownership. In the developed countries the General Motors-Toyota alliance is undoubtedly a harbinger of things to come. In the developing world the corporations see the LDCs less as pliable exporters of raw materials and more as expanding local markets and industrial partners or even potential rivals. Thus the relatively simple models of both liberal [modernization] and dependency theorists are becoming outmoded in the final quarter of the century.
>
> (Gilpin 1987: 256)

Data on these new forms of MNE that may or may not require direct investment are scarce but all observers appear to agree that they are developing much more rapidly than traditional TNCs. The reason appears to be that the cost advantages of TNCs have met their limits. Complex companies, producing wide ranges of products in multiple markets are extremely difficult and costly to manage and to service. For this reason traditional TNCs are tending to remain regional rather than global (Emmott 1993). There is an emerging triad of overseas investors each with its own regional specialization based on propinquity and imperial history: American firms tend to invest in Latin America and some parts of Southern Asia; Europeans in Africa, Brazil, Southern Asia and Eastern Europe; and Japanese firms dominate investment in East Asia and Australasia.

The emerging form of MNE is therefore not a TNC but an 'alliance', an arrangement between firms that may involve equity swaps, technology transfers, production licensing, the division of component manufacture and assembly, market sharing or 're-badging'.[1] Because there is no agency that collects statistics on alliances their precise extent is impossible to assess, but they are as Emmott (1993: 15) suggests a 'hot topic' in the business schools and the popular business literature. They might be expected in the transport industry. Forming a 'global alliance' appears to be the survival strategy for any national airline, e.g. Star (All Nippon-Ansett Australia-Air New Zealand-Air Canada-Lufthansa-Singapore-Thai-United-Varig) and Oneworld (American-British-Canadian-AirLiberte/DeutscheBA/TAT-Finnair-Iberia-Qantas), or telecommunications firm, e.g. Worldsource (AT&T-Kokusai Denshin Denwa-Singapore Telecom), BT-MCI, Deutsche Bundespost Telekom-France Télécom but they also occur in unexpected quarters. IBM, for example, once manufactured mainframe computers alone, but its famous PC was developed in conjunction with Microsoft, Intel and Lotus and it holds a significant cross-holding in Apple, with which it is co-operating to develop a common software architecture (Emmott 1993: 15). Indeed, alliances tend to be common in smaller postindustrial or postmodernized firms at the leading edge of scientific application including information technology, new materials technology and biotechnology. In 1990, around 40 per cent of such alliances were in information technology (including telecommunications), about 20 per cent in biotechnology and a further 10 per cent in new materials technology (Dicken 1998: 229). This may be because innovation in these areas occurs on such a broad front that firms must co-operate or be left behind. International inter-firm agreements on research co-operation among semiconductor firms, for example, grew from 43 in 1983 to over a hundred in 1989 (OECD 1992: 14).

Although these trans-national *keiretsu* might conceivably be hailed as the future globalized shape of world business organization, a truly globalized system might look quite different. We consider in an earlier section the liberalization of world trade. Emmott (1993: 8) argues that in a completely liberalized trade environment and where the marginal costs of transportation are low MNEs would cease to exist. This is because firms would obtain the best cost advantage by producing in one place so as to maximize economies of scale and licensing offshore production where such economies failed to offset transportation costs. In a truly globalized economic context then, the MNE would disappear in favour of local producers marketing globally.

CULTURAL ECONOMIES

Traditionally there have been wide variations in national organizational cultures, the set of norms and values under which firms operate. Under the current acceleration of globalization cultural differences are tending to be subsumed within a single idealization of appropriate organizational behaviour. This paradigm incorporates many of the ideas found in preceding versions but is constructed in terms of a single, newly recognised imperative – that an organization must have the capacity to make a flexible response to uncertain market conditions caused by commodity saturation. Such an organization might be described as postmodern because it is both internally and externally hyper- or dedifferentiated.[2] Internally management and workers shade into each other in an emerging professionalized work role; externally, organizations that can adapt rapidly to changing markets will have a 'shapelessness' and individuality that makes them appear structurally similar.

There are two main alternative explanations for the shift, what might be called the postmodernization and the globalization explanations. The first, best represented in Harvey (1989), is Marxisant in its orientation suggesting that capitalism moves in boom and bust cycles based on a pattern of capital investment–labour economies–unemployment–reduced demand–push for efficiency–further investment, etc. These cycles build towards periodic points of 'overaccumulation' in which large amounts of capital and labour sit unused. This is manifested in a crisis of unemployment, market gluts, spare industrial capacity and unsold inventories (1989: 180–1) that force a radical restructuring of capitalist accumulation. The crisis of the Great Depression of the 1930s opened a generalized transition to Fordism and Keynesianism. A similar crisis also occurred in about 1973 when Fordist productivity so outstripped demand that a new paradigm had to be sought that would reduce market dependency.

The globalization explanation for the shift (e.g. Marceau 1992) offers a more prosaic alternative – the explanatory factor is the impressive global success of Japanese industry in challenging American and European domination. This was in part accomplished by the effectiveness of the Japanese state in co-ordinating industrial strategy and of the new information and material technologies that were applied to production. However, the critical factor in Japanese industrial success is a novel combination of managerial practices. These were globalized partly by the activities of Japanese MNEs which transplanted them into branch operations outside Japan with considerable success. Local competitors have deliberately sought to match the efficiency advantages of Japanese organizational practices.[3] More importantly there has been a process of global cultural transmission in which the Japanese version of the best way has been carried around the world as a system of ideas. This transmission occurs in three arenas: first, in the popular mass media Japanese production systems are represented as a highly generalized but somewhat ambivalent ideal, discussed in terms of both fear and admiration; second, in universities, business school academics and organization theorists conduct comparative research on the Japanese advantage and these results are both published and incorporated into organizational design courses for potential managers; and third they are written up as easily digestible popular books that can be peddled to managers as manuals for organizational transformation.

We can now consider the elements of the Japanized organizational paradigm that specifies flexible specialization and accumulation, sometimes known as Toyotism (Dohse, Jürgens and Malsch 1985).[4] The general orientation of the paradigm is that the firm must become organization-oriented rather than being accountancy-oriented (Dore 1989), focusing on asset building and market share rather than on immediately calculated issues of cost and revenue. These elements are as follows:

1 *Strategic management*: strategic management practices aim to forecast and, if possible, to control the future relationship between the organization and its supplier and customer markets. A typical example is the way in which prices are set low early in the production life of an item in order to secure a market share of sufficient scale in the future to maximize not merely bottom-line profitability but overall gross profits (Swyngedouw 1987: 491–3). Another example is the practice of paying prices for raw materials at above current market defined levels in order to secure long-term supply contracts.

2 *Just-in-time (JIT)*: the basic principle of JIT is to minimize inventory at each stage of the production process since surplus inventory represents unrealized value. The production process is divided into a number of stages each organized as a team of workers. Each stage uses components on a 'go and get' basis and produces its own components on the basis of demand from the succeeding assembly stage (Swyngedouw 1987: 494–6; Wilkinson, Morris and Oliver 1992). This may be compared with the Fordist 'just in case' approach in which parts and

finished products are stockpiled. An important consequence is that control over workers must be established by alternative means than those given in the flow of an assembly line, including long-term incentives to continuous worker loyalty in terms of job security, promotion possibilities and family welfare. JIT implies multiskilling, so that surplus labour time can be employed, and localized decision-making about parts requirements and production.

3 *Total Quality Management*: JIT implies that supplies of components both from outside and inside the firm must be reliable in quantity and high in quality. The Japanese quality control system depends on all workers being involved in the maintenance of production standards. Workers meet in quality control circles (QCC) where they are provided with charts and diagrams which identify systematic, as opposed to unique sources of quality failure. QCCs diffused rapidly throughout Japanese industry from the 1960s and are now spreading with similar rapidity in Europe and North America.[5]

4 *Teamwork*: the imperatives of JIT and QCCs encouraged Japanese businesses to adopt the idea of autonomous work groups developed by the British Tavistock Institute in the 1950s and 1960s. Teamwork experiments were also common throughout Europe during the 1960s and 1970s, especially in Scandinavia. Teamwork involves the collectivizing and sharing of tasks for a small group of workers at a similar stage of the production process. In some instances tasks are mixed so that distinctions between skilled and unskilled work are broken down, in others workers maintain their individual skills but work together.

5 *Managerial decentralization*: this involves the displacement of inflexible, centrally controlled, multi-layered hierarchies in favour of a shapeless and flowing matrix of shifting and flexible exchanges, a federation of organizational styles and practices each surviving on their capacity to respond to demand. The extreme form of such a structure occurs where flexibility is externalized, that is where the production of components,

workers' skills and other assets are subcontracted outside of the organization.[6] The contracting organization typically uses advanced technology, is large in the scale of its production, and employs highly paid, multi-skilled, highly committed workers while subcontractors are smaller in scale and employ low-paid, frequently marginal labour.[7] The constellation of subcontracted firms cushions the core firm against market shock especially where this requires labour redundancy.

6   *A numerically flexible labour force*: the chief object of numerical flexibility is the possibility of laying off labour in market downturns or periods of lack of market success and of taking it back on when demand rises. The mechanisms include part-time and temporary work, outworking and homeworking, as well as subcontracting.

7   *Functionally flexible workers*: this involves three elements: task integration which involves a widening of job classifications, task rotation and, more importantly, the involvement of manual workers in some policy implementation and concep-tualizing processes; multi-skilling which involves the development of broad-based skills including both quality control and maintenance functions as well as direct operation of manufacturing equipment; localized responsibility in which middle-management functions are reappropriated by workers (Mathews 1989: 108–9).

The Japanization of organizational practices has had the important effect of culturalizing economic life. Under a liberal, nineteenth-century laissez-faire regime workers in organizations were regarded simply as motivated by the calculation of individual costs and benefits. As they began really to do their calculations and to realize the power provided by the possibility of the withdrawal of their labour, firms engaged in Fordist practices of maximum control by bureaucratic and technological means. The Japanese discovery is that this can only provide an organiza-tion with minimal performance in relation to rules. In order to develop a proactive commitment by workers one needs to develop a totalizing cultural environment that gives them a sense of belonging to a primary social group. This involves not only the security and material benefits of 'lifetime employment' but a reflexive attempt to reconstitute the firm as a quasi-familial community. Part of this discovery, as is indicated above, is that the coherence of such a community depends on restricting it only to those whose skills are absolutely necessary to the organization.

The culturalization of economic life exhibits a triple effectivity in relation to globalization. First, it is a reflexive process in which employers deliberately gaze on their firms with the intention of providing them with a particular culture. They pay attention to their employees seeking to involve them in a sense of shared belonging; they develop corporate symbols and rituals that heighten emotional engagement; they seek to develop the skills and abilities of their workers through training; they try to communicate directly with employees as much as is possible rather than having their communications mediated through a hierarchy (Thompson and McHugh 1990: 228–31). In a reifying formulation that might look a little odd to a sociologist, firms are classified as having 'strong' or 'weak' organizational cultures.[8] In seeking to develop strong cultures firms become receptive to ideas and seek them out. Global flows of business ideas have therefore increased very rapidly. This provides the second effect, which is that the very act of looking outside the company and outside the nation for ideas encourages a consciousness of global events and consequences. When organization was determined by technology managers could believe that their firms were shaped by local events – they no longer can. The third globalizing effect is that Fordism in its purest form was restricted to particular types of organization: business firms employing technologically sophisticated, large-scale capital equipment. Only here could the formula of technological control of workers plus high wages succeed. The new organizational paradigm can be operated in any enterprise and indeed can be exported beyond the business sector to other types of organization. Now not only firms but government agencies, churches, schools, hospitals, social clubs and, *horribile dictu*, universities all can exhibit the full panoply of symbolic trappings from the new cultural paradigm – mission statements, strategic plans, total quality management, multi-skilling and staff development. This constitutes globalization not only in its recent meaning of planetary inclusion but also in its older one of totalization.

Although it is common practice to focus on such material issues as trade, FDI and the operations of TNCs as prime movers in globalization, the key globalizing flows are less material and more cultural in character. The material flows merely render the global economy internationalized, that is, they elaborate connections between territories that remain bordered, separate and sovereign. Globalization implies the dedifferentiation of the planet, rendering irrelevant 'national' differences in economic practices so that borders and sovereignty will themselves become irrelevant and will expire. The key flows that produce this outcome are marketization and reflexive phenomenologies of globalization.

In the 1960s it was possible to speak of three types of economy: developed market economies dominated by monopolistic mass production firms serving protected home markets and often also operating as trans-national corporations; centrally planned economies producing only for intensively regulated domestic markets; and less-developed economies composed of subsistence agriculture, narrowly based primary production for global markets and protected infant industries. Each of these operated under a supporting ideology focused respectively on nationally sponsored corporatism, socialist welfare and economic sovereignty. There is now widespread acceptance that none of these practices will succeed in enriching populations. Rather, an ideology of marketization implies that the DMEs can only enrich their populations by consistently moving out of labour-intensive and into capital-intensive enterprises and that this can only be achieved by allowing markets to offer individual reward incentives. In the CPEs there is widespread acceptance that regulation and planning cannot deliver outcomes because economic behaviours are too complex to be subjected to regulation. LDCs, in turn, have come to rely on the principle of comparative advantage, the idea that they can compete within global markets in those economic activities in which the efficiency gap between themselves and others is at its lowest. The ideology of market-ization suggests that populations will be productive and enriched to the extent that political intervention is reduced and economic behaviours are liberated.

Ever since Levitt advised that 'The globalization of markets is at hand' (1983: 92) marketization has been linked ideologically to globalization. Indeed, many academic observers would argue that 'globalization' must principally be understood as an ideology that serves to reduce both the regulation of capitalism and the costs of government (see e.g. Mittelman 1996; Scott 1997) and thus advantages capital. Whether ideological or not, globalization has become a reflexive phenomenon, that is, managers now inten-tionally seek to reconstruct themselves and their organizations in globalized forms. In part this is the consequence of business-to-business advertising that often stresses the importance of global consciousness and it is in part a reflection of the preachings of business schools but it is also a response to feelings of relative powerlessness in the face of globalized events that appear to be beyond one's control. Whatever the cause, the effect is clear, that globalization is being accelerated by intentionality and:

> The process of globalization easily becomes a self-fulfilling prophecy, both a cause and effect of change. Globalization requires businesses to become more cosmopolitan, and the cosmopolitans who rise to leadership in these companies promote further globalization.
>
> (Kanter 1995: 60)

TIMELESS FINANCIAL MARKETS

In the preceding chapter we noted that the Bretton Woods system of international financial management hit a crisis in the mid-1970s because it had become awash in devaluing American currency. The key event that signalled the collapse of the Bretton Woods system was the withdrawal of the US dollar from the gold standard because the relationship to gold could no longer be maintained in the face of dollar inflation. Already the IMF had supplemented gold by so-called special drawing rights (SDRs) i.e. rights to borrow from the IMF as necessary, as the fiduciary support for the dollar and other currencies. Progressively, SDRs have replaced gold, sterling and the US dollar as the global standard of accounting and are constituted as a weighted mix of four currencies (US$, £Stg, €, ¥).

However, the SDR has not become global currency. Rather, moves towards a global currency are taking place by means of progressive aggregation at the level of trading blocs. The tendency is for harder currencies to replace softer and more unreliable ones. The American dollar is the closest to a global currency. In many parts of the world a dollar economy operates in parallel with the local currency economy especially, for example, in Russia, India, China and Latin America. The US dollar has become the official currency in Panama and Ecuador, and there is speculation at government level about extending its reach to Canada and Mexico, which are members of NAFTA, and Argentina, which is not. A second major development is, of course, the introduction of the common European currency, the euro, which has now displaced the local currencies in most of the countries of the EU and is based on the strength of the Deutschmark. It is possible to conceive of successive aggregations of this sort that lead to a unified global currency. However, their greater significance lies in the confirmation that this is a further set of tokens that is disembedding from local and national contexts and thus able to flow freely across the planet.

Returning to the issue of the international financial system, the normal expectation, given the collapse of Bretton Woods, would be a shift of the financial centre, perhaps to Frankfurt or Tokyo, but this did not happen. Rather, a genuine shift has occurred to what Germain calls 'decentralized globalization' where 'its central institutional nexus of credit networks has no definitive hub' (1997: 103). This 'fourth era' has emerged from the coincidence between the decline of New York, the development of instantaneous and computerized telecommunications, and the privatization of financial institutions.

The global financial market has developed in three directions. First, the elimination of space has accomplished the conquest of time. Because the opening times in particular localities overlap, 24-hour trading by electronic access has been made possible, and arbitrage much more technical and frantic. This continuous trading extends to dealing in currency, stocks, securities, futures and commodities. Second, financial markets have dedifferentiated so that banks have become stockdealers, building societies and credit unions have become banks, and so on. The relevance of this postmodernizing effect to the present argument is that the entire system has become more difficult to control. States are placed at the mercy of financial markets – the collapse of the European monetary system in 1992 was the consequence of persistent market attacks on its weaker elements, for example. All the power of the Bundesbank could not save it. Third, banks have become the main credit providers at the international level and these are clearly far less territorially linked than the state credit providers that they replaced.

Under decentralized globalization, the only way in which governments can affect financial markets is by intervening in them rather than regulating them or by collectively underwriting currencies. They often attempt to do this on a concerted basis, with occasional success, as in 1985 when the seven largest economies persuaded the markets to devalue the dollar by selling tranches of their holdings, but with frequent failure, as in 1987 when they bought 90 billion dollars but failed to protect the currency's value. The political leaders of the seven largest economies ('G7') and their central bankers do meet on a regular basis with a view to aligning their domestic economic policies and smoothing the effects of trade imbalances. In general this usually means putting pressure on Germany and Japan to reduce trade surpluses, and this is the current extent of global financial management.

The globalization of financial markets affects individuals as well as states. Its effect in linking distant localities is well captured in the following description:

> Banking is rapidly becoming indifferent to the constraints of time, place and currency . . . an English buyer can get a Japanese mortgage, an American can tap his New York bank account through a cash machine in Hong Kong and a Japanese investor can buy shares in a London-based Scandinavian bank whose stock is denominated in sterling, dollars, Deutschmarks and Swiss francs.
>
> (*Financial Times* 8/5/78, cited in Harvey 1989: 161)

Their effect in globalizing culture and consciousness must therefore be equally profound.

A GLOBALIZED ECONOMY?

A sequence of events that occurred in the late 1990s can illustrate just how globalized the international economy had become. As international credit provision became privatized and more fluid it sought opportunities. A major opportunity appeared in the DMEs, especially in South-East Asia, and a flood of money, largely short-term credit, chased those opportunities. In 1996 alone US$93 billion flowed into Indonesia, Malaysia, the Philippines, South Korea and Thailand. However, because these were DMEs, domestic supervision of credit in the form of modern banking and legal institutions had not yet taken hold. For example, in 1997, Thailand's ninth-largest bank collapsed because nearly half its assets were in the form of bad loans, many to associates of the bank's CEO. Meanwhile in 1995, the G7 decided to push up the value of the US dollar against the yen, in order to resolve balance of payments difficulties between the two countries. This dragged up South-East Asian currencies tied to the dollar, and priced them out of export markets.

The first domino to fall in this, the so-called 'Asian meltdown', was Thailand. Sales shrank, businesses failed, loans went bad, banks failed, short-term capital fled the country, the stockmarket fell. In July, under speculative pressure, Thailand floated the baht, at which point it fell dramatically, as did other currencies in the region. In October 1997 the IMF lent US$5 billion to bail out the Indonesian government. Austerity measures and bank closures led to rioting, leading to the downfall of the authoritarian regime of General Suharto. In November the crisis hit Korea and the country was on the brink of complete collapse. The IMF lent Korea US$57 billion, the largest loan in its history.

As Asian industries closed, demand for commodities dropped and commodity prices fell with them. DME commodity producers such as Australia and Canada weathered the storm by tolerating huge drops in exchange rates and by switching export markets. Such strategies were unavailable to LDCs and NICs. So in June 1998, the Russian rouble came under extreme pressure. It was devalued in August and stockmarkets around the world plunged. In January 1999 Brazil devalued the real by 35 per cent, setting up further panic and further IMF bailouts.

The Asian meltdown illustrates several features of the globalized economy under discussion here. First, it shows that globalization is a relatively complete phenomenon in that it connects the economies of the entire planet. The Great Depression of the 1930s illustrated interconnectedness, but it was more or less restricted in its impact to North America and Western Europe. Second, it demonstrates the connection of the global to the local – it led to street-level rioting in Asian cities, starvation and lesser hardships in rural areas, and employment losses in Australia and Canada. Third, it illustrates the impact of fluid movements of credit and capital that compressed time into an intensive flash of a crisis. Fourth, it confirmed that globalization was by no means a finished process – the crisis was 'solved' by IMF loans and regulations, bankrolled by the US government, with the IMF working closely with the US Treasury. The impact of the US hegemon cannot be overstated.

We are now in a position, as in each of these substantive chapters, to take stock of the process of globalization in each of the dimensions we have isolated. In a globalized economy, the factors of production are so fluid and mobile that they are detached from territory and circulate through space as if it is boundless. Under this scenario, land, that most territorialized and spatially fixed factor of production, reduces in its significance to an infinitesimal level. The declining proportion of economic effort devoted to agriculture, even in LDCs, and indeed to manufacturing industry, indicates that the planetary economy is indeed moving in this direction. However, this development must not be overstated. Even in MDCs, where agricultural production is most industrialized, and notwithstanding the introduction of hydroponics, agricultural capacity remains connected to fertile acreage. Equally, the fluidity of labour can be overstated. While it is true that economic migrants will risk razor wire and trigger-happy border guards, will travel thousands of kilometres in rust-buckets, risking storm, piracy and incarceration, and will commit their life savings to escape underpaid drudgery, it is also true that huge populations remain in poverty in some parts of the world while serious labour shortages are experienced in others. Territory still has a hold on labour.

The flow of raw and processed materials, that is trade and production, occupies an intermediate position. While the prices for many products are set in such globalized markets as the Chicago commodities exchange or the London metals exchange, most prices are determined by market conditions and state interventions in national markets. Trade is still largely an inter-national or at least an inter-trading-bloc issue, as the WTO Millennium Round development indicates. The price (and thus the flow) of coal is determined largely by negotiations between Japanese steel producers and nationally based coalminers in the Southern hemisphere, the price of wheat by American export subsidies and European price supports, and the price of oil by the level of production in Saudi Arabia and the Gulf states. These and similar trade flows are determined by nationally based decisions and policies but some others are not. Trade in consumer products, especially those with highly culturalized or symbolic significance, is much less susceptible to nationally based decisions. For example, the price and supply of Atsuro Tayama frocks or Manchester United soccer shirts is influenced mainly by the taste and choice of millions of individual consumers operating independently of national structures and responding to global mediations of their desirability. An even stronger case could be made for those most dematerialized of commodities, information and mass-mediated images.

However, globalization is most advanced in flows of the factors of production traditionally identified as 'capital' and 'entre-preneurship'. Under contemporary conditions the latter might easily be respecified as 'managerial knowledge'. Financial markets have almost become the paradigmatic example of economic globalization. And as one of the preceding elements of this chapter argues, managerial expertise is not only globalizing but is reflexively globalizing.

The critical differentiating factor here then appears to be mediation. Consumer goods markets, mass media and informatic markets, financial markets and ideological arenas are highly 'tokenized', that is the exchanges within them are symbolically mediated. At the risk of subscribing to the hacker reification, 'information wants to be free', symbolic goods cannot be con-strained within geographical and temporal boundaries in the way that material items can. Land, labour and some primary com-modities, on the other hand, remain resolutely material and largely controllable and so these markets remain subject to the organized regulation of individual preferences.

This argument can lead us back to an element of the paradig-matic proposal of this book. As is indicated in the introduction, speaking roughly, the theorem that underlies it is that, material relationships localize, power relationships internationalize, and symbolic relationships globalize. As a given sector of social life moves from a predominance of material through power through symbolic relationships the tendency will be towards globaliza-tion. In each of the dimensions of economic life we have inspected we can identify an approximate periodization of modern society that corresponds with this theorem. Between about 1600 and 1870 we find a period of 'capitalist economy', fading absolutist empires and emerging but weak nation-states. Trans-geographical links are established by entrepreneurial traders and merchants. Between about 1870 and 1970 we find a 'political economy', a system of inter-national or more precisely inter-organizational economic relations. The power of a state depends on the strength of its economy, on the capacity of its national enterprises to trade and invest and become multinational. States collaborate with MNEs to enhance their economies in the international system by steering flows of labour, trade and investment. Emergent hegemons can manage the international financial system through nominally international organizations.

With all the caveats expressed in the preceding paragraphs, it is never the less clear that the inhabitants of the planet now appear to be entering a third phase, a phase of 'cultural economy'. Here symbolicized markets are moving beyond the capacity of states to manage them and units of economic production are beginning to downscale to a more individual and humanized scale. The economy is becoming so subordinate to individual taste and choice that it is becoming reflexively marketized and, because tokenized systems will not succumb to physical boundaries, reflexively globalized. The leading sectors in this process are those whose commodities are themselves symbols, the mass media and entertainment industries and the postindustrialized service industries (Lash and Urry 1994). The economy can thus begin to turn on and penetrate the remaining defences of economic and political geography. It also follows that in a culturalized global economy, world class is displaced by a world status system based on consumption, lifestyle and value-commitment.

NOTES

1   Entering an agreement in which the allied firms sell each other's products under their own brand name. Possibly the best-known example is the re-badging of Honda cars produced in Britain as 'Rovers'.

2   Crook, Pakulski and Waters (1992) argue that hyperdifferentiation implies dedifferentiation.

3   The advantages and the branch-plant effect are most apparent in the motor vehicle industry. For example, in 1982 Toyota could produce 56 cars per employee per year whereas Ford could produce only 12. During the 1980s Toyota established major manufacturing capacity in Australia, Canada, Britain and the USA, often in alliance with GM (Wilkinson, Morris and Oliver 1992).

4   This section relies on Crook, Pakulski and Waters 1992: 178–92.

5   There is some variation in opinion about the extent of diffusion of QCCs. Swyngedouw (1987: 493) says that currently there are 100,000 operational in Japan, that is, in 71 per cent of all firms and in 91 per cent of firms with more than 10,000 workers. Mathews (1989: 81) says that there are about a million QCCs in Japan and that 100,000 had been formed in South-East Asia during the previous ten years. Although the growth of QCCs is doubtless exponential it is unlikely to have increased tenfold in two years, even in Japan.

6   54 per cent of Japanese firms with less than 300 employees are sub-contractors. 25 per cent of all such firms subcontract to only one core firm (Swyngedouw 1987: 496).

7   Wages of workers in Japanese firms with less than 100 employees average 62 per cent of those in firms with more than 500 employees, while those in firms with 100–500 employees average 81 per cent of the wages of those in large firms (Swyngedouw 1987: 497).

8   In the new culturalist language a Fordist organization has 'weak' culture because it relies for control on technology rather than commitment. Sociologically however Fordism was at least as effective in cultural terms as the new paradigm.

4

STATES OF FLUX:
INTERNATIONAL POLITICS

Globalization is what we in the Third World have for several centuries called colonization.

Martin Khor

One of the great paradoxes that any analysis of globalization must unravel is that the institutionalization of the nation-state is an integral and necessary element in its development. After all, the nation-state might be thought to be the chief victim of globalization, the source of territorial integrity, juridical sovereignty, cultural peculiarity, economic self-sufficiency and military aggrandisement and self-defence. Indeed, many would argue that the persistence of the state with its formal sovereign rights, and the clamour of local nationalities for states of their own is compelling evidence that claims about the march of globalization are, at best, overstated and, at worst, ideological.

This chapter confronts the paradox directly. Its underpinning arguments are as follows. First, globalization implies that social structure cannot be predicted on the basis of planetary geographical location. For this to be true, either each territory must have a similar structure or government, or governmental structures must be entirely randomized in their distribution. In fact, the nation-state has become a globalized structure, common to all parts of the globe. Indeed, as will be argued below, not only is that macro-political structure becoming common but so also is the type of regime that operates within it. Second, globalization implies relationships across great distances of space. Such relationships are only possible where there is a system of collective actors that can engage in them. Nation-states are the necessary actors for the global networks of relationships that we call 'international relations'. Third, the argument advanced in Chapter 2 about the development of globalization suggests that this development is phasic. The second phase, that of 'internationalization', the linking of global territories by means of colonization, trade, warfare and diplomacy is only possible where power is concentrated in institutions that specialize in its application. Nation-states are the institutions that accomplish this. Fourth, an absolutely globalized political system would encompass a system of global governance. Such a system might be possible on the basis of two developments – either a single hegemonic power might impose governance on the rest of the planet by force, by economic might or by cultural invasion, or the various powers on the planet might pool their sovereignty on a consensual basis. In either case the development of nation-states, or similar institutions, is a prerequisite.

This chapter examines the development of the nation-state and its rise to global predominance during the middle third of the twentieth century. That predominance had three expressions: first, it became the normal political institution and the primary point of political reference; second, the state was, in almost all circumstances, the predominant institution within the national society, actively governing and regulating civil society and culture; and third, global issues came under the thrall of superpower states whose interactions prescribed possibilities and risks for most of the inhabitants of the planet.

DEVELOPMENT OF THE NATION-STATE

States preceded nation-states. However, the feudal state was simply a federation of aristocratic landholdings loosely integrated by idealized service relationships between baronial vassals and a monarch and legitimated by reference to a universal religion. In practice seigneurial power predominated. In Europe certainly and in Japan possibly this fragile coalition was disturbed by religious differentiation and intra-aristocratic civil war in the seventeenth century. As Kossalleck (1988) points out, the result was a strengthening and extension of the central power of the monarch; in a word, the development of an absolutist state which could resolve conflicts by centralized domination. In an absolutist state the monarch is the sole source of secular law and governs with the aid of a bureaucracy and an army which is permanent, professional and dependent on the monarch (Mann 1986: 476). The monarch's power is thus rendered independent of religious or aristocratic control and was applied in an expedient and rationalized manner.

However, not all major European states followed the same absolutist path. The model for future development lay on the Western edge of Europe in England and Holland, particularly, which stand apart from the rest. These were distinctively constitutional states where monarchical power was constrained by law. Kossaleck attributes this distinctiveness to rapid economic differentiation which allowed a fast-emerging bourgeoisie to insitutionalize such limitations. Equally, for Anderson, England under the Tudors and early Stuarts was among the earliest absolutist states, but its development was 'cut off by a bourgeois revolution' in the mid-seventeenth century (1979: 142). Mann (1986: 478–9) also gives credence to the notion of an emerging capitalist class, but attaches great significance to the fact that England and Holland's military power was primarily naval and thus could not be used to establish state power internally. However, whatever the differences between state systems their relationship to the globalization process is similar – that is, state practices were primarily military rather than economic in character. The state did not own property, it extracted its revenues on a fiscal basis and it was the co-ordinator of class action for military purposes. The continuation of any state therefore depended on the monpolization of control of a particular territory in which it could raise both armies and taxes.

The development of an international system of states is often attributed to the Treaty of Westphalia, signed in 1713. That treaty brought an end to what is known as the the Thirty Years War, in which the Catholic empire of Austria-Hungary, a sprawling conglomeration of nationalities running from Holland to Spain to Bosnia, sought to impose Catholicism on the reformed Protestant areas of Northern and Western Europe. Westphalia established three principles: *rex est imperator in regno suo* (the king is emperor in his own realm), which meant that the state was not subject to external authority; *cujus regio, ejus religio* (the ruler determines religion), which meant that the state had absolute internal sovereignty; and that there should be a balance of power between states with no hegemon (Jackson 1997: 41). Essentially, Westphalia enshrined territorial sovereignty, established the importance of borders and institutionalized national citizenship. It also ensured that if sovereignty and the balance of power were to be maintained, states would need actively to engage other states in order to resolve mutual problems. It opened the possibility, then, for diplomacy to displace war as the main form of international action.

By the early nineteenth century the independent states of Europe had disposed of hegemonic threats from Austria-Hungary and Napoleonic France, and the nation-state had been transplanted to North America. For much of the nineteenth century Europe did indeed focus on diplomacy at the expense of war. In this international context, the emergence of the modern industrial state involved a set of related processes: the unification and centralization of power centres which overcame the resistance of formerly independent corporate bodies; the autonomization of state power, so that it rested on an internal principle of sovereignty rather than being derived from tradition or from 'external' sources; a broadening of the political community and popular support, achieved by an extension of suffrage and constitutional reform; the development of state-national symbols (flags, anthems, a national language, etc.) which increased the popular legitimacy of the state; and the activization of the state, so that the domain of its legitimate intervention extended beyond military and law and order functions, expecially to fiscal reform. These processes coincided with the rise of an industrial bourgeoisie which vigorously advocated principles of laissez-faire yet also promoted the development of the sovereign, authoritative state. The progressive constitutionalization of absolutist states became the instrument by which this capitalist class achieved its own technical and economic goals, not least by using the state to establish external colonies and thus to affect international competition by seeking to control global flows of resources. The modern industrial state became the vehicle for the export of the state idea beyond its European origins and for establishing the global flows of trade discussed in Chapter 3.

TRANS-NATIONAL CONNECTIONS

If globalization is a reality, it presents the discipline of political science with a considerable problem.[1] The chief focus of political science analysis is the nation-state, and if globalization genuinely takes effect, the nation-state will be its chief victim. The main vehicle for the political analysis of global trends is the subdiscipline of International Relations (IR).[2] IR, with its focus on diplomacy, imperialism and war has always taken a global view of politics. The traditional IR view of these processes takes the form of what we might, after Burton (1973: 28–32), call the 'snooker-ball model'.[3] Here each state is its own little globe and these balls are of various weights and colours. As they change through time – or move across the surface of the table – they interact with each other. Each ball has some 'autonomy' exerted upon it by the player (equivalent to the agency of its own government) but as it moves its autonomy is limited by the positions and actions of the other balls (other states). In an extension of this model, the white ball might be a superpower.

IR has gone through many changes as it has adapted to transformations in the shape of international politics. However, the most recent shift, the one that coincides with the recent acceleration of globalization, is the most significant. It is beginning to encompass relations between economies and cultures that bypass primarily political agencies. In so doing it is reconstructing itself as a proto-theory of globalization. It must be described only as a proto-theory because all of its instances are dualistic. They retain a commitment to the continuing saliency of relations between states but accept that economic and cultural integrations develop alongside them.

Perhaps the first signal that International Relations needed to change was given by Burton (1973) himself. In what is essentially an undergraduate textbook Burton enjoins his readers to study not international relations but world society, a layering of interstate relations with networks or systems relationships between individuals and collectivities that transcend or subvert state boundaries. In an ultimate extension of Burton's metaphors, this argument might lead us to conceive of the snooker table as being overlain by a cobweb of relatively fragile connections between the balls – when the balls move gently (as in diplomacy) they are guided by the strands, when they move violently (as in war) they disrupt them. The networks that Burton identifies are patterns based on such factors as trade, language, religious identification, ethnicity, ideology, strategic alliance, communications links, and legal and communications conventions. In a formulation that clearly prefigures true globalization theory he argues that we should replace a simplistic geographical notion of distance by one based on what he calls 'effective distance' (1973: 47). Here the more dense the systemic linkages between locations, effectively the closer they are. If we were to take Burton's argument to its extreme we would indeed have a genuine globalization theory – if the entire world is linked together by networks that are as dense as the ones which are available in local contexts then locality and geography will disappear altogether, the world will genuinely be one place and the nation-state will be redundant. However, for Burton, as for many other political scientists, this position remains much too radical because it denies the saliency of the state as a prime organizing priniciple of social life. He wants to insist that the world is dualistic, integrated at the substate level but still organized as segmented nation-states.

Burton is not alone – dualism remains the bottom line for political science and IR versions of globalization. Bull (1977), for example, insists on the continuing saliency of what he calls the states-system, a pattern of international relations in which there is a plurality of interacting sovereign states that accept a common set of rules and institutions. Bull identifies the clearest threat to the states-system that he values so highly as the emergence of what he calls a 'new mediævalism', a system of overlapping or segmented authority systems that undermines the sovereignty of states. He analyses this threat as four components that are generally consistent with the argument being offered in this book. They are:

- a tendency for states to amalgamate on a regional basis, e.g. the EU;
- the distintegration of states into constituent nationalities;
- the emergence of international terrorism; and
- global technological unification.

However, Bull asserts that there is no evidence for the emergence of a world society that displaces the states-system, but his criterion for the emergence of a world society is too severe by most standards embracing: 'not merely a degree of interaction linking all parts of the human community to one another but a sense of common interest and common values, on the basis of which common rules and institutions may be built' (1977: 279). No self-respecting globalization theorist would subscribe to such a straw-person condition (see especially the review of Robertson's work p. 106). It does allow Bull happily to conclude, in the face of a great deal of evidence that he adduces to the contrary, that: 'the world political system of whose existence we have taken note in no way implies the demise of the states-system'.[4]

Rosenau's analysis of emerging global interdependence is another example of what might be called a dualistic approach to the current transformation.[5] Rosenau's early work (1980) concentrates on what he calls 'trans-nationalization'. This is a process by which inter-governmental relations at an international level are supplemented by relations between non-governmental individuals and groups. Here Rosenau is a technological determinist much in the fashion of Kerr and his colleagues or Bell:

> Dynamic change, initiated by technological innovation and sustained by continuing advances in communications and transportation, has brought new associations and organizations into the political arena, and the efforts of these new entities to obtain external resources or otherwise interact with counterparts abroad have extended the range and intensified the dynamics of world affairs.
>
> (1980: 1–2)

So the proper study for a political science of world affairs is no longer simply 'international relations' but 'trans-national relations' involving complex extra-societal relationships between governments, governmental and non-governmental international agencies, and non-governmental entities. Non-governmental interaction rebounds onto states to produce an increasing level of interdependence between them and a disintegrative effect as it promotes intra-societal groups to the world stage. This involves: 'a transformation, even a breakdown of the nation-state system as it has existed throughout the last four centuries' (1980: 2). However, in what can only be regarded as a contradiction Rosenau insists that nation-states nevertheless remain the central actors. Some of their governments, he says, 'enjoy near total power to frame and execute policies' and all of them provide the main adaptive capacity for coping with change in the global system (1980: 3). We can only regard it as curious that they can manage to do this while simultaneously breaking down.

This dualism in Rosenau's analysis has not disappeared as it has matured. In his most recent work, in which globalization becomes much more explicit, he insists on what he calls the bifurcation of macro-global structures into 'the two worlds of world politics' (1990: 5). For this bifurcated system he now proposes to use the term 'postinternational politics' (1990: 6) implying that a simple snooker style pattern of international relations between states has now disappeared in the face of an unpredictable turbulence and chaos, that there is a very clear phase-shift under way.

Rosenau identifies five sources of this phase shift, beginning with his old friend, technology (1990: 12–13). They are:

- postindustrialization, forcing the development of micro-electronic technologies that reduce global distances by enabling the rapid movement of people, ideas and resources across the planet;[6]
- the emergence of planetary problems that are beyond the scope of states to resolve them;
- a decline in the ability of states to solve problems on a national basis;
- the emergence of new and more powerful subcollectivities within national societies; and
- an increasing level of expertise, education and reflexive empowerment in the adult citizenry that makes them less susceptible to state authority.

Among these, the first, the 'technological dynamic' remains paramount:

It is technology that has profoundly altered the scale on which human affairs take place, allowing people to do more things in less time and with wider repercussions than could have been imagined in earlier eras. It is technology, in short, that has

fostered an interdependence of local, national, and international
communities that is far greater than any previously experienced.

(1990: 17)

Rosenau can now make explicit the evolution of the bifurcated
global structure (1990: 14). International relations emerged from
world war in 1945 dominated by two superpowers, the USA and
the USSR, and their attached alliance blocs. This pattern was
subjected to a decentralizing dynamic forced by changes in the
planetary distributions of population and resources which led to
the emergence of third-world states; and simultaneously to a
centralizing dynamic forced by micro-electronic technological
development which led to the development of governmental and
non-governmental international organizations. By the 1960s this
had introduced enough instability into the system to set the
conditions for turbulence: individuals became more assertive and
ungovernable; insoluble global problems emerged; subgroups
and localisms were energized; and states began to appear incom-
petent. By the late 1980s the bifurcation had become manifest
between: a state-centric world comprising relations between
the USA, the USSR/Russia, the EC/EU, Japan, and the third
world, and their links to international organizations and subgroups; and a 'multi-centric world' focused on relations between
subgroups, international organizations, state bureaucracies and
trans-national actors (e.g. trans-national corporations). The
multi-centric world strives for autonomy from the state,
the state-centric world for the security of political institutions.
The contradiction between these principles pushes human society
inexorably towards a manifest turbulence.

By contrast, a rather more conventional effort to preserve the
saliency of the state is made by Gilpin (1987). Gilpin takes his
lead from Marx and Wallerstein, linking globalization to the
advance of capitalism. But it is a particular aspect of capitalism
which attracts Gilpin's interest. The world will become globalized, he argues, to the extent that the capitalist market, the
process of commodification, expands and penetrates every corner

of the planet: 'market competition and the responsiveness of actors to relative price changes propel society in the direction of increased specialization, greater efficiency, and . . . the eventual economic unification of the globe' (1987: 65). The market, which is Gilpin's equivalent of Burton's systems or Rosenau's multi-centric world: 'is driven largely by its own internal dynamic' but, and here the schizoid tendency returns, the pace and direction of advance are 'profoundly affected by external factors' (1987: 65). It will come as no surprise to learn that among the most significant of these external factors is the domestic and international political framework. Again, we must recognize that if Gilpin wants to say that the state *profoundly* affects the direction and pace of marketization then very little effectivity can remain for its own internal logic.[7]

For Gilpin the capitalist market, and its globalizing effects, advance most effectively under conditions of geopolitical stability. Stability is a function of the extent to which the international political economy is dominated by a hegemonic superpower. And if the market is to succeed that hegemon must be liberal rather than authoritarian in its orientation. So: 'the existence of a hegemonic or dominant liberal power is a necessary (albeit not a sufficient) condition for the full development of a world market economy' (1987: 85) Where there is no hegemon to impose the conditions of freedom and perfection on the market the global economic system dissolves into a nationalistic and mercantilist competition in which states seek to monopolize demand and monopsonize supply.

There have been two main phases in which a liberal hegemony has prevailed, and consequently two main bursts of marketization/globalization. The first covered most of the nineteenth century when Britain was, in global terms, the dominant hegemonic power by virtue of its industrial head start, its colonial empire and its naval military superiority. This was a period of relative international order and security, a period when international relations as a reflexive practice of diplomacy between states emerged. It was a period of treaties and alliances as well as an expanding global imperialism. The second was the briefer period between 1945 and 1970 when the USA was the global hegemon, drawing on its technological advantages, its mass production systems and its military might. Through the Bretton Woods agreement it set up the International Monetary Fund and the World Bank to stabilize exchange rates and curb international inflation; it set up the Marshall plan to underwrite the re-entry of the European economies into the world market; and it initiated GATT and the 'most favored nation' system to try to reduce international levels of tariff protection.

Gilpin now tries to turn conventional wisdom upon its head. That wisdom says that American hegemony declined with its inability to compete with Asian and European producers in world markets. Gilpin argues rather that America deliberately chose no longer to act as hegemon and in so doing opened up the international political economy to a triangular mercantilist dogfight. The international political economy is thus for him no longer truly globalized but rather consists of nationalistic attempts to succeed by beggaring neighbours through tax competition, migration prohibitions, investment subsidies, export subsidies and import restraints. Often the actors in this process are regional groupings of states (e.g. Andean Pact, APEC, ASEAN, EU, NAFTA) but these act much as did the mercantilist states of the seventeenth and eighteenth centuries.

In a thesis full of contradictions Gilpin's solution to current economic problems is especially paradoxical. He calls for pluralist intervention to restore economic liberalism, that is, for the triangle of dominating states to co-ordinate their policies in the direction of freedom of the market. Under the theory of hegemonic stability such a strategy cannot succeed. Indeed, the slow progress achieved within such attempts as G7 economic summits and the Millennium Round of WTO negotiations would tend to confirm this proposition.

Arguably, these four political science accounts of globalization remain at the same level as Wallerstein's world-system theory. They are prepared to admit the emergence of a world economic system but are unwilling to admit the possibility of the ultimate disintegration of nation-states and national cultures – indeed, they often resort to a theoretical dualism in which contradictory causal effects are allowed to reside in separate parts of the theory. The global political economy is, for them, organized by the interactions of states. This is despite the fact that it is impossible to deny that multi-national or trans-national corporations are frequently more powerful than the states whose societies they operate in and that the extent to which cultural currents can transsect national borders is now greater than it has ever been. This narrowness of vision extends to an unwillingness to recognize the extent to which states are now surrendering sovereignty to international and supra-national organizations as well as to more localized political units.

STATE FUNCTIONS

A key figure in the formalization and specification of the concept of globalization, then, is Roland Robertson. His early work with J.P. Nettl seeks to link modernization processes to the international system of states. The key formulation is the argument that such an international system palpably exists, at least *in statu nascendi*. The notion of system is borrowed from Parsons and is an application of his well-known AGIL scheme (first developed in Parsons and Smelser 1968). This argues that a complete system has structures or parts that function to resolve four system problems: adaptation to the environment (A); establishing practices for attaining goals (G); integrated exchanges between the parts of the system (I); and latent provision for reproduction of the system over time (L). In caricature then, in any social system there must be economic, political, community and cultural activities.

Nettl and Robertson (1968) are the first to admit that there is (or was in the 1960s) no completely formed international system. Rather, a process of system building was in train which proceeded from the 'G subsystem' (international interaction between states) but met resistance in the form of unresolved cleavages in the cultural arena (L subsystem) that prevented full system development.

This is confirmed by what they call 'a cursory empirical examination' (1968: 150). Organizations of states seek to push out and 'systematize' the other three subsystems on an international scale. UNESCO and WHO for example engage the L subsystem, the IPU and IATA the I subsystem, and the World Bank and ILO the A subsystem. At a higher level of abstraction, the international system of states was said to be actively engaged in:

- sharing power at an international, although normally continental, level to provide for collective security;
- establishing universal values and norms in, for example, the areas of political and social rights, the uses of nuclear power, and principles for the use of force;
- mitigating the distributional consequences of the international pattern of stratification by re-allocating economic resources; and
- co-ordinating exchanges between themselves in the areas of trade, migration, cultural performances, and so on.

But the development of the international system of states could only go as far as the cultural or L subsystem would allow, and here there were three signficant cleavages within it preventing global systematization (1968: 152–62).

- the religious cleavages between cultures that stress values of inner-directedness versus other-directedness, this-worldliness versus other-worldliness, theoreticism versus aestheticism, rationalism versus traditionalism, and linear conceptions of time versus cyclical conceptions;
- the legal-diplomatic cleavage between cultures for which international contact and 'the rule of law' are normal and regular on one hand and cultures that are internally oriented and absolutist on the other; and

- the industrial cleavage, between cultures that emphasise norms consistent with industry (e.g. rationality, individualization, impersonal authority) and those that do not.

Global unification was prevented by religious and more specific cultural discontinuities which cleave the world in two dimensions that can be characterized in terms of the compass points: East (e.g. China) cleaves from West (e.g. USA) in religious and legal terms, while North (e.g. USSR) cleaves from South (e.g. Ethiopia) in diplomatic and industrial terms. However, Nettl and Robertson view the three cleavages as a hierachy of levels with the highest degee of 'effectivity' or 'control' at the top. Religion, in the most general meaning of that term, is therefore the critical factor that must be overcome if globalization is to occur.

Parsons has long been identified as a consensus theorist, one who stresses subscription to common values as the basis of the integration of social systems. In basing their theory of the international states-system on Parsons, Nettl and Robertson might have overlooked what might be described as the defining function of the state, the aggregation and application of power and control. This issue is rather neatly addressed by Giddens (1981, 1985) who identifies the rise of the state with extensions of control over populations by means of surveillance.

Giddens explains the universalization of the nation-state in three sets of terms (1985: 255–7). First, those 'imagined communities', the European nation-states of the nineteenth century (especially Britain, France, Germany and Italy) were able successfully to marry industrial production to military action. This industrialization of warfare made them particularly successful in military encounters with tribal societies, which they colonized, and with absolutist empires, which they dismembered. Second, their rational-bureaucratic characteristics made them particularly effective in harnessing resources in the service of national development and in managing relations with other nation-states through diplomatic networks and trans-national political agencies. Third, a set of historical contingencies, the most important of which were the long peace of the nineteenth century, allowed the European states to concentrate economic resources on industrialization and colonization. A subsequent contingency, the destabilization of international relations by the world wars of the twentieth century forced the reflexive establishment of an international military order incorporating both superpower hegemony and international peacekeeping systems. However, the burgeoning development of international organizations during the twentieth century does not, Giddens insists, imply a loss of sovereignty for the nation-state but rather the securitization and institutional-ization of that sovereignty. The reflexive system of international relations affirms the territorial and ethnic integrity of individual nation-states. Indeed, it provides a secure environment in which new states, however small and weak, can emerge and to some extent prosper.

In his later work Giddens links the process of globalization to the development of modern societies. A modern society, that is, a post-feudal European society or any of its more recent copies, has four institutional characteristics or 'organisational clusters' (1990: 55–63; 1991: 15). The first two of these are broadly eco-nomic in character. Modernity involves, first, a *capitalist* system of commodity production that involves a social relationship between the owners of private capital and non-owners who sell their labour for wages. Enterprises compete in markets for capital, labour, raw materials and components, and products. Second, modernity implies *industrialism*, the multiplication of human effort by the application of inanimate sources of power channelled through machines. The scale of this technology implies a collective process of production in which the activities of a number of individuals are co-ordinated in the pursuit of an accumulation of material resources.

However, Giddens' main message is that a modern society is not defined entirely by its economic base but by the fact that it is a nation-state. A specific feature of the nineteenth-century European nation-state was its administrative competence, its capacity to establish co-ordinated control over a population within a defined territory. The main social technology that allowed the state to achieve this was the development of Foucauldian *surveillance* techniques. There are two varieties of surveillance: the ability to collect abstracted and coded sets of information about individuals; and the establishment of hierarchical systems of supervision that allow populations to be watched. A second specific feature of the modern nation-state is the centralization of control of the means of violence within an industrialized *military order*.

The surveillance process is also being extended in global directions in systems of military alliances. We have already considered the point that the sovereignty of a state is enhanced by mutual and reflexive recognition of sovereignty. International organizations fix sovereignty and allow the incorporation of former colonies into the nation-state system. Beyond this we find that co-operation between states in international organizations, the pooling of information and expertise, increases the capacity of a state to oversee its own population and, indeed, to interfere in the oversight of the populations of other states.

CONFLICTS OF INTEREST

Perhaps the central events that converted bilateral relations between nation-states into an inter-national system of states were the two 'world wars' of 1914–18 and 1939–45. The first of these was not truly a global war because, apart from a few naval engagements and colonial occupations, it was fought largely in the European theatre. Its significance lay, first, in the fact that it brought about the demise of the last major autocratic, multination empires of Europe, the Austro-Hungarian, Ottoman, Prussian and, most significantly, Russian empires. These were replaced by more ethnically homogeneous nation-states that could be integrated into the states-system more effectively. Second, it gave rise to attempts to establish an international order of states. This was partly a matter of necessity. The collapse of empires virtually forced the victorious states (principally Britain, France and the USA) into the position of redrawing national boundaries. But the Versailles conference that did this work was also obliged to recognise the existence of formally equal states in Asia, Africa and Latin America.

The Second World War was a truly international conflict, escaped only in Latin America and in a few neutral countries. Its main significance lay in the rise to dominance of two large, populous, industrially advanced and militarily effective federated states, the Soviet Union (Russia) and the USA. Each of these was able to develop constellations of client states, mainly in a divided Europe, by means of military occupation, economic aid, mutual security treaties and trade dependency. It was also significant in providing aspirations to independent statehood in the European colonies of Asia, Africa and Latin America. The post-1945 period was characterized by wars of independence and liberation struggles in these areas, often promoted or abetted by one or another of the two big states or their allied surrogates.

These international conflicts set up the inter-national states-system that immediately preceded the era of accelerated globalization. Inter-national relations focused on a rivalry between the two big powers which was expressed in sporting, cultural and scientific terms as well as in competition for influence and control in other states. This was the primary cleavage, between the alignments of the 'West' (North America, Western Europe, Japan and South-East Asia) and the 'East' (the Soviet Union, China and Eastern Europe). As state systems were established elsewhere and as economic disparities between these new states and the old ones became apparent, a new cleavage became established between the industrialized 'North' (Europe, North America, the Soviet Union and Australasia) and the developing 'South' (Africa, Asia, and Latin America). We can now consider political developments around these cleavages in some detail.

North versus South

The previous chapter specifies some of the details of the way in which the core of the world's economy is managed on an international scale – financial markets originally were managed through the IMF although they are now decentralized, trade is managed through the WTO (formerly GATT), and economic policy co-ordination through the G7. However, none of these co-ordinating agencies gave attention to what has often been viewed as the central problem of the global political economy, that of gross differences in income and wealth between its constituent sub-economies and the relations of domination and subordination that arise between them.

In previous eras international relationships of inequality were viewed as the non-problematic outcome of the superiority of the dominating race or society. In current circumstances they are often viewed as morally repugnant but more frequently as problematic in terms of their capacity to disrupt the global economy as a whole.

The first evidence that global inequality was viewed as a common political problem was the instutionalization of economic aid programmes established individually by most of the capitalist rich societies in the 1950s and 1960s. Aid programmes typically had one of three ostensive objectives: to 'band-aid' specific threats to human life and welfare such as temporary famine; to prime the local economic pump by financing such strategic projects as dams and steel mills; or to break down social or cultural barriers to development including the introduction of birth-control programmes. Financial transfers were often accompanied by teams of technical experts and volunteer aid workers, of which the US Peace Corps is the best-known example. Such development aid was only infrequently altruistic or recipient-controlled: it was often directed to ex-colonies or established spheres of influence; it was often linked with military aid as a way of maintaining a particular ideological cast on the host state; and it frequently insisted that aid monies be spent in purchasing items from the donor society. Almost everywhere, the donors had a clear commitment to maintaining markets for manufactured goods and stable and low-cost supplies of raw materials in the host societies.

Aid formed part of a spectrum of relationships, including trade and debt, between rich and poor states that appeared to reinforce global inequality. By the 1970s the development issue centred a crisis of legitimation in these relationships – claims to morality in the way in which rich states treated poor ones could no longer be sustained. Two social scientific theories effectively delegitimized the relationship (Gilpin 1987: 274–88). The first is the so-called Singer–Prebisch or structuralist argument. This suggests that rich states have dynamic economies committed to technological advancement in which monopoly corporations and effective labour unions can hold up the prices of manufactured goods. Meanwhile poor states have feeble investment patterns and a disorganized labour force which means that there is constant downward pressure on commodity prices and no incentive to industrial diversification. This produces a consistent tendency towards increasing disparity between the prices of manufactured goods and raw materials that makes development impossible. By contrast, dependency theory, as we see in Chapter 3, concentrates on the allocation of capital. International capitalists, it is argued, deliberately use capital allocation to control the pattern of development in LDCs, and indeed they argue that capitalism in the MDCs could not flourish unless there was a deliberate suppression of indigenous development.

These arguments led to the UNCTAD-sponsored conference of 1974, of which Prebisch was the general secretary, and which established the NIEO discussed in the next chapter. Here all states agreed in principle to improve aid, redress the growing disparity in the terms of trade and give LDCs more power within the organs of global economic management. Notionally, many of the goals of NIEO were realized. Between 1950 and 1980 GDP growth in LDCs outstripped that in MDCs. Even taking into account population growth, GDP per capita growth remained positive, and far more of that GDP was attributable to manufacturing industry. However, these gross figures mask the fact that development was uneven. While GDP of the South-East Asian and Latin American DMEs and in the oil producing states grew very rapidly, many parts of Africa and Asia experienced further decline into poverty, starvation and debt. Between 1960 and 1990 the proportion of global income going to the poorest 20 per cent of countries declined from 2.3 to 1.3 per cent while that going to the richest 20 per cent increased from 70 to 83 per cent (Thomas 1997: 456). In fact, then, few of the goals of the NIEO have come to be realized and, as we have seen, the international economic order in general has become more disorderly and decentralized.

East versus West

In the 1970s a cult of strategic gaming spread through the university campuses of North America. Two games, 'Diplomacy' and the more ominously named 'Risk' became commercially popular. In these games the participants would role-play nation-states and would act without morality or loyalty in furthering their interests, occasionally to the extent of subjective personal conflict. International relations in the nineteenth century operated much as these games did. Britain, for example, could fight against France in the Napoleonic War, then with France 40 years later in the Crimea, and stay neutral during the Franco-Prussian War of the 1870s. There were no stable blocs or alliances and even the Triple Alliance (Germany, Austria-Hungary, Italy) and the Triple Entente (Britain, France, Russia) that emerged at the end of that century were temporary and hasty marriages intended conveniently to manage specific problems.

The peace treaties that closed the First World War did little to move international relations in a truly global direction but rather confirmed its fragmentation. France and Britain sought to reassert a faltering international leadership; America isolated itself; Germany was plundered and excluded; and Russia was a pariah state. For all Western intents and purposes the rest of the world, including China and Japan, did not exist. Throughout that period international relations was without a world focus. States sought to manage their interests in terms of bilateral relations with other states rather than seeking to establish an international system in which these interests might prosper.

The Second World War changed this view by making three things very clear. First, that global conflict threatened every nation-state whether it chose to be involved or not (*vide* Pearl Harbor); second, that only the collective security of stable alliances could protect states from aggression; and third, that to exclude or to beggar other nation-states would often lead to instability. The Yalta and Potsdam conferences that occurred between the three main victorious powers (Britain, the USA and the Soviet Union) at the end of that war intentionally constructed a global system of international relations by explicitly dividing the world into spheres of influence and assigning them to the victors: Eastern and Central Europe to the Soviet Union; Western Europe to Britain, France and the USA; the middle East, Africa, South and South-East Asia to Britain and France; and the Asia-Pacific region and Latin America to the the USA. Eventually Britain and France proved to be too weak, economically and militarily, to sustain global influence and their spheres passed to the USA.

The world thus became divided between two superpowers or superstates that dominated it by three means. First, they armed themselves to the teeth with nuclear weapons, long-range delivery systems and rapid deployment forces that enabled them to give their power a global reach and place each other in a situation of mutual threat. Second, they established alliance systems in their spheres of interest that established protective buffer regions that could absorb aggression and aggregate national armed forces. The Soviet dominated system, the Warsaw Treaty Organization, included its 'satellite' states in Eastern Europe, while the USA dominated NATO, the Western European alliance, SEATO in South-East Asia and CENTO, a central Asian alliance inherited from Britain. Third, they intervened and competed in areas where their influence was in dispute, that is, in parts of Asia, Africa and Latin America. Often that intervention involved direct military aggression, as in the US invasions of Korea and Vietnam and the Soviet invasion of Afghanistan, but more frequently it took the form of advice, aid, military assistance to sympathetic regimes as well as covert and surrogate operations.

By these means the globe was divided into two worlds, East and West. The superpower system was, for the most part, stable. The superpowers agreed to respect each other's sphere of influence. When Soviet forces moved to repress anti-state forces in Hungary in 1957 and in Czechoslovakia in 1968, for example, the West merely expressed horror and took no action. This commitment was reinforced by the knowledge any pre-emptive nuclear strike on the opponent would not destroy its military capability sufficiently to render the aggressor immune – to destroy the opponent would be to destroy the planet. So convincing was this imperative that for much of this so-called 'cold war' period the superpowers practised a form of diplomacy known as '*détente*', in which they sought to establish bilateral norms for their competition.

As indicated above, that competition remained at its most intense in what became known as the 'third world', the ex-colonial states of Africa, Asia and Latin America. These sought to establish themselves as an alternative and neutral source of global influence. Being impoverished their only leverage came from their ability to play one superpower off against the other. This meant that each individual state tended at least to 'tilt' towards either the USA or the USSR, and the third-world movement was seldom cohesive. Nevertheless, many nations managed to maintain a moderately independent foreign policy.

INTERNATIONAL ORGANIZATIONS

In this section we examine the extent to which planetary society moved in the direction of unified global governance at the peak of the inter-states-system. To speak of global governance can invoke the image of a world government, a single unitary and centralized state similar to contemporary nation-states, or even a world-empire. This not need be the case. A globalized polity can have the characteristics of a network of power centres, including nation-states, co-ordinated by means other than command. In principle, such power centres might be co-ordinated because their controllers share common norms and common interests and seek to move towards consensus on such issues. Such a view is not as romantically optimistic as it may appear. Regional groupings of states, such as the EU, and a wide range of specialized interest associations already co-ordinate their activities on just such a basis. However, such an outcome is less likely than a polity organized as a market, or more precisely as multiple markets. Here processes of allocation (e.g. of welfare, economic development, peace and security, pollution, cultural performances) would be governed by competition between power centres much in the way that global flows of finance or of information are the consequences of multiple and complex decisions.

The vehicles within which these parallel processes of consensus building and competition can occur are international organizations. Political scientists normally make a distinction between two types of international organization: inter-governmental organizations (IGOs) and international non-governmental organizations (INGOs). Such organizations are not individually necessarily global in scope and indeed may cover as few as two national societies. However, taken together they constitute a web-like global network through which goal-setting and allocative decisions can flow. IGOs include not only the obvious organizations of whole states, such as the UN or ITU, but also links between the parts of governmental systems, between parliaments, or central banks, or environmental departments. Such links are greatest in the areas defined as common global problems. INGOs might be regarded as more important in globalization terms than IGOs because they outflank nation-states and threaten borders. They are unruly because their complexity defies command and their capacity to link diverse people in relation to common causes and interests undermines the saliency of the state.

Many date the initial development of international organizations at around 1920 (e.g. Archer 1983: 3; Giddens 1985: 261–2).

Prior to that date international relations had been conducted largely by means of the state-based systems of trade, diplomacy, colonialism, military alliance and war. Only in the areas of postal communications and health regulation was there serious previous IGO activity. A critical turning-point was the Versailles peace conference, which sought to impose an international order in the aftermath of the First World War. It took two critical measures: it gave states to the nationalities of the dismembered Austro-Hungarian, Ottoman, Prussian and Russian empires; and it set up a League of Nations to serve as an umbrella for the 30 or so IGOs that already existed and to act as a forum for consensus building on issues of peace and security. However, the League was to fail because the USA turned isolationist and, having originally promoted the idea, refused to join, because the Fascist and Communist states (Germany, Italy and the Soviet Union) were not members, and because the organization had no power of enforcement at its disposal. It collapsed with the outbreak of the Second World War in 1939.

By 1945 the international system had suffered the depredations of two world wars and of consequent revolutions and economic upheavals. The system of competing sovereign states, able to use force at will, established by the Treaty of Westphalia had now clearly failed – there was a dual hegemony rather than a balance of power. Moreover, techological developments in the area of nuclear weapons and their delivery systems meant that any further outbreak of global war represented a genuine threat to the survival of life as a whole. The world was no longer safe for capitalism or any other system of social power.

In that year, 51 nations, mainly the victors in that war, met in San Francisco and set up a new system that sought to constrain violence between states on the basis of a set of enforceable norms. The principles of that United Nations Charter to which they agreed were as follows (Cassese 1991: 263):

- war and the use of force between states was prohibited;
- a monopoly on the use of force was vested in the Security

Council of the United Nations Organization which was expected to use military means to maintain collective security and to constrain aggression; and

- states could only use force to defend themselves against aggression by another state.

Clearly the UN has never managed to enforce collective security other than in two doubtful cases: the 'defence' of South Korea against aggression from North Korea and its Chinese ally in the early 1950s, and the 'defence' of Kuwait against invasion from Iraq in 1988. In these doubtful cases the UN acted as a legitimizing umbrella for direct action by the USA and its allies. Otherwise it has engaged in 'peacekeeping' operations which merely serve to keep the protagonists apart. It has failed to prevent protracted wars in Israel/Palestine, Afghanistan and, most notably, Vietnam, as well as numerous minor conflagrations.

Nevertheless, the UN system represents a very clear advance on the Westphalian system and is clear evidence that peace and security is a shared global problem that can neither be left to private treaties between states nor to the dubious intentions of any hegemon. Moreover, the existence of the UN has established a communicative and normative framework for clearly positive developments in the control of the most destructive means of violence. These include the nuclear test ban treaty of 1961, the nuclear non-proliferation treaty of 1968, the various strategic arms reduction agreements of the 1970s and 1980s, and the Helsinki accord that set up the European Council for Security and Co-operation (ECSC).

GLOBALIZATION AND THE STATES-SYSTEM

By the end of the twentieth century the states-system had become the predominant form of political organization on the planet. Only the merest scintillas of territory and population lived outside the system, in such enclaves as Gibraltar, the Cayman Islands, St Pierre and Miquelon, and the Netherlands' Antilles.

Many of the tiniest specks of territory such as Nauru, Kiribati and Antigua had achieved the status, while other small but often colonial enclaves had been reunited with the nations from which they had been carved. Hong Kong, Macao and Goa are primary examples. The institution of the nation-state focused on unified sovereignty over a single territory and population had become globalized.

However, this was no longer a Westphalian system. Nation-states routinely surrendered sovereignty within military alliances. And the Westphalian system proposed a balance of powers between states that could occasionally coalesce in order to resist the advance of hegemons. In the superpower world of the mid-twentieth century, hegemony had become a fact of life. It had become divided into spheres of influence dominated by the Soviet Union and the USA, which routinely engaged in economic interference in their respective constellations of satellite states, and this interference frequently extended to military intervention. Occasionally, as in Korea in 1950, Vietnam in the 1960s and Cuba in 1960, this flared into direct and dangerous confrontation between the superpowers or their surrogates.

The United Nations, while having the appearance of a global system of governance was actually under the thrall of the superpowers. Its activities were subjugated to theirs in three ways: first, as is noted above, under certain circumstances it was possible for the USA to use the UN as a legitimizing front for its confrontations with the Soviet Union; second, it was otherwise largely prevented from maintaining peace and security in situations in which the superpowers were directly implicated; and third it operated peacekeeping ventures in contexts in which the superpowers had a common interest.

The emergence of this inter-national system of states represents the culmination of the second phase of what we refer to above as general globalization. The entire population of the planet lived and operated within a single set of institutional arrangements. However, these arrangements nevertheless continued to imply the division of the globe into bordered territories each with distinctive political practices, sovereign governments and local-ized party systems. Domestic issues dominated political activity and national politicians had the capacity and the authority, in the main, to manage and resolve such problems. So, although the processes under inspection here do indeed consitute an important phase in the general development of globalization they cannot be considered an instance of specific globalization.

NOTES

1   Indeed the discipline of International Relations is currently engaged in a paralysing debate between so-called 'realists' who argue that the state is the site of real power and so-called 'modernists' who argue more or less in favour of globalization.

2   'International Relations' (first letters upper case) will indicate the sub-discipline. The term without the upper case indicates the subject matter studied within the subdiscipline.

3   Burton calls this model a 'billiard-ball model'. However, billiards is a game played with three balls of two colours. Snooker, with its differentiation of colours and points values and greater complexity of interaction, might be a better metaphor. It is also a far superior game.

4   A similar but more recent argument is made by Luard (1990) although it appears, at first glance, to be more committed to a globalization thesis. National societies, he argues, are becoming attenuated by internal divisions and conflicts, not merely between minority nation-alities but by religious and ideological differences and class divisions. At the same time the multiplication of inter-state relationships supports the view that we should recognize that international society is almost equally as important. However Luard appears to remain not entirely convinced by his own claims. The list of key characteristics given for international society (1990: 6–10) is a list of the things that it lacks: it lacks centralized authority, a formal structure of relationships, a sense of communal solidarity, a sense of obligation to a legitimate order, and a consensus on common values. Nevertheless, Luard hesitantly suggests, it is a society 'of a kind'. The kind of society he specifies almost returns us to early theories of international relations. International society encompasses both relations between states and trans-national practices between non-state actors. However: 'The relationships which individuals can undertake across frontiers depend on the under-standings and agreements reached between governments. And the

general character of international society at any one time, including its characteristic "ideology", is thus determined by the actions and decisions of states more than by those of individuals or groups' (1990: 5).

5   A similar and equally influential version of the argument is given by Keohane and Nye (1973). However, their analysis matches Rosenau's so closely that it would add little to review both.

6   This technological version of postindustrialization is inconsistent with Bell's original formulation (1976) which insists on the importance of service production and of *intellectual* technology.

7   Gilpin has a technological cake in the oven to go along with the etatist one he is eating and the economic one he is keeping: 'Improvements in communications and transportation that reduce the cost of conducting business have encouraged the integration of once isolated markets into an expanding global interdependence. From the innovation of oceangoing sailing ships to contemporary information-processing systems, technological advances have been an almost inexorable force for uniting the world economy' (1987: 82).

5

WITHER THE STATE?
GLOBALIZING POLITICS

The nation-state is becoming too small for the big problems of life, and too big for the small problems of life.

Daniel Bell

The preceding chapters indicate that in many material dimensions there is an increasing interconnectedness and interdependence between previously separate societies. Inter-societal exchanges of management, capital, components, finance, labour and commodities are increasing relative to intra-societal exchanges. In Chapter 4 we examine the way in which the disciplines of political science and International Relations have sought to theorize the impact of these and other changes. It will be remembered that typically they theorize the world in dualistic terms – the world is argued to be globalizing at the level of economics and culture but states remain the primary location for sovereignty and decision making. In this chapter we can examine a radical counter-proposal, the argument that the state too is becoming subordinated to globalization processes and that political activity increasingly focuses on cross-societal issues.

The best and most explicit outline of the general argument is given by Held (1991: 207–9). He begins at the level of non-political inter-societal connections and then takes the argument through a series of steps which see the undermining of the nation-state and its eventual displacement by a world government. The steps in Held's argument are as follows:

- increasing economic and cultural connections reduce the power and effectiveness of governments at the nation-state level – they can no longer control the flow of ideas and economic items at their borders and thus their internal policy instruments become ineffective;
- state power is further reduced because trans-national processes grow in scale as well as in number – TNCs, for example, are often larger and more powerful than many governments;
- many traditional areas of state responsibility (e.g. defence, communications, economic management) must therefore be co-ordinated on an international or intergovernmental basis;
- states have thus been obliged to surrender sovereignty within larger political units (e.g. EU, ASEAN), multilateral treaties (e.g. NATO, OPEC, APEC) or international organizations (e.g. UN, WTO, IMF);
- a system of 'global governance' is therefore emerging with its own policy development and administrative systems which further curtails state power; and
- this provides the basis for the emergence of a supranational state with dominant coercive and legislative power.

Robertson insists that this process of globalization is not new, that it pre-dates modernity and the rise of capitalism. However, modernization tends to accelerate globalization and the process has moved to the level of consciousness during the contemporary period. Moreover, European civilization is the central focus for and origin of the development. He maps the path of globalization as a series of five phases (1992: 58–60)

1 *The germinal phase* (Europe, 1400–1750)
  - dissolution of Christendom and emergence of state communities,
  - Catholic (i.e. universal) churches,
  - development of generalizations about humanity and the individual,
  - first maps of the planet,
  - sun-centred universe,
  - universal calendar in the West,
  - European exploration of Africa, Asia and the Americas,
  - colonialism.

2 *The incipient phase* (Europe, 1750–1875)
  - establishment of the nation-state,
  - formal diplomacy between states,
  - citizenship and passports,
  - international exhibitions and communications agreements,
  - international legal conventions,
  - first non-European nation-states,
  - first ideas of internationalism and universalism.

3 *The take-off phase* (1875–1925)
  - conceptualization of the world in terms of the four globalizing reference points: the nation-state, the individual, a single international society and a single (masculine) humanity,
  - international communications, sporting and cultural links,
  - universal calendar,
  - first ever world war, so defined,
  - mass international migrations and restrictions thereon,
  - more non-Europeans in the international club of nation-states.

4 *The struggle-for-hegemony phase* (1925–69)
  - League of Nations and UN,
  - Second World War; cold war,
  - conceptions of war crimes and crimes against humanity,
  - the universal nuclear threat of the atomic bomb,
  - emergence of the third (part of the) world.

5 *The uncertainty phase* (1969–92)
- exploration of space;
- post-materialist values and rights discourses.
- world communities based on sexual preference, gender, ethnicity and race.
- international relations more complex and fluid.
- global environmental problems recognized.
- global mass media via space technology (satellite television, etc.).

The 1990s are uncertain he argues because *we* (the inhabitants of the planet) have little confidence in the direction in which *we* are heading and only a little more in the direction of the planetary environment.

These developments occur independently of the internal dynamics of individual societies. Indeed, globalization has its own logic which will inevitably affect these internal dynamics. This logic, Robertson insists, has its roots in the emergence of the culturally homogeneous nation-state in the middle of the eighteenth century: 'the diffusion of the *idea* of the national society as a form of institutionalized societalism . . . was central to the accelerated globalization which began just over a hundred years ago' (1992: 58, original italics). Robertson does not make explicit this logic but the steps might be: nation-states are bounded social systems; they will compete for resources and markets and they will not necessarily be materially self-sufficient; they will therefore engage in economic, military, political (diplomatic) and cultural exchanges across the boundaries that are both co-operative and conflictual; differential outcomes and therefore cross-national mimesis will ensue; states will seek to systematize international relations in order to secure the conditions of their own existence.

The critical point of debate is the issue of how far the world has gone and will go within the last three steps in Held's analysis or into Robertson's uncertainty phase. For many 'realists' (e.g. McGrew 1992b) the prevailing territorial sovereignty of nation-states and the meaning they have for their citizens makes them the undeniably primary context of political life. For 'modernists' such as Held or Robertson the sovereignty of the state is already in decline and 'world government', although not taking the same form as contemporary nation-state governments, is a real possibility. As might be expected on the basis of the previous chapters, this book tends towards the second of these positions.

Before making a case in that direction, however, it is worth reiterating a point made by Giddens (1990) and stressed by McGrew (1992b). It is not absolutely necessary to demonstrate that the nation-state is in decline in order support a case for political globalization. Indeed, the emergence of the nation-state is itself a product of globalization processes. As discussed in Chapter 4, the institutionalization of the nation-state occurred within the context of an elaborating system of international relations that began in the nineteenth century. Nations could survive and operate within that system only if they had a centralized and unified governmental system that could steer their affairs and manage their security. The demise of the feudally based and absolutist continental empires of tsarist Russia and Austria-Hungary and the later dismantling of the European colonial empires bear witness to the success of the nation-state in blending citizen commitment with administrative effectiveness and international security. We begin then with developments at the level of the state.

INTERNAL CRISIS

In the third quarter of the twentieth century the corporate welfare state hit a multiple and widely recognised crisis. Its components were as follows (Crook, Pakulski and Waters 1992: 92–7).

- Popular demands escalated beyond the capacity of the state to meet them. The right to make a claim against the state had been separated from the capacity to make an economic contribution to it. Moreover, the state had educated and politically enfranchised its population. The volume and effectiveness of collective claims against the state was clogging the political process.

- The locations of real state power became hidden. Politicians focused on mediating claims and cultivating support while the real power was exercised behind the scenes by bureaucrats and technicians.

- The administration of welfare was consuming an increasing proportion of the welfare budget. Moreover, the welfare system was cultivating its own clients by creating a culture of state dependency.

- The interventions of the state in economic matters tended to destabilize the markets which they were intended to preserve. Economies were populated by weak and failing industries and underemployed workers.

- The class-interest groups on which the corporatist state had been founded were decomposing in favour of new status groups, often with 'postmaterialist' value-commitments that the materialist strategies of corporatism could not meet.

- Lastly, through international alliances, the state was creating more danger than security. It divided the world into hostile camps whose commitments to the acquisition of military technology could only have one purpose.

The response to this multiple crisis was a process of disetatization or state-weakening. The corporate interest groups that previously had supported the state began to downscale and localize. Trade unions shrunk and were displaced by local interest groups and civic initiatives. State intervention by command was reduced but at the same time states sought to increase the scope and scale of the market. Many government services were opened to competitive tendering between the public and private sectors and, as is well known, many state-owned industries were returned to the private sector. Many states stopped providing welfare in certain areas and others moved towards demilitarization. They also partially surrendered their sovereignty by participating in global and regional organizations.

This crisis took its most extreme form in the most statist societies in the world. In the totalitarian societies of Eastern Europe and the Soviet Union the state had subordinated and absorbed civil society to such a degree that economy and culture were substantively indistinguishable from politics. Here, the state was all-pervasive and intensively regulative. So the crisis elements described above were amplified throughout civil society. Commitment drained away, economies grew weak, resources were diverted into increasingly ineffective defence activities and grandiose state projects. They staggered on by penning in populations, repressing dissidents, rationing, military occupation and transmigration into ethnic enclaves, constructing national achievments in sport, culture and space exploration, and intensive propoganda. By the end of the 1980s the veneer of legitimacy was cracked beyond repair. The Communist Party lost control of the state first in Poland, then progressively throughout the 'satellite nations' of Eastern Europe. In 1989 the Soviet Union broke up into a new constellation of nation-states in the Baltic, the Caucasus and in Central Asia. Russia, the dominant nation in the Soviet Union, itself became a chaotic and problematic liberal democracy, still wrestling militarily and politically with claims to statehood from ethnic minorities. In each instance the state was seriously weakened and rolled back in the face of a resurgent civil society.

The implications of the crisis of the state and consequent dis-etatization for globalization have both obvious and less obvious aspects. Clearly any breakdown in the nation-state system leaves an opening for political globalization. So long as the state persists a sovereign world polity is impossible. The less obvious aspects might be more important however. The crisis of the state contributes to the reflexivity of globalization. This is because the excuses of politicians for their failures have taken on a global hue: our economy is failing because of the recession in the USA or Europe or Japan or somewhere else; our currency is declining because of the activities of unidentified international speculators; our air is dirty because someone else has had a nuclear meltdown; we cannot solve the problem of urban crime because it is fed by international drugs syndicates; or, we cannot feed our people because the level of international aid is not adequate. In so far as politicians deflect blame onto the global arena, collective political actors will focus their attention on that arena and the nation-state will progressively become an irrelevance. We can now consider the globalized political issues on which they are focusing and their effects on the sovereignty of the state.

EXTERNAL SOVEREIGNTY

One of the key features of the system of international relations set up by the new nation-states of the nineteenth century was the principle of sovereignty. This principle asserts that the state has the absolute right to determine autonomously the internal fate of the nation for which it consititutes the set of political arrangements. Under this principle, interference by one state in the internal affairs of another is regarded as pathological.[1] Under current globalized circumstances this principle is frequently breached on a multilateral basis on the grounds that the inhabitants of the planet experience a set of common problems that can be exacerbated by the actions of an individual nation-state. This development represents, at the minimum, a 'nationalization' of global issues, an expectation that national policies must address the common problems of the planet.

Human rights

The institutionalization of human rights norms that transcend state boundaries originally took place under the auspices of the UN (see Weissbrodt 1988). When it was signed the Universal Declaration of Human Rights of 1948 was a purely nominal document, a commitment to a set of principles that was unenforceable. The Declaration, its covenants and protocols, some dealing with such specific threats to human rights as apartheid (racial separation), genocide, gender discrimination and torture, now however have the status of treaties. Some 90 governments have ratified protocols that allow individuals to bring complaints to the UN's Human Rights Committee (HRC) against those governments themselves. The treaties oblige governments to amend legislation to conform with HRC judgements.

The institutionalization of human rights is most secure in Europe where governments have ceded the power to enforce the conditions of the European Convention for the Protection of Human Rights and Fundamental Freedoms to supra-national bodies. The European Commission on Human Rights, like the HRC determines whether complaints have any foundation in fact; and the European Court of Human Rights can make decisions that are binding on states. The European Court has established a considerable jurisprudence, having heard over 100 cases since its foundation in 1961 (Weissbrodt 1988: 16). Perhaps the best-known of its judgements is that of 1976 in which it found that the British Government had employed inhuman and degrading methods to punish and interrogate prisoners in Northern Ireland.

The Treaty of Westphalia (see Chapter 4) established that states were the only actors in the international arena, that they had the right to defend themselves against territorial aggression from other states, that they could act in that arena free from regulative constraint, and that they had the sovereign right to govern and indeed to act free from interference by other states in governing their subject populations. In the blunt words of Cassese, in this international community, 'peoples and individuals [did] not count' (1990: 13; italics deleted). The key domestic feature of this state system then was that each state was 'absolutist' in so far as all rights were vested in the sovereign and that subjects received only revocable privileges from the monarch's hands. However, it was different from the feudal state that preceded it because it also established a centralized administrative system that could extend sovereign power across a broad territory and a large population (Giddens 1985: 88, 93–4).

The nation-state was a liberal system based on a constitutionalization process that established the rights of citizens against the state. Citizenship is a social construction in which a rising class can claim certain political and civil liberties against the state – it is a curtailment of absolutist power. We should not be confused by the flowery phrasing of Paine's *The Rights of Man* or of the American Declaration of Independence. These were not claims made on behalf of all men, much less of all humanity, but merely expressions of the limits of state power as against economic power. Certainly in the first instances, citizenship rights were rights to engage in contract, to own and to alienate private property and to a share in state power. They were expressions of a class structure and not its ameliorations (see Barbalet 1988). On this analysis, the emergence of citizenship institutions is a social construction arrived at on the basis of a balance of interests between state power-holders and a rising class.

That all too briefly said, we now have the two main dimensions of the liberal nation-state: external sovereignty and an internal rule of law regulating the relations between rulers and citizens. A key development that disrupted this pattern was global war in the twentieth century. During the nineteenth century peace had been accomplished on the basis of an uneasy equipoise between more or less equal powers with defined spheres of interest. The First World War profoundly altered this balance of power, weakening and impoverishing civil society in two key states, Germany and Russia, and leading in each instance to an enhancement of state power at the expense of citizenship rights. Equally it established a new economic and diplomatic hegemon, the USA, that had been founded on an elaborated civil society and a weak state. These developments set up conditions for the development of a new set of interests in the relationship between state power and individual rights that was to emerge after the Second World War. These conditions involved the defeat of the fascist states by an alliance of liberal democracies and state socialism, and subsequent competition between the superpowers that emerged from that alliance.

The critical breach in state sovereignty came from an expression of state interests, and human rights was the vehicle that allowed these interests to be expressed. The victorious states of the Second World War sought to legitimize their victory and to stigmatize the vanquished by putting the defeated political leaders on trial as war criminals. In order to do this they needed to breach the Westphalian principle that each state had the right to govern subject populations free of external interference. The only way in which that could be achieved was by an appeal to Kantian principles, that is, to try them on grounds of crimes against humanity (Held 1991: 220). The International War Crimes Tribunal that sat at Nuremberg established then an entirely new principle of international relations. It decided that when state laws are in conflict with international humanitarian standards, individuals are obliged to disobey the state. It did so in the military arena in particular, an arena in which obedience to the state is normally regarded as an absolute requirement. 'Just following orders' was no longer an adequate defence against a failure to exercise a humanitarian moral choice.

War-crime trials can therefore partly explain the emergence of the 1948 Declaration but only partly so. The emergent 'cold war' between the superpowers included a propaganda campaign of mutual castigation and vilification, partly to encourage commitment among subject and allied populations and partly to cultivate support among the non-aligned states. The proposal from the West, the main movers in establishing the Declaration, was a re-expression of citizenship rights, that is, it emphasised the civil and political rights of individuals [while not extending as far as the Lockeian right to rebellion] (Cassese 1990: 35). The West therefore had in its hands a libertarian document by which it could justify an opposition to state socialism. But the Declaration also includes prescriptions for economic and social rights that were proposed by the Soviet Union – these would allow the East to depict the Western states as exploiting their populations and tolerant of extreme class and racial inequality. The key feature that allowed both sides to accept the Declaration (the USSR and its allies participated in the drafting but abstained from the voting, as did the racist state of South Africa and the pre-modern Islamic state of Saudi Arabia) was that the treaty was non-binding so that, 'human rights were to be realized by each state in the context of its national system' (Cassese 1990: 37). Each state was responsible, then, for the administration of human rights and there were to be no means of collective enforcement.

Human rights thus entered the arena of superpower politics, now not simply as a means by which states could heckle each other but also as a legitimation for superpower hegemony. The Declaration established a set of grounds that could reference interference by one state in the affairs of another, even to the extent of military intervention. The superpowers could control their spheres of influence to protect rights specified in the Declaration. The USA, for example, justified its intervention in theatres as diverse as Vietnam and Haiti by reference to threats to political and civil rights; the USSR could justify its interventions in Hungary or Afghanistan by a need to protect revolutionary gains in the sphere of material equality. Equally, the USA could encourage subversive organizations in Eastern Europe, while the USSR could demand the economic and cultural isolation of racist states in Africa that were allied with the West. This conjuction of superpower interests was partly responsible for ensuring that the effects of the Declaration have not been entirely nominal. The expanding set of UN arrangements for human rights judgements and findings is testimony to the extent to which human rights served the shared interests of the superpowers that dominated the UN by establishing the grounds, if not the rules, for the contest.

But superpower politics is not the only element in this story, because the Declaration unleashed a whirlwind. Governments were no longer entirely sovereign and could no longer govern their populations in an authoritarian fashion but rather were required to negotiate in relation to popular sovereignty. In an era of rising expectations claimant groups could now demand entitlements that were previously not available. This had not been possible under the preceding institutions of citizenship.

First, citizenship had always prescribed exclusions against non-citizens, often women, racial or ethnic minorities, indigenes, children, the mentally and physically less able, resident aliens, *Gastarbeiter*, prisoners, members of the nobility, and so on. Citizenship rights offer no protection for non-citizens (e.g. Jews in Nazi Germany, Aborigines in pre-1967 Australia, blacks in apartheid South Africa) because citizenship is a legal status that can be denied. By contrast, under a human rights regime, all of these excluded groups are instances of humanity and humanity is a moral status that is non-deniable. Second, citizenship can offer firm protection only for civil and political liberties because only these are constitutionally prescribed (Barbalet 1988; Roche 1992). Citizenship guarantees only the libertarian and not the egalitarian aspects of rights.

The social movement is the main mechanism for the expression of expectations for the redress of material disadvantage by the establishment of entitlements. The Declaration and its descendents proved to be the constitutional reference point for activist social movements seeking to advance claimant interests on behalf of second-class or non-citizens. In the West these claims have been mainly egalitarian in character, the principle examples being the civil rights, women's liberation, gay rights, indigenous land rights and anti-apartheid movements. In the East, social movement claims have been primarily libertarian in orientation with the main examples here being Solidarity, Charter '66, and the Chinese student democracy movement. In each instance the claim can be made that state laws or provisions are illegitimate because they violate international standards of human rights.

The planetary environment

The above discussion of human rights can confirm the point made in Chapter 2 that one of the most important aspects of globalization is that it connects the local with the general. Human rights connects the individual with humanity by asserting that each individual is an instance of humanity. Another 'planetary problem' achieves this just as effectively – the issue of environmentalism connects subjective lifestyles with the physical condition of the planet. Many of the inhabitants of the planet, especially those fortunate enought to be affluent, are beginning to see the earth as a common home that needs to be maintained and tended if they and their individual descendents are to have a comfortable, prosperous and healthy life. A particularly globalizing aspect of this conceptualization is the view that human society cannot infinitely be expanded beyond the physical limits of the earth and its constituent resources. The environmentalist architect Buckminster Fuller's 1980s characterization of the planet as 'spaceship earth' neatly conveys the notion that it is bounded in space.

There are two main environmental impacts on the sovereignty of the state (see Goldblatt 1997). First, environmental effects on domestic territory and population can originate in other states and territories beyond domestic governmental control. Pollution can be borne across borders by the atmosphere, by water, by trade and by transportation. Indeed, there can be long chains of chemical or biological reactions that link distant territories. Second, certain sectors of the planetary environment have been relocated outside the territorial sovereignty of nation-states – they have been redefined as 'global commons' (Vogler 1992). They include, to varying degrees and with varying levels of enforcement, the high seas, the seabed, fisheries, marine mammals, satellite orbits, the moon, the airwaves, the atmosphere, the entire continent of Antarctica and, for good measure, the rest of the universe. These commons, once established, require management on an international scale if they are to be conserved against the prospect of unlimited economic exploitation. They are also subject to environmental degradation that can impact on states not responsible for that degradation.

Beck (1992) gives us perhaps the most compelling analysis of the first of these issues, that of cross-border pollution. From the viewpoint of the most economically advanced sectors of the world, Beck argues, we are already living in a post-scarcity society. Contemporary society has moved out of the phase in which it was predominantly oriented to technological applications that would maximize the flow of material resources and in which the main practices of the state were to effect a fair and just distribution of these material returns through a welfare system. In that modernization phase people had been prepared to accept medical and ecological side-effects in return for an increase in material welfare. But now things have changed:

> In the welfare states of the West a double process is taking place now. On the one hand, the struggle for one's 'daily bread' has lost its urgency as a cardinal problem overshadowing everything else, compared to material subsistence in the first half of this century, and to a Third World menaced by hunger. For many people problems of 'overweight' take the place of hunger. . . . Parallel to that, the knowledge is spreading that the sources of wealth are 'polluted' by growing 'hazardous side effects'.
>
> (1992: 20)

These side-effects constitute risks, and the distribution of these risks is becoming the central feature of affluent societies. An important defining feature of risk is its social reflexivity. It is not the hazards themselves that are new and special but the way in which they are socially constituted: 'Risk may be defined as a systematic way of dealing with hazards and insecurities induced and introduced by modernization itself' (1992: 21, italics deleted). The risks of which we are becoming increasingly conscious, both scientifically and politically, include threats from radioactivity, toxins and pollutants that cause long-term, irreversible and invisible damage to organisms.

These risks, argues Beck, are qualitatively different from the hazards and dangers experienced in previous periods of history. First, the current risks are the direct consequence of industrialization and are implicit and unavoidable within it, they are not the risks of intentional adventure. Second, the risks we currently experience in the forms of trace toxins or radioactivity are no longer perceptible to the senses. Third, they do not derive from undersupply of technology or wealth but from overproduction. Indeed, as industrialization intensifies on a global scale, the risks multiply. Fourth, the contemporary experience of risk is scientifically and politically reflexive. Society is intentionally recast as an attempt to reduce risk but cannot deal with 'the threatening force of modernization and its globalization of doubt' (1992: 21). Fifth, contemporary risks are not tied to their local origins but 'By their nature they endanger all forms of life on this planet' (1992: 22, italics deleted). Such ecological and 'high-tech' risks as nuclear accidents and acid rain admit of no boundary in time or space – once present they are continuous and general. Sixth, the globalization of high-risk industries means that the scientific calculation of risk and of its consequences has become impossible.

Risk has a double saliency in relation to globalization. As is clear from the above, Beck reckons modernization to be the primary globalizing force. Global risks are the product of global industrialization. But because risk is itself inherently globalizing, the advent of risk society accelerates the globalization process. It is in terms of this effect that Beck makes his contribution to the conceptualization of globalization. Risk globalizes because it universalizes and equalizes. It affects every member of society regardless of location and class position. Moreover it respects no border:

> [F]ood chains connect practically everyone on earth to everyone else. They dip under borders. The acid content of the air is not only nibbling at sculptures and artistic treasures, it also long ago brought about the disintegration of modern customs barriers. Even in Canada the lakes have become acidified, and forests are dying even in the northern reaches of Scandinavia.
>
> (1992: 36)

The reflexive character of risk, combined with its lack of boundedness in space, forces consciousness in the direction of globalization. The only possible solutions to risk are supra-national solutions: strategic arms reduction talks, earth summits, international agreements on emission reduction or the use of CFCs, nuclear weapons proliferation agreements, etc.

Risk distribution in the globalized system follows a pattern that Beck calls the 'boomerang curve'. Here, the hazardous consequences of risk return to their sources and adversely affect those who produce them. In the previous period of modernization risk had been a latent side effect from which the rich and powerful could insulate themselves but now risk returns to haunt the very centres of production. This is especially apparent in industrialized agriculture, where the use of artificial irrigation, fertilizers and pesticides can actually destroy land and increase the immunity levels of pests. The universalizing–localizing paradox of globalization theory is present here too then: 'under the roof of modernization risks, perpetrator and victim sooner or later become identical' (1992: 38). The paramount risk in this syndrome is the (albeit receding) risk of a global nuclear war in which there can only be losers.

However, the boomerang effect is not restricted to risk-production zones but can be generalized to other social valuables including money, property and legitimation. A principal effect is on property. Wherever an ecology-threatening change is made to a particular locality, such as the construction of a power station, airport or highway, property prices fall. Beck calls this ecological expropriation. The globalizing effect of ecological expropriation is progressively to make the planet uninhabitable: 'everyone is pursuing a "scorched Earth" policy against everyone else – with resounding but seldom lasting success' (1992: 38). Equally, ecological expropriation can destroy the money-making capacities of agricultural land, forests or sea fisheries, as well as the legitimacy of corporations and governments.

At one level then, the advent of risk society reduces inequality. In particular, it mitigates against class inequality because it neither respects class boundaries nor, in its afflictions, establishes zero-sum relations of exploitation. In a contradictory formulation, however, Beck also argues that class disadvantage can lead to risk disadvantage, that poverty and risk attract. However, his formulation is clearly novel in that it argues for an international class system in which clean industries are retained in the economically advanced societies while dangerous and highly polluting industries are exported to the third world: 'In the shunting yard where risks are distributed, stations in 'underdeveloped provincial holes' enjoy special popularity. And one would have to be a naive fool to continue to assume that the responsible switchmen do not know what they are doing' (1992: 41). NICs effectively purchase economic independence by their acceptance of risk. Here safety regulations are weak and unenforced and populations are insufficiently literate to be aware of the risks they run even where they have a choice about whether to be engaged in the risky endeavours of, say, spreading fertilizers and pesticides by hand. The managers of trans-national corporations know that their capital is a necessity and that if a catastrophe should occur their resources will allow them to resist legal redress.

What they cannot resist, says Beck, is the boomerang effect and the contagion of risk: the pesticides and the toxins will return in imported foodstuffs; sulphur emissions will turn rain to acid; carbon dioxide emissions will alter the climate of the entire planet; and exported atomic power stations can melt down and emit radioactivity or their products can be used for the local construction of nuclear weapons. The boomerang effect puts the poor and the wealthy in the same neighbourhood. In his most pronounced statement of globalization Beck affirms that: 'The multiplication of risks causes the world society to contract into a community of danger' (1992: 44).

Another characterization of that risk addresses the second of the environmental threats to sovereignty under discussion here, that is, impacts on the global commons. These impacts can be understood in terms of Hardin's model of the 'Tragedy of the Commons' (1968) which is a variant games modelling of 'the free rider'. The model proposes that where a relatively large number of actors has access to a common resource, the only rational course of action for any individual is to exploit that resource to the maximum. For any individual to practise restraint would be simply to transfer exploitative advantage to others. Under conditions of rapid escalation of consumption and/or of technological change, over-exploitation is likely to destroy the resource. These conditions can be argued to apply to the global commons.

Perhaps the first popularized attempt to specify these impacts was the first report of the 'Club of Rome', a group of concerned public intellectuals (Meadows et al. 1976). The report pointed out that both population and economic growth are limited by the capacity of the planet to accommodate them. The limits are threefold: food, mineral and energy resources, and pollution. The Club's Malthusian arguments about them were as follows:

- Food production is based on the availability of arable land. Even if the productivity of arable land were doubled, because the supply of arable land is falling, the world population will be unable to be fed at some point prior to 2050 AD. In some parts of the world that point has already arrived.
- The crisis is even more severe with respect to non-renewable resources of minerals and energy.
- A rapidly increasing population with an increasing economic growth rate also produces pollutants – heat, carbon dioxide, nuclear waste, and chemical waste – which can seriously impede its own capacity to survive. The rate of outputs of pollutants is increasing exponentially along with population size and economic growth.

On these arguments the world finds itself in what may be called a *population–resources trap* in which a feedback system operates to exacerbate an already problematic situation. The more population increases, the more it uses up non-renewable resources and increases pollution. Resource shortages and pollution costs reduce international capacity to engage in sustained long-term economic growth. Yet economic growth is the engine which modernizes societies and alters traditional values about family size and age of marriage and thus has a constraining effect on fertility. If these traditional orientations do not change then population will continue to increase and the cycle will begin again.

The issues identified by the Club of Rome, problems of starvation, resource depletion and pollution, remain salient. More recently public attention has focused on two specific areas in which these problems are having a particular and pressing effect: biodiversity and global warming. So pressing have they become that they were the central topics at the first 'Earth Summit' intergovernmental conference in Rio in 1992.

Biodiversity is the issue of the maintenance of multiple species of plants and animals on the planet. There are two threats to biodiversity. The most obvious is economic exploitation – this has led to the depletion of such publicly prominent species as the rhinoceros, the African elephant and the great whales. The second and more significant threat comes from the destruction of habitat. As human populations expand they extend urban environments, extend agricultural activity and expand their exploitation of natural resources of minerals and timber, thus destroying natural habitat. And as they migrate humans carry with them exotic species and introduce them to new environments. All of these activities can upset delicately balanced ecosystems in such a way as to make it impossible for many indigenous species to survive. Such activity is reponsible for the probable extinction of the Tasmanian tiger (Thylacine) and other species currently threatened include the Kouprey (10 left), the Javan rhinoceros (50), the Iriomote cat (60), the black lion tamarin (130) and the pygmy hog (150) (*Melbourne Sunday Age* 31/5/92).

'Global warming' is a catch-all phrase which covers four developments: depletion of the ozone layer, atmospheric pollution, deforestation and climatic change.

- The ozone layer is a high-level stratum of the atmosphere which screens the surface of the planet from intense ultraviolet radiation. It was discovered to be thinning over Antarctica in the mid-1980s and by 1991 had suffered a depletion of 3 per cent in temperate regions (*The Economist* 30/5/92). It is of particular concern to human beings because high levels of ultraviolet radiation are associated with high levels of skin cancer. The main cause of depletion of the ozone layer is the emission of the inert gases called chloro-fluoro carbons (CFCs) used as propellents in aerosol sprays and in refrigeration systems. An international protocol signed in Montreal in 1987 has effectively reduced CFC emissions but it is unclear whether the ozone layer will recover and how long it will take to do so.

- Scientists have long been aware of the effects of both hydrocarbon emissions from cars and industrial sulphur dioxide pollution which returns as acid rain to destroy forests. A more recent concern has been industrial emissions of carbon dioxide from the burning of fossil fuel. The level of such emissions is associated with the level of industrial development of a society. The USA emits about 5.5 tonnes per head per year, for example, while Brazil emits less than a tonne per head (*Economist* 30/5/92). Carbon dioxide and methane (produced by pastoral production) are 'greenhouse gases' – they prevent reverse radiation of solar heat, thus raising the temperature of the planet.

- The effects of greenhouse gases are exacerbated by progressive deforestation in the wet tropics. Trees extract carbon from the atmosphere, trap it and emit separated oxygen. Deforestation reduces the amount of carbon dioxide taken up and also releases previously trapped carbon by burning. Since 1850 about 7.7 million square kilometres of forest (about 12 per cent of the total, or an area the size of the USA) have disappeared (*Melbourne Sunday Age* 31/5/92).

- Many scientists agree that the above developments will lead to a raising of the temperature of the planet. However, there is widespread disagreement about the extent and speed of the warming process and about its effects on different areas. The most recent United Nations estimate suggests that the surface temperature will rise between 2 and 4.5 degrees in the next century (*Melbourne Sunday Age* 31/5/92). The consequences may well be serious for food production and sea levels.

Public consciousness of these problems has been raised by a series of popular scientific publications that seek to raise the alarm and thus accelerate the reflexivity of the globalization process. The first Club of Rome report is an early example but consciousness of planetary problems has come a long way since then. Perhaps the most extreme statement of the earth as a single entity is Lovelock's 'Gaia hypothesis' (named after the Greek goddess of the earth) which proposed that:

> the entire range of living matter on Earth, from whales to viruses, and from oaks to algae, could be regarded as constituting a single living entity, capable of manipulating the Earth's atmosphere to suit its overall needs and endowed with faculties and powers far beyond those of its constituent parts.
>
> (1987: 9)

This stunning piece of gynomorphism was embellished by the claim that if Gaia was threatened by human action she would turn on and eliminate them. If believed, this argument would be alarming enough, but at least Gaia is a predictable system. By contrast 'chaos theory' (Gleich 1987; Hall 1992) asserts that global and other systems are interconnected but inherently disorderly. As they evolve, minute peturbations can amplify very rapidly. The condition of the planet is not only full of danger but this danger can rapidly be exacerbated by inadvertent individual events, perhaps a single nuclear melt-down or oil-spill.

The response to environmental danger often takes the form of a panic, a widespread tendency to overblown and irrational fear and emotive responses of flight or aggression to that fear. O'Neill indicates that such panics are both the product of and contributors to globalization:

> By a *globalizing panic* I understand any practice that traverses the world to reduce the world and its cultural diversity to the generics of coca-cola, tourism, foreign aid, medical aid, military defence posts, tourism, fashion, and the international

money-markets. Since these practices are never quite stabilized, their dynamics include deglobalizing tendencies which will be reinscribed by the global system as threats to the 'world order'.

(1994: 332)

O'Neill's example of a globalizing panic is Aids, which might itself be considered an 'environmental' threat in the technical sense that the organic body is part of the physical environment of the social.[2] Aids first appeared in 1981 and about 400,000 people had contracted the disease within 10 years. During the same period about 10 million people contracted the Aids-indicative HIV virus (data from Scholte 1997: 25). Global networks of afflicted people transcend borders, intergovernmental conferences seek solutions, and multi-national drug companies search for cures. Such panics undermine the legitimacy of problem-solving states, not only because they do not respect territorial boundaries but because they are in principle insoluble by any state. They disempower state systems.

There are two possible political solutions to the tragedy of the global commons (Greene 1997). One possibility is to convert collective ownership to privatized ownership, itself a threat to the sovereignty of the state and a contributor to internal processes of disetatization. Privatization will place limitations on over-exploitation but has other possible downsides in that it institutionalizes inequality and opens up the possibility of resource monopolization. In many instances privatization of global commons, e.g. in the case of the airwaves, is literally impossible. A second possibility is inter-governmental regulation. Here states surrender sovereignty to international agencies of regulative governance that allocate access to the commons to users under an agreed set of principles.

The main regulative regimes that have so far been established are as follows (Greene 1997):

- *Antarctica*: the Antarctic Treaty of 1959 suspended the territorial claims to the continent and established it as a global

commons. Subsections of the Treaty prevented nuclear proliferation and laid down conditions for economic exploitation
and environmental protection.

- *Ocean resources*: the International Law of the Sea signed in 1982
  was one of the last attempts at privatization. It established
  Exclusive Economic Zones extending 200 miles from shore of
  any state.
- *Ozone depletion*: the regime as established under the Vienna
  convention of 1985 and the Montreal protocol of 1987. This
  prescribes reduction of CFC emissions by industrialized
  countries and the progressive elimination of certain types of
  CFC.
- *Biodiversity*: The Convention on Biological Diversity signed
  in Rio in 1993 obliges signatories to develop plans to protect
  species, ecological niches and habitats.
- *Global warming*: the main convention is the Framework
  Convention on Climate Change (FCCC) signed in Rio in 1993.
  Established non-legally binding agreements to reduce hydrocarbon emissions. Binding reduction targets and procedures
  for trading carbon credits were established at the Kyoto
  Conference of 1995.

The political leaders of nation-states have thus responded to the
fears of their panicked constituencies in the only way possible,
that is by reducing the sovereignty of their states relative to
international arrangements

NEW GLOBAL POLITICAL ACTORS

Under contemporary conditions the three-world or superpower
system is hyperdifferentiating. We can no longer identify three
worlds or two superpowers but rather a singular system in which
the critical basis for international relations is no longer the
ownership of military hardware but both economic muscle and
the ability to influence ideas and commitments. The sources of
these changes are the following:

- As is indicated above, the Soviet system proved unable to provide its citizens with a standard of living similar to that found in the West while simultaneously maintaining a command economy and a globally active military force. In 1989 the USSR gave up its attempt to control Eastern Europe, where market democracies rapidly emerged. The USSR then itself democratized and defederated and Russia can no longer be regarded unambiguously as a superpower. Poland, the Czech Republic and Hungary have now joined NATO and many ex-satellites and ex-Soviet republics seeking to join. Many have also joined a queue for accession to the EU.
- The USA is unable economically to sustain its military influence in Europe and the far East. Deficit financing of military budgets during the 1980s has been resolved by cutbacks in military commitments. Nevertheless, the USA, remains an essential, if not quite sufficient, partner in any global security action of serious scale.
- New power centres have emerged in Japan and the EU. This power was originally economic in character but is now extending to diplomatic and military arenas.
- Third-world states are experiencing rapid economic differentiation so that they no longer constitute a homogeneous community of the disadvantaged. This differentiation began with the development of OPEC (see Chapter 4) which ensured the escalation of the GDPs of oil-producing states. More recently, the rapid industrialization of the NICs has placed them closer in their interests and commitments to the first world than to the third.

A specific outcome of these developments has been the merging of military actions undertaken on behalf of such defence alliances as NATO, with peacekeeping operations carried out on behalf of the UN. The most important instance was the intervention of an American-headed expeditionary force that recovered the state of Kuwait following an Iraqi invasion in 1988. While the force was clearly an alliance of Western capitalist with traditional middle

Eastern interests it operated under UN auspices and with the sanction of the Security Council. Equally, it is unclear whether the European peacekeeping troops operating in the former Yugoslavia in the early 1990s were acting on behalf of the UN, NATO or the EU. The NATO intervention to protect the Yugoslav province of Kosovo was more clearly NATO governed but it predicated a UN administration of that province. Certainly, such developments indicate that in many instances national interests are becoming merged into global ones.

There are three possible theoretical interpretations of these developments. The first suggests the emergence of a 'new world order', a liberal construct that implies the disappearance of the superpowers and the emergence of a highly differentiated yet relatively consensual family of nations that punishes the deviant and protects the defenceless. This is a clearly ideological conception that seeks to obscure very real differences of interest and inequalities of military power. The second is the suggestion that the USA won the cold war and that the world is dominated by an unchallenged hegemon. Curiously, this view appears to be the property both of leftist critics and rightist triumphalists. It fails in the light of American impotence in Vietnam, Iran and Somalia. The USA succeeded in Kuwait and in Yugoslavia but only with allied military support, UN legitimacy, tacit Russian acceptance and European, Japanese and Arab financial assistance. This suggests that a third interpretation, that of the emergence of a multi-polar world, has much to offer as a realistic assessment. The domination of the superpowers has disappeared to be replaced by a fluid and highly differentiated pattern of international relations that exhibits much of the chaos and uncertainty that is also found, for example, in financial markets.

A specific outcome that can confirm the arrival of this newly disorderly world is the way in which the territoriality and sovereignty of states is being reinterpreted. The ex-Soviet republics are universally recognised as states yet they have extremely porous borders and precious little substantive independence. The key point of pressure here is the issue of nationality – the Baltic states, for example, cannot remain entirely separate from Russia so long as they include substantial Russian minorities. National pressure has been felt in a different way in ex-Yugoslavia and ex-Czechoslovakia leading to their dissolution into almost borderless nationalities. This development is paralleled in a spectacular way by the formation of the EU and to a lesser extent by NAFTA. The former is seeking to remove customs barriers and inspections and passport controls as well as seeking to aggregate such state norms as citizenship rights at a continental level. Equally, its constituent nation-states are experiencing a resurgence of minority nationalisms in such diverse locations as Scotland, Flanders, Catalonia and Lombardy. In general, the firmness of the linkage, state-societal community-nation-territory, that had been imposed by the realpolitik of the superpower order is widely being called into question

The globalization of the states-system has rendered international relations between states more complex and unpredictable. More states and fewer hegemons bring uncertainty and unpredictability. As we have seen, political elites have responded to the insecurity that such developments bring by entering into international regimes of governance. The last quarter of the twentieth century saw a rapid growth in the number of international governmental organizations (IGOs) that pooled state sovereignties. However, the burgeoning growth of International non-governmental organizations (INGOs or NGOs) has been even more remarkable. Some examples given by McGrew (1992b: 8) can illustrate their importance and the breadth of their activities. They include environmental pressure groups (e.g. Friends of the Earth, Greenpeace, WWF), professional and academic associations (e.g. Association of Commonwealth Universities, International Sociological Association), religious forums (e.g. World Council of Churches, World Moslem Congress), sports organizations (e.g. International Olympic Committee, International Cricket Conference), and welfare organizations (e.g. International Federation of Red Cross and Red Crescent Societies, Caritas). By 1992 there were nearly 15,000 such organizations, excluding MNCs and

BINGOs (business INGOs). Together they constitute a complex and ungovernable web of relationships that extends beyond the nation-state.

An examination of the growth pattern of states IGOs and NGOs can confirm the pattern of periodicity in the globalization process that is discussed throughout this book. As Figure 5.1 shows, the international system was, until the First World War, numerically dominated by states and their mainly bilateral relations. IGOs were very few in number and NGOs almost non-existent. An expansion of the global system began in the first quarter of the twentieth century when all three types of organization grew rapidly in number and importance. However, in the second half of the twentieth century the world was dominated by IGOs in which states surrendered a considerable

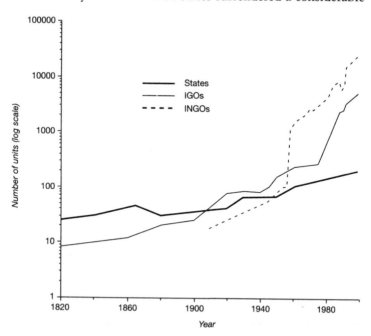

Figure 5.1 Growth of states and international organizations, 1820–1999
Sources: Giddens 1985: 264; McGrew 1992b: 8, 12; UN; Union of International Associations

measure of their sovereignty. A key feature of the accelerated phase of globalization, since about 1960 has been the rapid growth of NGOs which lends support to the claim that the main thrust of this phase is cultural, rather than material or political, in character.[3] The question of how much power the INGOs actually have will obviously be a major point of debate, but their existence and expansion should at least convince us that their value and effectiveness is in little doubt for those individuals who construct them. It is also clear that national governments are obliged to take IGOs and NGOs seriously and treat with them.

If counts of IGOs and NGOs are hazardous then counts of global social movements are impossible. Nevertheless there is widespread agreement on their growth and importance. They are both an indicator and cause of the decline of the nation-state. They are doubly effective in bringing about that decline in that they provide an alternative focus for political commitment and because they tend to be oppositional, to deny the legitimacy of the state as the focus for political action. They assert the predominance of super-state issues, human rights, the planetary environment, international inequality, peace and gender issues, over national interests. They also establish global communities linked together by mass-mediated protests and electronic communications.

The intersection of these developments can be inspected in a series of arenas but nowhere more forcibly than in the case of gender issues. One of the key features of the nation-state has been its capacity to exclude women from public political participation. Even at the lowest level of participation, that of voting for representatives, women were included relatively late and only by dint of pressing claims on their own behalf. Participation in state elites by women has been highly variable but in no nation-state can it be argued to be equivalent to the participation of men. Women have thus been obliged to both oppose and circumvent the state, to develop collective political actors of their own. The key forms of such action are social movements and NGOs. The key issues are participation levels, women in development, and equal rights and freedoms. The arenas in which these issues are promoted include the UN and its human rights subsidiaries and global conferences and networks that seek to exert pressure on other political actors.

UN-sponsored global women's conferences have taken place in Mexico in 1975, in Copenhagen in 1980, in Nairobi in 1985 and, most notably, in Beijing in 1995. Beijing was qualitatively different from the earlier conferences because in each of those women tended to argue with each other from the point of view of their own nation-states. They represented the cleavages discussed in Chapter 4 characterized by East vs. West, and North vs. South (Dickenson 1997: 106–13). Beijing established a platform for action which established targets for participation and norms for gender rights and for sexual and corporeal freedoms. The *Platform for Action* was endorsed by all 189 delegations which meant that claims to the cultural specificity and necessity of acts of oppression (e.g. polygamy, female genital mutilation, purdah) were no longer acceptable. The Beijing conference was also noteworthy because the community of politicized women who attended did much of their preparatory work globally by means of electronic communication. Importantly, some 4,000 NGOs were accredited to the conference, far outnumbering the governmental delegations and constraining the application of diplomatic pressure to the conference's resolutions by the Chinese government.

A NEW POLITICAL CULTURE

There is an intimate connection between borderless political organization and the extent to which there is a common political culture across societies. To the extent that governments share ideological commitments and interests they will be more prepared to see aggregation or decentralization of state sovereignty and also to dismantle protective and defensive barriers between one another. So the degree of commonality of political culture is itself an indicator of globalization.

The case for the emergence of a single political culture is made most strongly by Fukuyama (1992) and Huntington (1991). Fukuyama's thoretical explanation for commonality is a version of Hegelian essentialism that asserts that the human desire for individual 'recognition' drives a universal history in the direction of such a singularity. The empirical case that he sets out in support of this view is that the national societies of the world have moved or are moving towards a political culture of liberal democracy. The central ideas of such a culture are: first, that individuals should have rights to autonomy in certain spheres of thought and action, including for example, due process under law, speech and publication that expresses political or religious ideas, control of the body, and ownership and disposal of property; and second, that the members of any polity should have the right to choose and to participate in their own government by means which roughly give them an equal influence in that choice and an equal chance to participate (1992: 42–3). Contentiously, Fukuyama is quite clear that liberal democracy implies a commitment to market capitalism because these guarantee individual rights in the economic sphere. He also stresses that it is the culture rather than practice of liberal democracy that is critical. In triumphalist tone, he asserts: 'What is emerging victorious . . . is not so much liberal practice, as the liberal idea. That is to say, for a very large part of the world, there is now no ideology with pretensions to universality that is in a position to challenge liberal democracy' (1992: 45, original italics).[4]

The global predominance of liberal democracy was accomplished in a series of waves punctuated by fallbacks that began with liberal revolutions in Europe and America in the seventeenth and eighteenth centuries. However, the main developments occurred within what we have come to recognise as the accelerated phase of globalization, the last third of the twentieth century. In this period authoritarian regimes, first of the right and then of the left, began to collapse. In the 1970s fascist or military dictatorships folded in Spain, Portugal, Greece and Turkey. In the 1980s liberal democracies were established in the former dictatorships of Latin America. Korea, the Phillipines, Taiwan, and Thailand also moved in that direction. Fukuyama's proposal is even more convincing if we consider the emergence of democracies in Eastern Europe and the former Soviet Union, and its establishment in South Africa as well as in other parts of that continent. It must be admitted, however, that not all of these regimes are as liberal as they might be. Fukuyama argues that the dictatorial regimes were toppled by a crisis of legitimacy, their governments were no longer seen as representing society as a whole. Both Fukuyama and Huntington give weight to the inability to deliver economic prosperity without the liberal institutions of capitalism but equally stress the problem of the legitimacy of authoritarian regimes in the face of prevailing global democratic norms (see especially Huntington 1991: 106).

The outcome of these developments is shown in Figure 5.2, which gives the number of liberal-democratic states in the global system. This number doubled between 1975 and 1991 so that about 60 of the world's large societies are now liberal democracies. The main exceptions are the remaining socialist states of East Asia and Islamic theocracies, monarchies and military dictatorships. Many of the latter also display some of the characteristics of liberal democracy – Iran, for example, is democratic in that it has relatively free and fair elections but not liberal in that the citizen is without rights; China is clearly undemocratic but is liberalizing in the economic sphere. Nor do the data include the effects of recent developments in ex-Yugoslavia, the ex-USSR or South Africa. Depending on measurement criteria these would account for perhaps another 25 or 30 democratic states, about a dozen of which might be counted as liberal.

However, we must also consider the possibility of cultural variation between liberal democracies – for example, in Sweden a high level of state intervention and personal taxation has historically been more positively valued than in the USA, which tends to value personal autonomy above equality of condition. However, here too there is evidence of cultural convergenge. A shift is under way towards a culture described by Inglehart

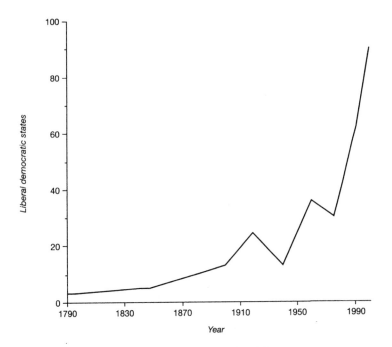

Figure 5.2 Number of states estimated to be liberal democratic, 1790–1999
Sources: Fukuyama 1992: 49–50; Freedom House

(1990) as the rise of postmaterialist values. The traditional focus of politics in liberal democracies was material values, issues to do with the distribution and redistribution of goods and services. The typical division in this politics was between a 'right' or conservative side that stressed the preservation of property ownership and freedom of contract in markets, often coupled with a paternalistic welfarism, and a 'left' or social democratic side that stressed the redistribution of property and income on a more egalitarian basis, a state-interventionist welfare system and the regulation of markets. Postmaterialist values emphasize community, self-expression and the quality of life. Here, a political value division emerges between a 'new right' that stresses individual autonomy, the right to consume and governmental minimalism and a 'new left' that stresses the empowerment of minorities and a mutuality of interests among human beings and between them and their environments. Inglehart estimates that by 1970 postmaterialists outnumbered materialists in the core group of liberal democracies in Western Europe, North America and Japan.

The question now arises as to why this value shift should be regarded as a globalizing trend. The answer is that it contributes to many of the developments discussed above. In materialist value conflicts the key issue is the role of the state and the way in which it represents the interests of one class or another. Here the state is the focus of political attention and its structures will be extended in so far as political parties can enhance their support by so doing. In postmaterialist politics the state is problematic across the political spectrum: the new right regards it as a transgressor against individual freedoms and a distorter of markets; the new left views it as an agency of rampant materialism and a means for the juridical control of populations and their minorities. More importantly postmaterialism focuses political attention on trans-societal issues, the planetary problems discussed above. It indicates such phenomenologically globalizing items as 'the individual', 'life', 'humanity', 'rights' and 'the earth' that indicate the universality of the condition of the inhabitants of the planet rather than the specific conditions of their struggle with an opposing class about the ownership of property or the distribution of rewards.

CONCLUSION

A critical and striking feature of political globalization is that it does not in any area exhibit the extreme level of globalization found, for example, in financial markets. Political globalization is most advanced in the areas of international relations and political culture. However, the state remains highly resistant, largely sovereign, at least in formal terms, and a critical arena for problem solving. A possible explanation is that politics is a highly territorial activity and that the organized nation-state is the most effective means for establishing sovereignty over territory that human beings have yet devised The state might therefore just be the final bastion of resistance to globalizing trends and the key indicator of their ultimate effectivity. If states survive globalization then it cannot be counted the force that it currently appears to be.

The undermining of the state, and indeed such disetatization as has already occurred, must, on the arguments offered in this chapter, be counted as a cultural development. The theorem that material exchanges localize, power exchanges internationalize, and symbolic exchanges globalize can thus receive a good measure of confirmation. The expansion of the nation-state /international relations system organized the territorial surface of the planet with political entities of a single type. That process contributed to globalization but it was not truly globalizing because it also maintained borders and barriers to social intercourse between its inhabitants. These borders are now being subverted by transcendent cultural items that will not respect them because they can be transmitted by symbolic media. The spread of liberal democracy and of postmaterialist values is not a *sui generis* development in each society where they occur but are transmitted from one society to another. Those who doubt the effectivity of culture might wish to compare the bloody and violent revolutions that established nation-states from the seventeenth to the nineteenth century with the almost bloodless coups and 'velvet revolutions' that have occurred in the last third of the twentieth. These suggest that the prospect of complete political globalization emerges as a genuine possibility.

However, the globalized polity that is likely to emerge is unlikely to resemble previous visions. The spread of liberal democracy is perhaps not quite as irreversible as some commentators propose, but it is both effective and resilient precisely because it combines the transparent governance with modest participation that most postmaterialist populations seem to seek. This means that threats of dictatorial global domination, represented by fascist and communist ideologies, if they ever existed, now have very little prospect of success. However, the utopian visions of a harmonious and consensual world government that attended the formation of such IGOs as the UN are equally unlikely to be realized. In a world in which every political opinion is of equal worth, consensus is unlikely to emerge. Nor, in view of its resilience and formal sovereignty, can one imagine that the state will, to use an outdated expression, 'wither away'. The more likely outcome is that the state will wither somewhat. The current indication is that the state's effectivity will recede from being the predominant form of political organization to being a dominant form and from there to being one of a number of players jockeying for position in political arrangements. It will continue to surrender powers and sovereignty, much as it has been doing since the middle of the twentieth century, so that it becomes one political system in a fluctuating hierarchy of systems operating at local, national, regional and global levels. States will become more numerous, focusing on natural ethnicities, and therefore more globalized but less powerful.

NOTES

1   This is enshrined in two legal principles: 'immunity from jurisdiction' – 'no state can be sued in courts of another state for acts performed in its sovereign capacity'; and 'immunity of state agencies' – 'should an individual break the law of another state while acting as an agent of his country of origin and be brought before that state's courts, he is not held "guilty" because he did not act as a private individual but as the representative of the state' (Cassese 1991: 218).

2   The *pan-ic* (i.e. totalizing) status of Aids is critical to the present argument. Unlike bubonic plague it is not merely *pandemic*. Victims and therapists alike view the disease as an aspect of a world-wide human community in a way that medieval sufferers from bubonic plague probably rarely did.

3   The growth of IGOs and INGOs may have surprised even the most expert observers. In 1983 Archer estimated that by the turn of the twenty-first century IGOs would remain at about 300 and INGOs might number 9,600 (1983: 171). By 1992 the respective figures were 3,188 and 14,733 (UIA 1992: 1671).

4   Fukuyama argues against Islamic theocracy as a serious challenge to liberal democracy on the grounds that it applies only in societies that have long been religiously and culturally Moslem. It cannot expand beyond these boundaries and is active and virulent partly because many of its adherents are tempted by liberal democracy (1992: 45–6).

6

CLASHING CIVILIZATIONS: INTERNATIONAL CULTURES

He's got the whole world in his hands.

African-American gospel song

The previous chapters make the claim that globalization proceeds most rapidly in contexts in which social relationships are mediated through symbols. Economic globalization is therefore most advanced in the financial markets that are mediated by monetary tokens and to the extent that production is dematerialized, and political globalization has proceeded to the extent that there is an appreciation of common planetary values and problems rather than commitments to material interests. These chapters also make the supplementary argument that material and power exchanges in the economic and political arenas are progressively becoming displaced by symbolic ones, that is, by relationships based on values, preferences and tastes rather than by material inequality and constraint. On these arguments globalization might be conceived as an aspect of the progressive 'culturalization' of social life proposed by theories of postmodernization (e.g. Crook, Pakulski and Waters 1992).

However, this, the first of two chapters concentrating more specifically on culture, focuses on the cultural equivalent of the emergence of trans-national corporations and international trade in the economic sphere and of nation-states in the political sphere. This is the emergence of idea systems that, while claiming the appeal of universality, could not individually manage to generate sufficient appeal to become globally dominant and universal. These idea systems took two main forms: universal religions that managed to missionize and proselytize so successfully that they were able to overwhelm or at least to syncretize local and native religious expression; and political ideologies that sought to unify diverse collectivities of people in the pursuit of common goals. The earliest and most important of these ideologies is nationalism but its competitors and interlocutors include liberalism, democratic socialism, fascism and communism. Such religious and political ideologies underpinned the institutionalization of the internally consistent but externally incompatible totalizing cultural systems that we call 'civilizations'.

The more such civilizations expand, the more likely they are to come into contact and therefore into conflict. Huntington (1993) argues that clashes between civilizations are, under conditions of globalization, likely to supersede conflict between classes or conflict between such Western political ideologies as socialism and liberalism. This book takes a rather different view, arguing that civilizational clash has a long history running from the eighth through to the twentieth centuries. Under conditions of low technological development and low geographical mobility, such clashes usually occurred at civilizational peripheries rather than at centres. Before turning to the story of what happens to civilizations and cultures under accelerated globalization, we can examine here the global spread of civilizing ideas and some of the conflicts that have been produced by them.

CRUSADES AND JIHADS

While it is clearly not the case that culture, as an arena differentiated from economics and politics, has ever been totally globalized it has nevertheless shown a greater tendency towards globalization than either of the other two arenas. This is particularly evident in the area of religion. For many centuries, the great universalizing religions of the world, Buddhism, Christianity, Confucianism, Islam and Hinduism offered adherents an exclusivist and generalizing set of values and allegiances that stood above both state and economy. In the medieval world, for example, Christendom was conceived as the kingdom of God on earth, and Islam has always been conceived as a social community of material and political interests that supersedes the state. Indeed, in the thirteenth and fourteenth centuries these two theocratic units came into generalized conflict over the possession of one of their common sacred sites. These religions in particular have had a globalizing sense of mission in which they sought to convert those defined as heathen or infidel by whatever constraint was possible. One strategy was to align themselves with expansive empires that had global ambitions (e.g. the Arabian, British, Holy Roman and Ottoman empires) and thus to export the belief system beyond its original point of adoption.

The claims of universalistic religions that the world was created by a single god and that humanity is a common form of existence in relation to that god is a primary long-run driving force in the direction of globalization. It leads to the argument that humanity constitutes a single community that disvalues geographical localities and political territories. Among the universalizing religions the derivative Abrahamic faiths of Christianity and Islam have proved the most effective globalizers because of their missions of proselytization and conversion. This is most explicit in Islam. The earthly objective of Islam is the establishment of a community of the faithful (*Umma*) which is ruled hierocratically, in which practices specified by the Qur'ān are followed to the letter and which engages in a holy struggle (Jihad) against unbelievers (Turner 1991: 169). The expansion of the Arab empire from the eighth century and the Ottoman empire from the twelfth through the fifteenth centuries under the aegis of this theology not only placed the 'nations' they conquered under a unified cultural system but brought Islam into contact with Christianity and forced some measure of relativization on each faith and its associated culture. The Ottoman capture of Constantinople in 1453 and its onward march to the gates of Vienna shook the confidence of Christendom. Indeed, the failure of Christendom successfully to control its Holy Land by means of successive and bloody military campaigns known as 'Crusades' and its incapacity to missionize beyond Europe may have contributed to the Protestant reformation and thereby to a further spurt in the Western globalization process.

For many, that process begins in the highly universalistic though exclusivist seed-bed faith of Judaism. As Long (1991) indicates, Judaism could not itself promote globalization because its particularisms (especially the covenant between God and his chosen people and the notion of a promised land) were so intense and because it had no mission of conversion. The universalisms it contributed to Christianity and Islam were, however, critically important. These included the ideas that there was indeed a singular and abstract god, a single value-reference for every person in the world, and that this god proposed a single set of legal and moral laws. Only these universalistic elements were adopted by early Christianity which in fact syncretized Judaic monotheism with Greek humanism (hence the deification of Christ) and Roman imperialism (Strange 1991). Indeed, two critical elements in the expansion of Christianity were its use of Greek, the *lingua franca* of the period, and its eventual alignment with the the Roman imperial dynasty.

Thereafter and for the next thousand or so years Christianity ceased to be a purely religious movement and more closely approximated a political ideology. Its globalizing consequence was the legitimation of the incorporation of tribal peasants into large-scale political systems. It achieved this by specifying that social order was ordained and that the relationship between any individual and God had to be mediated through a priestly hierarchy. Under this religious regime the conscience was truly collective and the earthly orientation was almost entirely towards the maintenance of internal societal order. It was not until after the establishment of the Iberian colonies in the Americas in the sixteenth century that Christianity, or Catholicism as it had become, again began to develop a conversion mission (Muldoon 1991). By that time, however, a newer and far more important globalizing religious force had emerged.

The Protestant Reformation was critical in the development of Western globalizing trends in two important respects. First, Christianity had always fudged the issue of the relationship between the powers of state and church (e.g. in the very notion of Christendom) so that there had been a long series of jurisdictional conflicts between kings and the popes to whom they nominally owed spiritual allegiance. The Reformation resolved this dispute either by subordinating the church to the state, as in England, or by secularizing the state, as in the USA and republican France. The state could now rely on the political legitimations of nationalism or liberalism rather than religious legitimation, and the stage was thus set for the emergence and enhancement of its powers which was itself the prerequisite for internationalization (see Chapter 5). Second, medieval Christianity also maintained some significant particularisms in so far as some people were regarded as closer to God than others (e.g. monarchs received their tenancies directly from God) and in so far as relationships to God had to be mediated through priests. Protestantism raised universalism to a new level by asserting the possibility of a direct relationship between every individual and God by the mechanisms of prayer, conscience and faith. It therefore asserted that all were equal in relation to God and that salvation did not depend on one's inclusion within a religiously ordered political community. Any inhabitant of the planet could now become a Christian simply by an act of faith so that by the nineteenth century Protestant missionaries were fanning out across the planet to give its inhabitants the good news. Catholic missionaries were not far behind.

Thus, the religion, whether Protestant or reformed Catholic, that is associated with Western modernity is highly secularized and privatized. It specifies that the morals of state and economic action, for example, are governed not by general and public principles but by the consciences of their individual practitioners. War and economic exploitation can thus equally be condoned because Christianity assumes that politicians and business leaders have exercised an individual moral calculus in advance of the act. In so far as capitalism and the nation-state are crucial configurations within globalization the Protestant reformation liberates them then from cultural constraint. But Beyer (1990) encourages us to stress that Protestantism carries with it its own positive contribution to globalization. Under medieval Christianity or Islam a territorial distinction could be maintained between good and evil, the saved and the damned, or the believers and the infidels – the good lived in a common space inside the community and the bad outside. To the extent belief or goodness is a matter of individual conscience, the fact that a person is a neighbour need not imply that they are as morally sound as oneself. The community of the faithful is dotted across the world and not confined to a locality, and so too are the morally feckless. In embracing individualism, Protestantism thus challenges spatial constraints.

REVOLUTIONS AND REVIVALS

In its embrace of secularization theory, social science has generally taken the view that the 'irrational' influence of religion on society would be tamed within an enlightened modernity. A second aspect of social life which might equally be regarded as threatening and irrational is ethnicity and its political expression, nationalism. From one point of view ethnic allegiances and commitments might be held to have been 'civilized' within the rationalistic structures of the nation-state, but a more compelling argument might be that the nation-state actually unleashed the forces of nationalism into the world by harnessing ethnicity to the state project (Hobsbawm 1992).

In the premodern world ethnicity was a taken-for-granted component of identity associated with tribalism – the Durkheimian notion of a mechanically solidaristic segment is an appropriate formal conceptualization. It was also politically unproblematic because there was no social technology that could connect successfully the large-scale political systems of empires and feudal monarchies and large-scale religious cultures with local practices. Medieval culture was in fact highly disunified so that political units were loose confederations of minority ethnic affiliations and the large-scale European continental empires could only survive so long as ethnic diversity was tolerated. Local segments owed formal allegiance to the centre and owed levies of troops and taxes to it, but economic activity and cultural expression in particular were organized on a local basis. Moreover, territory was not formally allocated as ethnicities flowed into each other at the boundaries.

The connection between *ethnie* and nation is a deliberate human construction by rising political classes seeking to displace the feudal autarchy. From the end of the eighteenth century there were specific attempts across Europe and in other parts of the world to raise national consciousness in favour of that new and modern form of political organization, the nation-state. Anderson's Marxist interpretation of nations as 'imagined communities', in contradistinction to the 'real communities' of class, has become an orthodox conceptualization in this regard (1983). Hobsbawm (1992: 188) argues that the objective of early nationalist movements was to invent a coincidence between four reference points, people (ethnie)-state-nation-government, that is, between a common identity, a political system, a community and an administration. To these we can also add the important component of territory, especially in so far as nationalism sought to establish the exclusive occupation of a territory by the nation. However, this nationalism was almost always ideological in character because there was seldom an exact homology between the four reference points. Only such very extreme forms of nationalism as German fascism could seek an exact correspondence by trying to incorporate into the state external members of the ethnie and by subordinating or even exterminating internal minorities. Hobsbawm (1992: 186) estimates that not more than a dozen of the 180 or so contemporary nation-states coincide with a single ethnic or linguistic group. Hall would think this an overestimate: 'Modern nations are all cultural hybrids' (S. Hall 1992: 297; italics deleted).

The political and intellectual elites that led the nationalist challenge engaged in a series of ideological practices that sought to represent the nation as a social, spatial and historical fact that is real, continuous and meaningful. Hall (1992: 293–5) outlines five such practices:

- They told stories or histories of the nation indicating commonalities of experience, of triumph and struggle. Among a multitude of examples we can mention stories of the American West, the Irish struggle against famine and British absentee landlords, the Great Trek of the Boers, and Australian military defeat at Gallipoli. These stories give people a sense of a common and continuous heritage.
- They make assertions about national character, about British fair play, or Japanese honourability, or Chinese industry and respect for authority, or Canadian decency, or Irish martyrdom, or Australian mateship. A national character gives a sense of timelessness to the nation that is independent of history.
- They invent new patterns of ritual, pageantry and symbolism that give collective expression to the nation. These include flags, heroes, systems of national honours, special days, national ceremonies, and so on. Some elites – Israel and Ireland are examples – invent or revive languages.
- They establish foundational myths and legends that locate the nation 'outside' history and give it a quasi-sacred character as well as a sense of originality or non-derivativeness. Examples include the Camelot stories of the English, the German revival of teutonic mythology, the Rastafarianism of Jamaicans and the claimed connections between modern and ancient Greece.
- They promote ideas of common breeding or even racial purity. The obvious example is the Nazi promotion of the idea of a

German *Volk* but the British speak of themselves as *the* island race and Malays as *bumiputra* (sons of the soil).

It must be stressed that these practices are evident not only in the emergence of the nineteenth-century European nation-states but in the contemporary attempts of emerging nations to free themselves from Western political and economic imperialism. Foster (1991) notes the promotion of ideologies of *kastom* (i.e. custom) in Pacific island nations that gives an anti-Western emphasis to mystical wisdom and social and environmental harmony but is actually built upon Western conceptions of the 'noble savage'.

The last example should tell us that nationalism is both a globalized and a globalizing phenomenon. It is one of the components of culture that has been transmitted around the globe as part of the process of political 'internationalization' discussed in Chapter 5. The establishment of nation-states everywhere provides a basis on which societies can be connected with one another. But nationalism carries with it a broader political culture that, as we have seen, is also subject to widespread adoption. This culture includes a commitment to rational and dispassionate administration, to political representation and accountability, and to steering in the direction of enhanced collective material welfare.

The great universalizing religions have generally been threatened or eclipsed by modernization and the rise of capitalism as well as by nationalism. But the emergence of the liberal-democratic state and of the capitalist economic system also carried with them universalizing values. The state carried a set of commitments to democracy, citizenship, patriotism and welfare, while capitalism carried commitments to instrumental rationality, aquisitiveness, individualism and the privacy of person and property. During the twentieth century the conflicts between the various aspects of these value-systems were played out in the context of the equally universalizing and often expansionist politico-economic ideologies of communism, conservatism, fascism, liberalism and socialism. Like Christianity and Islam these claimed global relevance, and their adherents campaigned and activized in order to establish them as the sole principle for the organization of individual values and preferences and for the legitimation of social organization across the planet.

As in the case of religion, nationalism and other political ideologies can set up civilizational boundaries and exclusivities that can result in conflict. The probability of conflict is increased to the extent that nationalism intersects with other ideologies. For example, the incorporation of nationalism into fascism prescribes that the will of the national collectivity is concentrated in the single historic destiny of a unique leader, the only person who can bring the nation out of chaos and restore it to its former glory. The ideology prevailed most effectively in Italy, Germany, Spain and (in a modified imperial-militaristic form) Japan from about 1925 to 1945 but it persisted far longer in some countries in South America, and it continues to define the political regimes in Syria and Iraq in the year 2000. The linking of the destiny of the leader to the nation often leads to a political commitment to the view that the glory of the nation can only be achieved by the domination of other nations by means of military conquest. The Second World War was a conflict between fascist regimes on one hand and communist and liberal ones on the other.

While that conflict can be regarded as an intersection between an extreme form of nationalism and of resistance to it, the super-power conflict that succeeded it was much more civilizational in character. Here, American nationalism and the nationalism of its allies was bound up with liberalism. To be opposed to capitalism or democracy or private property was, during the 1940s and 1950s often held to be 'un-American'. Similarly, communism was closely interlinked with Soviet nationalism. In the Soviet Union, the Second World War was called 'The Great Patriotic War' and the non-Russian republics of the Union and the satellite nations were intensively dominated.

CULTURE CONTACT

Modernization in particular generates media that can permeate and dissolve boundaries between localities and between political entities and thus allow cultural transmission to take place at an increasingly rapid rate. Token money was an obvious and important medium that we have discussed at several points. It had several effects. First, it allowed trade between localities to be transacted across a wide and generalized range of products. The more trade was extended, the greater was the probability of geographical specialization by product, which would further promote trade and so on. The global product market began to develop quite early. Second, it allowed capital to be translated into the exchangeable form of finance and also to be exported and invested across distances. The marketization of capital eroded localized, kinship-based concentrations of capital and allowed its accummulation on an ever-widening scale.

However, other media were also significant in linking cultural localities. The development of military sailing vessels in the fifteenth and sixteenth centuries coupled with an increasing level of macro-climatic and geographical knowledge which their use required increased the possibility of discovery and exploration as far as planetary limits would allow. This was but a first step in the liberation of the medium of transportation from the limits of animate power, but it was genuinely significant. Although the Phoenicians, the Venetians and the Vikings had achieved much using human rowers, the distant contacts that they made could not be sustained precisely because of an insufficiently developed technology of energy. Only the multi-masted sailing vessel, the Spanish galleon, the British clipper, the Arab dhow or the Chinese junk, could sustain a pattern of global economic colonization. Indeed, only such vessels could carry more people than the number needed to power them and thus, for example, move settlers from Europe *en masse* to the far-flung reaches of the globe. The medium received a further boost with the discovery and application of steam power. Not only did steam power further multiply the effectiveness of marine transport but it also enabled the conquest, by railways, of vast continental distances in the Americas, Africa, Australia and Siberia. The internal combustion, diesel and jet engines and their associated technologies clearly multiplied globalizing possibilities.

The third significant globalizing medium provided by modernization is electrical, electronic and photographic means for the communication of information. Transportation improvements could themselves improve communication by mail. However, perhaps the most significant event in nineteenth-century globalization occurred during the Crimean War of the 1850s when the war correspondent of *The Times*, a Mr Russell, was able to telegraph his reports instantly back to London, for the first time, so that descriptions of the events were available a mere day or two after they happened. The rest, as they say, is history – by about the turn of the century communication could be achieved by telephone, by wireless, by cinematography and even by television. Distant events could be known about, even 'witnessed' without leaving one's own locality.

A significant spurt of internationalization occurred in the nineteenth century, partly as a consequence of the development of these transportation and communication media. The invention of the social technology of administration (and surveillance) allowed power to be extended across territories and their inhabitant populations in a direct and centralized way. The key location of power for any individual member of one of the new nation-states was no longer a local kinsman or potentate but a distant bureaucratic system. The hierarchical organization of bureaucracies could be extended across such territories by the use of reporting systems. So effective were these bureaucracies that trans-global colonial systems involving territories and populations many times greater than those of the colonizing power could be administered and thus controlled from the European centres.

One of the consequences of these contacts was the consolidation of taste preferences across civilizations, particularly across Western Christian civilization and its colonial extensions. Consumption-based cultural globalization actually began in the nineteenth century but in the arena of elite or bourgeois culture. At that time, what previously had been courtly preferences in music and art trickled down to the nouveaux riches who established public art galleries, museums and libraries, civic symphony orchestras, national opera, ballet and drama companies, and open and secular universities to institutionalize (and socialize the costs of) their newly found sense of taste. As capitalism expanded across the globe these cultural institutions were carried by its dominant class so that no new society and no newly industrialized society, even if state socialist, could regard itself as having an autonomous national culture without them. By the end of the nineteenth century a global but mainly European cultural tradition had been established in which the same music, the same art and the same literature and science were equally highly regarded in many parts of the globe. Indeed, new methods of transportation allowed world tours by master practitioners and performers and allowed students to study at international centres of excellence, all of which served to consolidate a homogenized global high culture.

However, popular culture remained nation-state specific until the development of cinematographic and electronic mass mediation. A long-term effect of these media has been to democratize culture because they refuse to respect the 'specialness' or auratic quality of high cultural products. The early twentieth century saw the development of media machines using the complex technology of electricity and the opportunity for exports of popular cultural taste. The phonograph, the telephone and the moving picture were the first such developments to attain widespread popularity but radio and television were also physically invented quite early in the century. Radio, the first true electronic mass medium, became well established in the 1920s and 1930s. Television began to penetrate mass markets only after the Second World War, both hailed and feared as a more powerful and pervasive medium than radio, with an even greater potential to affect the minds of those consuming its contents.

In a world in which the minds of individuals are so resolutely focused on mass-mediated images it is surprising that so much social scientific attention should have been paid to global integration by means of economics and so little to culture or consciousness. This may well be because, as they stand, both sociology and political science are nonglobalized and modern, as opposed to postmodern, disciplines. The main source of an alternative is the literary and communications theorist, McLuhan. Although much of McLuhan's work is unsatisfactory from the point of view of a positivistic or even an analytic social science, his ideas although formulated over 30 years ago, are so perceptive and insightful that they have insinuated themselves into many of the accounts that we now regard as groundbreaking. Indeed, Giddens' recent statements on globalization (see this volume *passim*) clearly owe a substantial, though largely unacknowledged debt to McLuhan.

For McLuhan (1964) the determining principle of culture is the medium by which it is transmitted rather than its content. Media include any means of extending the senses and therefore include technologies of both transportation and communication. It follows that McLuhan's position anticipates the technological determinism of both Rosenau (see Chapter 5) and Harvey (see Chapter 4). This allows a periodization of history into two principal epochs that roughly correspond with Durkheim's mechanical and organic solidarity. The first is what might be called the tribal epoch which is based on the technologies of the spoken word and the wheel. In this oral culture human experience is necessarily instant, immediate and collective as well as subtle, sensitive and complete. The second is the industrial epoch based on technologies of the written word and of mechanization. In this literate culture, human experience is fragmented and privatized. Writing or reading a book is isolated and individualized, even lonely. Moreover, it emphasizes the sense of sight at the expense of sound, touch and smell which leaves the viewer distant and unengaged. Print also constructs thought into connected lineal sequences that allow societies to rationalize and thereby to industrialize.

This transformation also had globalizing effects. The use of paper, wheels and roads allowed the first moves in the direction of what Giddens is later to call time–space distanciation. In their capacity to speed up communication, they started to connect distant localities, to reduce the consciousness of the tribe or village. They also allowed power centres to extend their control over geographic margins. Again anticipating Giddens and Harvey, McLuhan shows that this reorganization of space through time is accompanied by the development of two other important universalizing devices. First, the mechanical clock disrupted recursive and seasonal conceptions of time and replaced them by a durational conception where time is measured in precise divisions. Measured, universal time became an organizing principle for a modern world divorced from the immediacy of human experience. As McLuhan says, the division of labour begins with the division of time by the use of the mechanical clock (1964: 146). The second device is money (Giddens' 'symbolic tokens'), which increases the speed and volume of relationships.

Current circumstances constitute a further epochal shift. The predominant industrial and individualizing media of print, the clock and money are being displaced by electronic media that restore the collective culture of tribalism but on an expansive global scale. Its key characteristic is speed. Because electronic communication is virtually instantaneous it drags events and locations together and renders them totally interdependent. Electricity establishes an international network of communication that is analogous to the human central nervous system. It enables us to apprehend and experience the world as a whole: 'with electricity we extend our central nervous system globally, instantly interrelating every human experience' (1964: 358). Lineal sequencing and thus rationality are dispatched by electronic speed-up and the synchronization of information – the world is experienced not simply globally but chaotically.

The accelerating effects of electronic communication and rapid transportation create a structural effect that McLuhan calls 'implosion' (1964: 185). By this he means that they, as it were, bring together in one place all the aspects of experience – one can simultaneously sense and touch events and objects that are great distances apart. The centre–margin structure of industrial civilization disappears in the face of synchrony, simultaneity and instantaneousness. In what has become an evocative and iconic formulation, McLuhan asserts that: 'This is the new world of the global village' (1964: 93).[1] Just as members of tribal society had been aware of their total interdependence with other members so members of the global village cannot avoid a consciousness of human society in its entirety. But global space is not at all similar to a tribal neighbourhood.

> Electric circuitry has overthrown the regime of 'time' and 'space' and pours upon us instantly and continuously the concerns of all other men. It has reconstituted dialogue on a global scale. Its message is Total Change, ending psychic, social, economic, and political parochialism. The old civic, state, and national groupings have become unworkable. Nothing can be further from the spirit of the new technology than 'a place for everything and everything in its place.' You can't go home again.
>
> (McLuhan and Fiore 1967: 16; original italics)

GLOBETROTTERS AND JETSETTERS

Contact between cultures can be achieved not only in the mediated form of technologized communications but by more direct means. In Chapter 3 we note an expansion in the mobility of labour, at first forced, but then increasingly voluntary, that often ensured the transplantation of one (usually Western) culture into another. Indeed, the history of Western colonialism involves the imposition of European values and preferences on sub-ordinated societies which often involved the establishment of colonial bureaucracies, missionary churches and garrisons. The insertion of these foreign populations into local contexts often involved the permanent inculcation of previously foreign values, tastes and preferences. We might thus explain preferences for

Catholicism in Rio, baguettes in Hanoi and bagpipes in Lahore. Similarly, the expansion of trans-national corporations in the twentieth century represented a further overlay of American and European taste but now carried by business executives as well as by advertising. The twentieth century has seen an unprecedented expansion of permanent and temporary migrations of business-men (*sic*), officials, academics, soldiers, workers and students who are themselves the agents of culture contact.

In this section, however, we mainly focus on the emergence and internationalization of tourism, which was to become, through mass temporary mobility, a major agent of culture contact. Tourism is itself a historical peculiarity and to under-stand its development we need to return to issues of time and space. Western phenomenologies of time and space were re-organized at around the middle of the second millennium. The mechanical clock disembedded time from natural diurnal and seasonal rhythms and the mapping of the globe dislocated space from place. Many were confronted with the fact that for the first time their perceptions of the physical context were not limited to their experience of it. The consequences were profound. Time could now be divided into segments and specific activities could be assigned to these different segments. In particular, public activity or 'work' could be separated in time from domestic activity, which meant that to the extent that the latter was undemanding it could be defined as leisure or recreation. Previously leisure could only occur in the ritual or carnivalesque atmospheres of feasts and holy days, when whole days or weeks could be put aside. Now it was possible for leisure to become a universal and general expectation with the time and place decided individually. Equally, as Marx tells us, work could be separated from home in space. For medieval and early modern people travel was an unusual practice, undertaken in relation only to such biographically unusual events as military service, pilgrimage, trade or diplomacy. Partly because transport was slow, it was costly in terms of time. It was also regarded as risky, and those who travelled (explorers, crusaders, pilgrims, etc.) were regarded as courageous or saintly or perhaps foolish. The conceptualization of space normalized travel by routinizing travel between home and work and increasing notions of an opportunity for trade.

These phenomenological developments then, insitutionalized two new and modern human possibilities as general features of social life, leisure and travel. This is not to suggest that in the early stages of capitalist industrialization either of them were generally accessible in any society. Rather, it suggests that both were available to some sections of industrialized societies and that it was possible for any member of society to imagine themselves engaging in such an activity, in however utopian a fashion. These developments also gave rise to a new possibility, something that would have seemed quite bizarre to a medieval, the idea of travel for leisure, indeed of travel for pleasure or at least for its own sake. This possibility became a reality for the first time in the eighteenth century, when aristocrats began to make what became known as the 'Grand Tour' (Turner and Ash 1975: 29–50). The Grand Tour was conceptualized quite explicitly as a civilizing process in which the elite from the cultural backwaters of England and France could rub up against the sumptuous splendour of post-Renaissance Italy. Accordingly, it could last up to five years. By contrast, by the time the industrial bourgeoisies of England and the USA had cottoned on to the act in the late nineteenth century both time and space had already shrunk, not least because of their time commitments to capitalist management. Tours lasted at most for a year but often for a few months and would attempt to take in Western and Central Europe in its entirety, within a more distant visual experience, rather than as a process of cultural immersion.

Nevertheless, foreign travel in the nineteenth century was still regarded as a culturally uplifting experience rather than a pleasurable one, if only because it was conceived romantically to improve one's sense of the sublime (Urry 1990: 4). This was true even for the middle-class package holidays organized by Thomas Cook and later by American Express to such uplifting spots as Constantinople, Luxor and tribal New Guinea.[2]

Travel for pleasure emerged from a different context altogether as working-class families sought to escape the grimy drudgery of industrial cities. Although the development of British seaside resorts as working-class pleasure zones has attracted much sociological interest (Urry 1990; Shields 1991), the phenomenon was much more universal including such diverse examples as Coney Island, Bondi beach, and Varna on the Black Sea. Here 'holy days' were transformed into secular 'holidays' during which people became deeply committed to having a good time, and wishing that others were there with them, by doing things that they would not normally have done – breathing fresh air, eating sweet junk food, riding animals, wearing silly clothes, taking thrilling fairground rides, taking walks for no reason at all, and playing carnival gambling games. Equally, at around the turn of the nineteenth century the more privileged sections of society established their own pleasure zones further afield. They converted an energetic Nordic means of personal transportation into an Alpine thrill, largely by mechanizing the remount, and they established their own upmarket version of 'housey-housey'.[3] The emergence of winter sports and of the French Riviera and its jewel, the Casino at Monte Carlo, marked a turning point in the internationalization of tourism.

Riviera and Alpine tourism indicate an upsurge in the reflexivity of tourist travel, the point at which tourism began to be consumed for its symbolic value, as a sign of affluence and cosmopolitanism. Signalling that one had holidayed could be accomplished by the possession of certain clothes worn outside the vacation, the ski jacket or the bikini, but more effectively by changes in the appearance of the body by allowing the sun to burn the skin (popular especially among the Anglo-Saxon, Celtic, Gallic, Teutonic and Scandinavian people of the North Atlantic rim) or even by having a broken limb encased in plaster-of-paris. Such bodily mutilation could only legitimately be accomplished in particular climatic and environmental niches so tourists began to search the planet for duplicates. Importantly, these could not be achieved at British seaside resorts and their equivalents. In the post-Second World War period we therefore see a new combination of Riviera and Alpine tourism with the seaside holiday in the form of the 'package holiday' (packaging air travel with accommodation and activities at a single price), an opportunity for the newly affluent working and middle classes to sample a Mediterranean or tropical climate without the uncertainties of the negotiation of travel arrangements with foreigners.

There is a sharp difference of opinion about whether this move constitutes or is the consequence of globalization in any absolute sense. For Urry (1990: 47–63) the movement of tourists between European countries or between, say, Japan and Thailand was indeed an internationalization of tourism that can be called globalized. For Turner and Ash (1975: 93–112), by contrast, it represents the creation of a 'pleasure periphery' that surrounded industrialized areas. Here, the local culture was displaced in favour of tourist encapsulation where walled hotels offered familiar consumption patterns in a familiar language. North European societies created theirs in the Mediterranean; the pleasure periphery for North America is Florida, the Caribbean, Mexico and Hawaii; for Australia it is tropical Queensland, Bali and the South Pacific; for Japan and Korea it is South-East Asia; for Russia, the Black Sea; and for Brazil and Argentina it is Punta del Este in Uruguay. The argument here is that tourist operators will take punters just far enough to provide them with the prospect of the 'four Ss' of tourism (sun, sea, sand and sex) and no further because transportation costs will limit markets.

CONCLUSION

Not all theorists accept the view advanced in this book that the cultural cleavages that might prevent globalization have now been closed. Many emphasise the long-term cultural processes that are canvassed in this chapter in which mutually incompatible civilizations maintain an uneasy global co-existence that can easily flare into a major conflagration. Kavolis (1988), for example, would argue that claims to rampant secular globalization represent a peculiarly Western version of culture in which religion is conceived to be an increasingly subordinate subset of it. Rather, under Islam for example, culture (understood as political and social values and material tastes) is enclosed by and is subordinate to religion. To the extent, then, that religion determines the moral-cultural sphere and to the extent that religions offer differential moral codes we can identify separated civilizational structures that constrain individual action. World culture is, for Kavolis, divided into at least seven such incommensurable civilizational systems: Christian, Chinese (Confucian-Taoist-Buddhist), Islamic, Hindu, Japanese (Shinto-Buddhist-Confucian), Latin American syncretist, and non-Islamic African (1988: 210–12). Huntington (1991) recognises a similar set of civilizational cultures (Western, Confucian, Japanese, Islamic, Hindu, Slavic-Orthodox, Latin American, and African) although, as we have seen, these represent for him an emerging system of political blocs, a new multipolarity to replace the bipolar, superpower system that folded with the collapse of the Soviet Union in about 1990.

These are adequate descriptions of the global condition on the eve of accelerated globalization at about the end of the third quarter of the twentieth century. Global culture was divided into civilizational traditions. These traditions were in contact with one another and there was some evidence of conflict. That conflict was the outcome of relativization, the reflexive comparison of one's own culture with that of others. However, rather too much was made of the Islamic relativization to Western culture and the so-called Islamic revival. It is true that there frequently was hostility between some elements of Islam and the West, but much of this was a politics of nationalism and much more was a politics of South vs. North. As the next chapter will show, much of this Islamic-Western conflict had faded by the turn of the millennium and conflicts between other civilizational blocs have failed to materialize.

The pattern does indeed parallel that found under internationalization processes in the economic and political spheres. Civilizations (and nations) competed with one another, established relationships with one another, communicated with one another, colonized one another, formed alliances with one another, and even, occasionally, understood one another. But they remained culturally sovereign, even to the extent of mutually recognising the legitimacy of their differences, and they occupied geographically specific territories. It was precisely at points of territorial confusion, such as in the Middle East, the Balkans or the Caucasus, that civilizational conflict occurred and reoccurred. Only the de-territorialization of nations and religions can provide for the diminution of such conflict.

NOTES

1   The term 'global village' was actually introduced apparently accidentally in the introduction to an earlier anthology: 'Postliterate man's electronic media contract the world to a village or tribe where everything happens to everyone at the same time: everyone knows about, and therefore participates in , everything that is happening the minute it happens. Television gives this quality of simultaneity to events in the global village.' (Carpenter and McLuhan 1970: xi). The term achieved wide currency and appeal. In the second edition of the *OED* it occupies much more space than 'globalization' (*OED* 1989, *s.v.* global village).

2   Cook took his first group to America in 1866, he took 20,000 people to the Paris exhibition in 1867, and he organized his first round-the-world tour in 1872. Globalization had apparently proceeded apace because he was able to boast that: 'This going round the world is a very easy and almost imperceptible business' (Turner and Ash 1975: 55–6).

3   An English working-class name for a numbers gambling game known in other versions as 'bingo', 'lotto' or 'keno'.

7

NEW WORLD CHAOS:
GLOBALIZING CULTURES

There will be no 'there' any more. We will all be here.

Advertisment for MCI Telecommunications

The general theoretical thrust of this book emphasises an acceleration of globalization in the 1970s. In one sense this acceleration is the consequence of the internationalization phase that precedes it. As material interpendence increases and as political sovereignty is whittled away, trans-national, inter-societal connections eventually become more dense and important than national, intra-societal ones. The central features of this acceleration are compression of time and its elimination of space, and an emerging reflexivity or self-conscious intentionality with respect to the globalization process.

We can draw on Robertson (1992) to characterize this emergent holistic consciousness. In his analysis, globalization involves the relativization of individual and national reference points to general and supranational ones. It therefore involves the establishment of cultural, social and phenomenological linkages between four elements (1992: 25–31):

1 the individual self,
2 the national society,
3 the international system of societies and
4 humanity in general.

Taken together, these constitute the 'global field', the range of objects we need to consider in analysing globalization. Under globalization the following phenomenological linkages and relativizations start to be made between these elements:

- the individual self (1) is defined as a citizen of a national society (2) by comparison with developments in other societies (3) and as an instance of humanity (4);
- a national society (2) stands in a problematical relationship to its citizens (1) in terms of freedom and control, views itself to be a member of a community of nations (3) and must provide citizenship rights that are referenced against general human rights (4);
- the international system (3) depends on the surrender of sovereignty by national societies (2), sets standards for individual behaviour (1) and provides 'reality checks' on human aspirations (4);
- humanity (4) is defined in terms of individual rights (1) that are expressed in the citizenship provisions of national societies (2) which are legitimated and enforced through the international system of societies (3).

These interactions produce processual developments at each of the four reference points, namely: *individualization* the global redefinition of each person as a complete whole rather than as a subordinate part of any localized collectivity; *internationalization* the multiplication of inter-state interdependencies and arrangements; *societalization* the establishment of the 'modern' nation-state as the only possible form of society; and *humanization*, the global establishment of the view that humanity cannot be differentiated by race, class, gender, etc. in terms of its possibilities and rights (1992: 282–6). Taken together these constitute the social processes of globalization. These developments occur independently of the internal dynamics of individual societies. Indeed, globalization has its own 'inexorable' logic which will inevitably affect these internal dynamics.

SEEING THE WORLD AS 'ONE PLACE'

Globalization has become, then, not only a major historical process that impacts on culture but the central substance of contemporary culture. In Robertson's terms this means an increasing probability that individual phenomenologies will be addressed to the entire world rather than to a local or national sector of it. This is true not only of such straightforwardly cultural phenomena as the mass media and consumption preferences, in which a globalization of tastes is readily apparent, but also in so far as we culturally redefine or relativize all the issues we face in global terms. For example: we redefine military-political issues in terms of a 'world order'; or economic issues in terms of an 'international recession'; or marketing issues in terms of 'world' products (e.g. the 'world-car'); or religious issues in terms of ecumenism; or citizenship issues in terms of 'human rights'; or issues of pollution and purification in terms of 'saving the planet'.

This rise in global consciousness, along with higher levels of material interdependence, increases the probability that the world will be reproduced as a single system. Thus, Robertson (1992) claims that the world is becoming more and more united, although he is careful not to say that it is becoming more and more integrated. While it is a single system, it is riven by conflict and there is by no means universal agreement on what shape the single system should take in the future.

This argument can be linked to some of Giddens' ideas about the character of high modernity (1992). As is confirmed in the chapters above, modern people trust their societies and their lives to be guided by impersonal flows of money and expertise. However, this does not mean that they allow such developments to proceed in an unmonitored way. Aware of risk, they constantly watch, seek information about and consider the value of money and the validity of expertise. Modern society is therefore specifically *reflexive* in character. Social activity is constantly informed by flows of information and analysis which subject it to continuous revision and thereby constitute and reproduce it. 'Knowing what to do' in modern society, even in such resolutely traditional contexts as kinship or childrearing, almost always involves acquiring knowledge about how to do it from books, or television programmes, or expert consultations, rather than relying on habit, mimesis or authoritative direction from elders. The particular difficulty faced by moderns is that this knowledge itself is constantly changing, so that living in a modern society appears to be uncontrolled, like being aboard a careening juggernaut, as Giddens has it.

The particular outcome that separates globalization in the contemporary period from its earlier manifestations, then, is its reflexivity: 'the world "moved" from being merely "in itself" to the problem or possibility of being "for itself"' (Giddens 1991: 55). Injunctions from the diverse viewpoints of both business consultants and environmentalists to 'think globally' mean that the inhabitants of the planet set out to make it, in the terms Robertson borrows from Giddens, to structurate it as a whole, to apprehend it as 'one place' (Robertson and Garrett 1991: ix). On this argument, people conceptualize the world as a whole, so they reproduce it as a single unit and in turn increase the probability that this is the way in which it will be conceived.

Robertson states numerous careful reservations about this argument. He claims that globalization, for example, is neither necessarily a good nor a bad thing – its moral character will be accomplished by the inhabitants of the planet. He is also not saying that the world is, as a consequence of globalization, a more integrated or harmonious place but merely that it is a more unified or systematic place. He means by this that while events in any part of the world will increasingly have consequences for, or be referenced against events in other distant parts, this relativization may not always be positive. Indeed, the world as a system may well be riven by conflicts that are far more intractable than the previous disputes between nations. However, he is saying the following: first, that world is experiencing accelerated globalization to such an extent that it can be regarded as an accomplishment; second, that we need new concepts to analyse this process; third, that the process is fundamentally cultural and reflexive in character; and fourth, that globalization follows the path of its own inexorable logic.

This discussion can therefore confirm that the current accelerated phase of globalization does not refer to the triumph and sovereign domination of any one state or superpower or of any one civilizational 'metanarrative' (Lyotard 1984) but rather to their dissipation. A globalized culture is chaotic rather than orderly – it is integrated and connected so that the meanings of its components are 'relativized' to one another but it is not unified or centralized or harmonious. Flows of resources (material objects, people, ideas, information and taste) sweep rapidly across the planet connecting up the components of this culture. These flows, as Featherstone (1990: 6) argues, give a globalized culture a particular shape. First, they link together previously encapsulated and formerly homogeneous cultural niches forcing each to relativize itself to others. This relativization may take the form of either a reflexive self-examination in which fundamental principles are reasserted in the face of threatening alternatives or the absorption of some elements of other cultures. Second, they allow for the development of genuinely trans-national cultures not linked to any particular nation-state-society which may be either novel or syncretistic.

Appadurai's increasingly influential argument about the global cultural economy (1990) identifies several of the important fields in which these developments take place. The fields are identified by the suffix 'scape', that is, they are globalized mental pictures of the social world perceived from the flows of cultural objects. The flows include: ethnoscapes, the distribution of mobile individuals (tourists, migrants, refugees, etc.); technoscapes, the distribution of technology; finanscapes, the distribution of capital; mediascapes, the distribution of information; and ideoscapes, the distribution of political ideas and values (e.g. freedom, democracy, human rights). Some of these flows have been discussed in the previous chapters and others will be discussed here, but we begin by examining what Appadurai might have called 'sacriscapes', the distribution of religious ideas and values.

The more rapid these flows, the more accelerated globalization becomes. So for Harvey, the last two decades represent: 'another fierce round in that annihilation of space through time that has always lain at the center of capitalism's dynamic' (1989: 293). He writes of the way in which satellite technologies have made the cost of communication invariant with respect to distance, the reduction in international freight rates, the global rush of images via satellite television which provides a universal experience, and the way in which mass tourism can make that experience direct. Spatial barriers have collapsed so that the world is now a single field within which capitalism can operate, and capital flows become more and more sensitive to the relative advantages of particular spatial locations. Paradoxically, as consumption becomes universalized through globally available brands, production can become localized according to cost advantages – so, for example, Levi jeans are available globally but are produced in the low-labour-cost environment of the Phillipines, and many of the 'Big Macs' sold in Europe contain Australian shredded lettuce, airfreighted overnight.

FRAGMENTATION AND SYNCRETISM

Until the third quarter of the twentieth century, religion under Western modernity followed the individualized Protestant pattern. Traditionally, sociologists interpreted it under what has become known as secularization theory, the thesis that religious beliefs and practices are trending towards separation in time and space (i.e., only in church and only on Sunday), that they are decreasingly oriented to narrative mythologies and more to abstract philosophical principles, and that individuals are becoming more non-religious or even irreligious. Two related empirical developments are now challenging secularization theory: first, there are signs that in many societies the decline in religious beliefs is stabilizing or even reversing (see Duke and Johnson 1989); and second, a wave of fundamentalist transformation is revitalizing the old universal religions.

The sources of these developments are modernization/post-modernization and globalization (Lechner 1989, 1992; Robertson 1992: 164–81). Modernization tends to disrupt the solidarity of meaning systems because it isolates individuals and families, rends communities and denies the relevance of the sacred and of substantive values. However, postmodernization (Harvey 1989; Crook, Pakulski and Waters 1992) has displaced even the certainties offered by modernization in so far as the pathways to material success are no longer clearly defined and in so far as its collective social arrangements (classes, firms, states) are attenuating. Postmodernization therefore accelerates the search for a single, often mythologized truth that can reference all social mores and practices. Fundamentalist religious and ethnic movements thus respond to these hyperdifferentiating tendencies of postmodernization.

Globalization also contributes both directly and indirectly to the world-wide development of fundamentalism. Globalization carries the discontents of modernization and postmodernization to religious traditions that might previously have remained encapsulated. Religious systems are obliged to relativize themselves to global postmodernizing trends. This relativization can involve an embracement of the postmodernizing pattern, an abstract and humanistic ecumenism, but it can also take the form of a rejective search for original traditions.

However, there are also direct effects. Lechner (1991: 276–8) shows that globalization has characteristics that are independent of modernity and that force religious and other forms of relativization. These include:

- the universalization of Western cultural preferences that require local particularisms to be legitimated in their terms e.g. the Islamic *Umma* must now be defended and reinforced in the face of Western claims about human rights, market democracy, and the position of women;
- the globalization of the nation-state-society that denies the legitimacy of superior allegiances to a church or its gods;
- the secularization and abstraction of law as the basis for social order; and
- the claim that the world is pluralistic and choice-driven, that there is not a single and superior culture.

However, fundamentalism is not the only possible religious response to globalizing and postmodernizing pressures. During the 1960s and 1970s Christianity experienced an ecumenical movement in which dialogue between its denominations and ecclesia increased in an attempt to discover common principles and commitments and with a view to unification. Indeed, some Protestant denominations did re-amalgamate. The general consequence was a further abstraction and thus secularization and privatization of religious belief that many 'traditionalists' found both threatening and offensive. So this ecumenical movement itself promoted such fundamentalist schisms as the Lefevbre group of Tridentinist Catholics. However, the most important revitalizing, fundamentalist religious movements were much larger in scale and we can now review the globalizing aspects of some of the most important of these.

Perhaps the most influential example is the development of what is known as the New Christian Right in the USA. In fact, this is a loose term for a coalition of genuine fundamentalist Protestants with traditionalists from the Episcopalian and Catholic churches that seeks directly to influence politics in the direction of reduced moral and sexual permissiveness, explicit references at the state level to Christian symbols, 'creationist' education, the criminalization of abortion, and a repressive attitude to crime and other forms of 'deviance'. The core of the movement is a

Protestant group called the Moral Majority led by Jerry Falwell, which parallels Paisleyite Protestantism in Northern Ireland and Fred Nile's 'Call to Australia' movement. Although its membership is small its effects are magnified by the successes of Televangelism, which mass mediates the fundamentalist messages of such charismatic figures as Billy Graham, Oral Roberts, Jimmy Swaggart and Jim Bakker, although their messages are seldom directly political.

The New Christian Right made a significant contribution to the establishment and the ideological tinge of the Reagan-Bush presidencies of 1980–91. More importantly, evangelical broadcasting has found its way beyond the borders of the USA by means of short-wave radio and satellite television. The three largest international Christian broadcasters produce 20,000 hours of programming a week in 125 languages, which makes them the largest single element in trans-national broadcasting (Hadden 1991: 232, 240). While it is difficult to assess its impact such broadcasting can do little but enhance the conversion work of new wave American fundamentalist Protestant missionaries in Latin America and Africa.

There is no better example of the relativizing effect of globalization than the fundamentalist revival in Islam that began in the 1970s. Until that time the Islamic world, as Turner (1991) notes, had been dominated by the issues introduced by secular nationalistic and socialist political movements. However, Western modernization in either its capitalistic (e.g. Libya, Iran, Pakistan) or Marxist (e.g. Algeria, Egypt) forms failed to deliver either material benefits or a coherent system of meanings. Indeed, rapid industrialization and urbanization appeared to offer only radical inequality between the populace and the politically dominant elite. Islamic fundamentalisms, particularly those associated with the Iranian cleric the Ayatollah Khomeni, the dictatorship of General Zia ul-Haq in Pakistan, the Islamic revival in Malaysia and the activities of the Moslem brotherhood and Hezb'Allah in the Middle East all mark a rejection of Western modernization and secularism. They call for 'Islamization', the creation of a hierocratic *Umma* in which education centres on the holy book, in which the economic system is oriented to redistribution rather than to acquisition, in which Sharia law displaces secular law, and in which cultural products (music, television programmes) are puritanized (Turner 1991: 175). At the same time globalization has made a pan-Islamic movement possible in which transfers of money, military intervention, terrorism, mass-mediated messages and Haj pilgrims connect the elements of a world community.

A Far Eastern fundamentalist movement with an explicitly globalized theology is Sun Myung Moon's Unification Church, a Christian fundamentalism that originated in Korea in the 1950s and spread to the West in the 1970s (Barker 1991). In its own terms it aims to restore, at one fell swoop, the Kingdom of God on Earth. This community will be a theocracy with the following characteristics:

> [It] will have no place for atheistic communism; there will be no pornography; sexual activity will be confined to marriage; crime will have been drastically reduced . . .; wars will be eradicated; exploitation . . . will be a thing of the past; racial prejudice will have disappeared – and there will be no need for passports.
>
> (Barker 1991: 202)

In connecting the local to the global, Moon's theology appears almost to reify sociological theories of globalization. Unification is not to be the consequence of grand political action but of changes in the hearts and the family practices of individuals. To ensure compatibility and God-centredness Moon matches spouses. To the extent that God-centred families are created global unification will proceed.

Just as in the case of religion, the current acceleration of globalization might be seen as destabilizing in relation to ethnicity. The previous chapters discuss the increasing integration of economic processes and the increasing interconnectedness of political practices, and the subsequent sections of this chapter discuss the emergence of a common global lifestyle and the rapid mediation of ideas by electronic communication and personal mobility. One might ask how it is possible for ethnic identification to survive such an onslaught. To answer this question one must bear in mind a point stressed throughout this book, that globalization does not necessarily imply homogenization or integration. Globalization merely implies greater connectedness and de-territorialization. The possibility arises, therefore, of an increased measure of ethnic pluralism but in which ethnicities are not tied to any specific territory or polity.

The impacts of globalization on ethnicity and nationhood are as follows (see Arnason 1990; Hall 1992).

- Globalization is in general a differentiating as well as a homogenizing process. It pluralizes the world by recognizing the value of cultural niches and local abilities.
- Importantly, it weakens the putative nexus between nation and state, releasing absorbed ethnic minorities and allowing the reconstitution of nations across former state boundaries. This is especially important in the context of states that are confederations of ethnic minorities.
- It brings the centre to the periphery. In so far as globalization is sourced in Western modernity, it introduces possibilities for new ethnic identities to cultures on the periphery. The vehicles for this cultural flow are elctronic images and affluent tourism.
- It also brings the periphery to the centre. An obvious vehicle is the flow of economic migrants from relatively disadvantaged sectors of the globe to relatively advantaged ones. It is also accomplished in so far as the mass media engage in a search for the exotic to titillate audiences in search of variety. Previously homogeneous nation-states have, as a consequence, moved in the direction of multi-culturalism.

Hall (1992) drawing on Robins identifies two possible adaptive responses on the part of ethnic groups to these globalizing trends, translation and tradition, which indeed parallel developments in religion. Translation is a syncretistic response in which groups that inhabit more than one culture seek to develop new forms of expression that are entirely separate from their origins. Tradition is ethnic fundamentalism, an attempt to rediscover the untainted origins of an ethnic group in its history. Tradition involves a search for the certainties of the past in a postmodernizing world where identity is associated with lifestyle and taste and is therefore constantly shifting and challengeable. Paradoxically, the search for tradition can contribute to this postmodernistic ambience by mixing the symbolic contents of the past into the present as everyday life becomes an historical and ethnic Disneyland.

Perhaps the best example of a translationist ethnicity is the emergence of the new identity in the 1960s and 1970s signified by the term 'black' (now 'African-American' in the USA) (Hall 1992: 308–9). In the USA this involved not only the translation of the disrupted and irrevocably mixed tribal identities that slaves had carried with them from Africa but also the translation of a class identity into an ethnic one that could become a source of pride. Although there has always been some ambivalence between translationist and traditionalist strategies, signified by the term 'African-American', only the former could allow black Americans not only to assert their identity but to divest themselves of their association with the urban lumpenproletariat, the outcome of their migration to the Northern industrial cities in the early twentieth century. Black identity can also offer other political advantages. In Britain, for example, it has allowed coalition across populations with origins in the Caribbean, South Asia and Africa. Here again, though, the traditionalistic/ fundamentalist elements of Rastafarianism and Hindu and Islamic revivalism also interweave the process.

Another syncretistic ethnogenesis is the emergence of Quebec nationalism, which Hobsbawm describes as: 'a combination of intensified petty-bourgeois linguistic nationalism with mass future shock' (1992: 171). Québécois culture had survived since the seventeenth century on the basis of being ignored as too troublesome by the Anglophone power centres and its own unification around the Catholic Church and local political patronage. In the 1960s and 1970s Quebec was penetrated by the global currents of industrialization and secularization and it also received an influx of 'third language' migrants anxious, in a globalized world, to learn the *lingua anglia*. The emerging nationalism was frequently defensive, relativized in self-references to 'white niggers' and claimed associations with the colonized third world, but often securely confident – the Quebec revolution had been a 'quiet revolution'. Above all, though, it laid claim to a new identity. The new Quebec society did not regard itself as a Parisien colony. Indeed, until the late 1960s the European French regarded Québécois as primitives. Rather, it claimed to represent a fusion of European origins with North American experience, of the cultivated with the rational. Quebec was probably the first of many such nationalisms. Other examples, often with similar ambivalences about nation-state formation, include Bangladesh, Bougainville, Catalonia, Eritrea, Flanders, Kashmir, Kurdistan, Lombardy, Palestine, Scotland, Tamil Elam and Wales.

A rich source of traditionalistic ethnic revivals is the dismemberment of the state-socialist confederations of Eastern Europe and Asia that began in the late 1980s. Two interpretations are possible of the emergence of such entities as Estonia, Slovakia, Bosnia-Hercegovina, Kazakhstan, Moldova and Kirghizia. Hall (1992: 312–13) views them as a continuation of the nationalistic movement that began at the end of the eighteenth century: 'These new would-be 'nations' try to construct states that are unified in both ethnic and religious terms, and to create political entities around homogeneous cultural identities' (1992: 312). By contrast, for Hobsbawm the attempt is bound to fail:

> That ethno-linguistic separation provides no sort of basis for a stable, in the short run even for a roughly predictable, ordering of the globe is evident in 1992 from the merest glance at the large region situated between Vienna and Trieste in the West and Vladivostock in the East.

(1992: 184)

For him, the creation of these small states is merely a step in the creation of a world of nations organized regionally and globally rather than on a state basis. He predicts moves towards supra-nationalism and infra-nationalism, that is, towards political and economic organization on a continental or global scale and to the organization of culture and identity on a local scale. The evidence is the ambivalence with which emerging nations approach statehood – Scotland and Catalonia seek independence not within the framework of a new state but within a new relationship with the EU, and the Baltic states no sooner are detached from the Soviet Union than they are seeking membership of NATO and the EU.

In summary, the effect of globalization on ethnicity is to revive it and to differentiate it from politics and economics. It enables the view that all ethnic identities are legitimate and not merely those successful ones that managed to establish states in the nineteenth century. In some instances this means the disruption of confederations of nations (e.g. Canada, Czechoslovakia, UK, USSR, Yugoslavia). However, all political entities are coming to be regarded as legitimately, even positively, multi-cultural. Developments in the two fundamentals of sex and food can confirm this. All the evidence suggests that ethnicity is a declining barrier to love and marriage, a development that nationalistic barriers cannot conceivably survive. Moreover, recipes for food consumption are becoming decreasingly localized both in terms of the diversity of so-called 'ethnic' restaurants and in the heterogeneity of domestic consumption. The postmodernization as well as globalization of ethnicity, that is its decoupling from locality, is confirmed by the development of ethnic theme parks in Japan to allow foreign tourism at home. They include 'The German Happiness Kingdom', 'Canadian World', 'Venice of Japan', 'Holland Village', 'Niigata Russian Village' and 'Cannonball City', a recreation of life in the USA (*The Economist* 22–28/1/94).[1]

The ultimate outcome of the globalization of religion and ethnicity would involve the creation of a common but hyperdifferentiated field of value, taste and style opportunities, accessible by each individual without constraint for purposes either of self-expression or consumption. Under a globalized cultural regime, Islam, for example, would not be linked to particular territorially based communities in the middle East, North Africa and Asia but would be universally available across the planet and with varying degrees of 'orthodoxy', as indeed it has tended to become. Likewise, in the sphere of political ideology, the apparently opposed political values of private property and power sharing might be combined to establish new ideologies of economic enterprise, as indeed they have. A globalized culture admits a continuous flow of ideas, information, commitment, values and tastes mediated through mobile individuals, symbolic tokens and electronic simulations.

CONSUMER MONARCHS

The above discussion of religion and ethnicity should confirm that it is possible to oversimplify and thereby to over-demonize the process of globalization. It argues that globalization can revive particularisms in so far as it relativizes them and in so far as it releases them from encapsulation by the nation-state-society. But cultural globalization does not simply imply a revival of difference. It implies a complex interweave of homogenizing with differentiating trends. In this section we concentrate on the homogenizing trends that are summed up in the phrase 'global consumer culture' and for which such value-laden terms as 'Americanization', 'Western cultural imperialism', 'Coca-colonization' and 'McDonaldization' are often employed, and not without good reason. These terms imply that the consumer culture that was developed in the USA in the middle of the twentieth century has been mass mediated to all other parts of the world.

In general, consumption patterns have experienced a similar temporal compression to those experienced in production. If taste is the only determinant of utility then that utility can be ephemeral and subject to whim. Product demand can be determined by fashion, and unfashionable products are disposable. And the most instant and disposable of products are mass-mediated images that are lost the moment that they are consumed. In so far as images have no past and no future, human experience becomes compressed into an overwhelming present shared with the other inhabitants of the planet.

We need to stress that consumer culture means more than simple consumption (Featherstone 1991). An interest in consumption is historically and cross-societally universal. However, in a consumer culture the items consumed take on a symbolic and not merely a material value. It arises in societies where powerful groups, usually those seeking to accummulate capital, in caricature, encourage consumers to 'want' more than they 'need'. Indeed, such marketing often involves confounding the meanings of these two terms. Under a consumer culture, consumption becomes the main form of self-expression and the chief source of identity. It implies that both material and non-material items, including kinship, affection, art and intellect become commodified, that is, their value is assessed by the context of their exchange rather than the context of their production or use. An advanced or postmodernized consumer culture experiences hypercommodification (Crook, Pakulski and Waters 1992) in which minute differences between products or minute improvements in them can determine variations in demand, and in which consumption is differentiated on the basis of the signifiers known as 'brand names'. Here consumption, or more precisely a capacity to consume, is itself reflexively consumed. This tendency is captured in such terms as 'taste', 'fashion' and 'lifestyle' that become key sources of social differentiation, displacing class and political affiliation. The consumer culture is created through the advertising and simulatory effects of the mass media. In its original form it was probably a deliberate creation[2] but under postmodernized conditions it is 'hypersimulated' (Baudrillard 1988), having a life of its own that is beyond the control of any particular group.

If the original American version of consumer culture depended on mass-mediated advertising and simulation, that process entered a global phase with the expansion of communications technologies beyond the nation-state-society. The examples are numerous, but a few may suffice to illustrate the point. In the 1930s the German car industry built a *Wagen* for its own *Volk* and the Model T and the Austin 7 were similarly conceived of as cars for the people of their respective nations, but now manufacturers build and market 'world cars'. The 'many colours of Bennetton', stressed presumably because colour is one of the few minute variations offered in their standardized clothing products, Nike and Reebok casual shoes, and Levi jeans infuse global popular culture. The expansion of the products of major fashion houses into such downmarket but associated brands as Armani Emporium, DKNY and YSL ape this global marketing strategy as well as illustrating postmodernizing declassification. A particular example of the local-global connection might be the way in which such peculiarly Australian products as Akubra hats, Drizabone wet weather gear and Blundstone boots (not to mention Foster's lager) have become internationally recognized brands, but recognized because they are specifically Australian. In food and beverage products global branding has been so effective that the examples are almost too obvious to mention: Coca-cola and its rival Pepsi are the paradigm case, now doing battle in China, the last sector of the globe that they have failed to dominate; McDonalds and its rivals, Pizza Hut, Sizzlers and KFC fast food restaurants engorge the world with vast quantities of sanitized and homogenized food; and kitchens are stocked, as occasionally are the walls of art galleries, with Campbell's soup, Pilsbury instant bread and Birds Eye frozen peas. Nor is global branding restricted to mass markets. Global yuppiedom is equally susceptible to the attractions of Rolex watches, Porsche cars, Luis Vuitton luggage, Chanel perfume, AGA kitchen stoves, Dom Perignon champagne and Perrier mineral water.

The globalization of popular culture has apparently paradoxical but actually consistent effects in simultaneously homogenizing and differentiating. Certainly, it can homogenize across the globe in that what is available in any locality can become available in all localities but at any particular locality it increases the range of cultural opportunity. For example, New Yorkers would be in a sorry condition if the only wine they could drink was that produced in their own state. In fact, that particular city, like many 'global cities' (King 1990b) offers a dazzling variety of consumption possibilities drawn from across the globe in terms not only of imported products but of imported cultural practices.

There are two broad views of the way in which consumer culture pervades the globe and invades and controls the individual. The most common explanation is one in which individual identity is conflated to culture. Capitalism transforms people into consumers by altering their self-images, their structure of wants, in directions that serve capitalist accumulation (e.g. Friedman 1990; Sklair 1991). This view is contestable in terms of the impressive example of Eastern Europe and the former Soviet Union where many, perhaps a majority, of the populations embraced consumer culture on the basis only of glimpses of life in the West and despite massive propaganda about the evils of consumerism. The 'velvet revolutions' of the late 1980s can be viewed as a mass assertion of the right to unlimited privatized consumption, a right which might also be viewed as a central issue in the third world.

A second and more interesting argument is Ritzer's view (1993) of consumer culture as an extension of the process of Western rationalization first identified by Weber. Weber had broadly been interested in the ways in which the rational calculability of capitalism was extended beyond material issues to human relationships, specifically those to do with production in its broadest sense of goal-attainment. Ritzer's view is that society, and thus the world, is afflicted by a process of 'McDonaldization': 'the process by which the principles of the fast-food restaurant are coming to dominate more and more sectors of American society as well as the rest of the world' (1993: 1, italics deleted). The principles are as follows (1993: 7–13):

- *Efficiency*: McDonaldization compresses the time span and the effort expended between a want and its satisfaction.
- *Calculability*: it encourages calculations of costs of money, time and effort as the key principles of value on the part of the consumer, displacing estimations of quality.
- *Predictability*: it standardizes products so that consumers are encouraged not to seek alternatives.
- *Control of human beings by the use of material technology*: this involves not only maximal deskilling of workers but control of consumers by means of queue control barriers, fixed menu displays, limited options, uncomfortable seats, inaccessible toilets and 'drive-through' processing.

Clearly, to the extent that the social technology of McDonaldization can penetrate the globe and to the extent that it can induce consumers to enter premises, it can convert apparently sovereign consumers into docile conformists. McDonaldization of course travels with the restaurant chain that gave it its name. By the end of 1991 there were 12,000 of them and in that year for the first time it opened more outlets outside the USA (427) than inside (188). But the formula has been extended to other fast food brands (Burger King, Pizza Hut, Taco Bell), to more up-market restaurants (Sizzlers) and to the marketing of a wide range of products including car servicing (Mr Muffler, Jiffylube), financial services (H&R Block, ITP), childcare (Kinder Care, Kampgrounds of America), medical treatment, university education, bakery products (Au Bon Pain) and many more (Ritzer 1993: 2–3). In summary, McDonaldization represents a re-ordering of consumption as well as production, a rationalization of previously informal and domestic practices, that pushes the world in the direction of greater conformity.

The paradox of McDonaldization is that in seeking to control it recognizes that human individuals potentially are autonomous, a feature that is notoriously lacking in 'cultural dupe' or 'couch potato' theories of the spread of consumer culture. As dire as they may be, fast-food restaurants only take money in return for modestly nutritious and palatable fare. They do not seek to run the lives of their customers, although they might seek to run their diets. They attract rather than coerce, so that one can always choose not to enter. Indeed, advertising gives consumers the message, however dubious, that they are exercising choice.

It might be argued that consumer culture is the source of the increased cultural effectivity that is often argued to accompany globalization and postmodernization. In so far as we have a consumer culture the individual is expected to exercise choice. Under such a culture political issues and work can equally become items of consumption. A liberal-democratic political system might be the only possible political system where there is a culture of consumption precisely because it offers the possibility of election. But even a liberal democracy will tend to be McDonaldized, that is, leaders will become the mass-mediated images of photo-opportunities and juicy one-liners, and issues will be drawn in starkly simplistic packages. Equally, work can no longer be expected to be a duty or a calling, or even a means of creative self-expression. Choice of occupation, indeed choice of whether to work at all, can be expected increasingly to become a matter of status affiliation rather than of material advantage.

COMPUNICATIONS[3]

Nowhere is time–space compression more evident than in the technologization of the mass media. The most recent technological trends involve extensions and re-combinations of the basic artefacts – telephone, record-and-playback machine, radio, and television. They can be summarized as follows:

- *Miniaturization*: All technologies have reduced in size. This is in part due to design criteria which apply in the Japanese consumer electronics companies that are pace-setters for the industry. Among these companies, Sony was the first effective miniaturizer when it bought out the patents of an American invention, the transistor, and built the portable radio. The trend applies to cassette players, disc players, TVs, telephones and computers. Miniaturization affects transmission as well as reception – a key factor in the satellite news broadcaster CNN's 'scoop' of Iraqi reactions to the attack on their territory by the USA and its allies in 1988 was the capacity of its journalists to set up a 'backpack' satellite transmission station in Baghdad.

- *Personalization*: There has historically been a general reduction of the scope of the audience for electronic mass communications. The music hall or the cinema could entertain several hundred, the television a family, but the PC is literally a 'personal computer', although it is not actually quite as personal as a lap-top computer, which is itself not quite as personal as a palm-top computer. The Sony 'Walkman' and its imitators represent the ultimate in personalized consumption – the sound becomes all-encompassing and internal.

- *Integration*: The various technologies of text, sound, visuals and response via keyboard or microphone are progressively becoming integrated with one another. This centres on the technology of the microchip which organizes computers. The microchip provides an enormous capacity to process information.

- *Diffusion*: Access to technologies of mass media is becoming more widespread in terms of both reception and transmission. The former is the consequence of the declining relative cost of receivers; the latter of such technological leaps as the exploration of space and fibre optics. Such diffusion implies not only that virtually every inhabitant of the planet has access to mass communications but an increasing range of choice within mass communications. It also implies it is now impossible to maintain national sovereignty in mass communications so long as the members of a society have access to satellite dishes.

- *Autonomization*: Fears that audiences might simply be the victims, or at least the passive receptors, of mass-mediated information appear to be receding. Consumers have an increasing potential for autonomy in so far as: they have a greater choice of products, e.g. via cable and satellite TV; they have increased 'talk-back' capacity via telephones and interactive computer networks; they have increased access to production facilities via home recording equipment and community studios; and they can control the timing and content of what they watch and hear by means of compact discs, cassettes, and video cassettes.

All of this technology originates in advanced capitalist societies, as does much of its content. In terms of cultural globalization it has three principal effects. First, it exports what Sklair (1991) calls the 'culture-ideology of consumerism' from the centre to the periphery of the world-system. This is because most of the news, information, entertainment programming, sport, information and advertising flows in that direction (Anderson 1984; Hoskins and Mirus 1988; Mowlana 1985; Sklair 1991). Not only the programme producers but the advertising agencies and news agencies as well as the companies that manufacture consumer products are owned in advanced capitalist societies. Advertising, in particular, seeks to sell products by depicting idealized Western lifestyles, often under the universalizing themes of sex, status and the siblinghood of humanity – the world sings a hymn of harmony to a soft drink of doubtful nutritional value. They mimic the opportunities for simulation already given in soap operas, sitcoms and action thrillers.

Second, as well as absorbing new nations into what some might call the network of cultural imperialism, cultural flows via the mass media dissolve the internal boundaries of that network and help to knit it together. These cultural flows are primary examples of trans-national connections, links between collective actors and individuals that subvert state frontiers. As we note above, satellite broadcasting in particular denies the possibility of national sovereignty over the airwaves. A specific consequence is that, in so far as much of the hardware is American-owned and much of the programming is American in origin, English is becoming the *lingua franca* of the global communications system. This has proved a particular problem for the territorially small nations of Europe, but the failure of Euronews, a multilingual satellite news channel, to dent the market shares of CNN and Sky News that broadcast exclusively in English, indicates that English may well become the common public language of the globalized system and that vernaculars may be restricted to localized and domestic contexts.

However, the mass media knit the global culture together by means of content as well as by means of language. They do this not merely by offering common simulation opportunities but by magnifying global problems and global events. We can say, with appropriate apologies, that we now look at the world through global spectacles. When a Canadian fighter pilot bombs a building in Belgrade we are there with her seeing what she sees and war becomes a spectacle; the demolition of the Berlin wall, a major political event, becomes a rock concert; the Olympic games expands its range of sports to include artistic rather than athletic events, however kitsch (rhythmic gymnastics, synchronized swimming, freestyle skiing) in order to reach a wider global audience; and the 'A Team' can scarcely compare for thrills with the Tianenmen Square massacre of 1988 or Yeltsin's conquest of the Russian parliament in 1993. These media events are of a qualitatively different order from, say, the television coverage of the first human landing on the Moon in 1968. They are deliberately constructed as stylized mass entertainments and they are, in Durkheimian terms, collective representations of global commitments to democracy, consumption, capitalism and a liberal tolerance of diversity.

The third globalizing effect of the mass media is the one originally noticed by McLuhan and argued further by Harvey and by Giddens. In so far as the mass media convert the contents of human relationships into symbols or tokens they can connect people across great distances. So effective can this process become that communities of interest or value-commitment can develop between people who have never met, much less joined together in a political event. These are elsewhere described as simulated communities or simulated power blocs (Crook, Pakulski and Waters 1992: 131–4) because they are based on behavioural cues given only in the mass media. For example, many women feel a sense of global sisterhood in relation to patriarchal oppression, even if they are not participants in the women's movement. Further, in so far as symbols can be transmitted very rapidly the compression of time eliminates the constraints and therefore the social reality of space.

The influence of the telephone and television in this respect is well established, but the newest, and possibly the most effective medium in accomplishing time–space compression is the 'Internet', an international network of direct links between computers. Internet originated in the USA, where it grew out of a merging of local area networks originally under military sponsorship. It then morphed into an academic and research network, but by the 1990s the commercial opportunities became apparent. The Internet is global[4] in its reach but not total in its coverage – it has 15 million users, growing at a rate of 20–30 per cent every three months. In its early development it simulated global space because users needed to conceptualize and find other 'places' in order to use the information there. However, in about 1990 new hypermedia software became available (e.g. Netscape, Internet Explorer) that could act as an agent for the user, independently searching the network, finding bits of information in different parts of it, combining them and presenting them back to the user without any reference to location. Equally, the software rendered the Internet increasingly user-friendly and thus generalized its use. The chief importance of such a development is that it will provide an opportunity for the realization of simulated communities that can now develop out of trans-global patterns of interaction. McLuhan's global village was perhaps misnamed, because a village without circuits of gossip would be strange indeed. Such globalized circuits of gossip are now becoming possible, as is the reality of McLuhan's vision.

TOURISM AT HOME

A new and more globalized form of tourism has emerged since the establishment of the pleasure periphery (see Chapter 6). It has several aspects. First, the package tour has achieved global extension. Mass tourism has moved beyond the pleasure periphery in order to provide more exotic and 'risky' environments for the jaded tastes of metropolitan tourists. Europeans and North Americans now swarm across the planet as one after another destination becomes fashionable in Africa or Asia. For example, Bali, once the preserve of the colonial Dutch and nearby Australians, is now knee-deep in Italians, French, Japanese and Americans; the cruise up the Nile achieved a fleeting popularity in the early 1980s and was then dropped; Sri Lanka was popular with Germans and Scandinavians prior to its civil war; and anyone flying from Australia to Britain on the 'Kangaroo route' via Bangkok is likely to find the aircraft filled by package-holidaying Britons weighed down with duty-free goods and bunches of orchids, as well as perhaps the occasional STD. Second, the middle-class tourist niche has been filled by 'new age travellers' and ecotourists. These are independent travellers seeking out the last morsels of authentic and exotic culture or of pristine environment. They blaze the trail to the remaining untouched corners of the planet for mass tourism and so, inevitably, consume the planet in the fullest sense.

A third aspect of the recent globalization of tourism is conceivably the most interesting. This is the postmodernizing declassification of tourist and non-tourist areas and the accompanying declassification of cultures. This is most manifest in a decline of the pleasure peripheries to follow the decline of the seaside resorts. Kuta and Torremolinas are now as passé as Coney Island and Blackpool. Moreover, the 'funfairs' of the pleasure periphery and their accompanying cultures, Disneyland and the like, are now replicated in the heart of industrial Europe and Japan where, seemingly, every town has a local theme park. More importantly, there is no non-touristic space from which one can escape. One can no more escape the tourist gaze by living in Glasgow or Hobart or Guangzhou than by living in Orlando or Cannes or Florence, perhaps less so because in the former one is part of the object of attention while in the latter one is merely incidental to the main event.

All of the above history indicates a rapid growth in international tourism in the second half of the twentieth century. Indeed, international tourism, measured by arrival from another country, expanded seventeenfold between 1950 and 1990 (*New Internationalist* (245) 7/93) (see Figure 7.1). Most of this expansion has been European and North American, but a significant feature of the period we have previously identified as the phase of accelerated globalization, from 1970 onwards, is the expansion of tourist arrivals outside Europe and the Americas. Tourism in the Asia-Pacific region is a central element in the transition outlined above. These data might also obscure the impact of tourism on individual societies outside the North Atlantic orbit. For example,

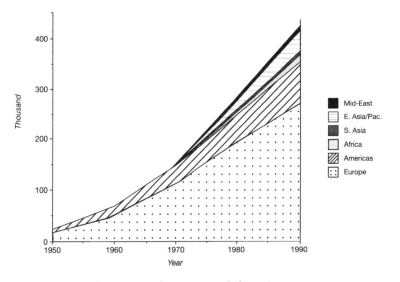

Figure 7.1 Annual international tourist arrivals by region, 1950–90
Source: *New Internationalist* (245), July 1993

in 1990 tourism receipts accounted for 67 per cent of Egypt's foreign exchange earnings, 55 per cent of Jamaica's, 43 per cent of Kenya's and 30 per cent of Morocco's (*New Internationalist* (245) 7/93).

The cultural impact of globalized tourism is multiple and complex but we can outline a few of the key dimensions here:

• the extent of globalized tourism indicates the extent to which tourists themselves conceptualize the world as a single place which is without internal geographical boundaries;
• globalization exposes tourists to cultural variation confirming the validity of local cultures and their differences;
• the objects of the tourist gaze are obliged to relativize their activities, that is, to compare and contrast them to the tastes of those that sightsee (in certain circumstances this may imply local cultural revival, if only in simulated form); and
• tourism extends consumer culture by redefining both human practices and the physical environment as commodities.

CONCLUSION

Like the conclusions of the previous chapters this one also is guided by the theorem that material exchanges localize, political exchanges internationalize and symbolic exchanges globalize. The contemporary accelerated phase of cultural globalization is directly attributable to the explosion of signs and symbols that many have come to associate with the denouement of modernity. Human society is globalizing to the extent that human relationships and institutions can be converted from experience to information, to the extent it is arranged in space around the consumption of simulacra rather than the production of material objects, to the extent that value-commitments are badges of identity, to the extent that politics is the pursuit of lifestyle, and to the extent that organizational constraints and political surveillance are displaced in favour of reflexive self-examination. These and other cultural currents have become so overwhelming that they have breached the levees not only of national value-systems but of industrial organizations and political-territorial arrangements.

In each of the dimensions of culture, globalization is highly advanced. Religious ideas must now be understood and often reinforced by fundamentalism in relation to the religions and the secularisms of all others. The commodification and marketing of religious ideas as a set of lifestyle choices is highly advanced and thus highly de-territorialized. Ethnicities are similarly relativized, dispersed and differentiated so that the modernist link between nation, state and territory appears permanently to have been disrupted. The pattern of exchange of valued items is now dominated by the consumption of signs, images and information. The mass media are increasingly dominated by global production and distribution companies that offer common images across the globe. Tourism is reaching its limits. Every corner of the globe is subject to its infestation and every person is a potential tourist and the potential object of tourism. Lash and Urry (1994) go so far as to project an 'end of tourism', a world so globalized that travel is a commonplace chore and where leisure and thrills are accessed through a video screen. This may not be such an immediate prospect as universal tourism, but it is a clear possibility.

NOTES

1 *The Economist* explains that: 'many Japanese prefer to see the West without having to leave Japan. The real West is too far, too dangerous and, quite honestly, too foreign.' (22–28/1/94).

2 The images created by the Hollywood movie industry, for example, doubtless represented an 'America of the desire' that the central European Jewish emigrés who ran it aspired to.

3 See Bell (1991: 38–43) for the origin of this term.

4 A measure of the general acceptance of global imagery might be the title of the most popular manual for the Internet, *The Whole Internet User's Guide and Catalog* (Krol 1992) that is based on the title of a much earlier manual for environmentally friendly consumption *The Whole Earth Catalog*.

8

REAL WORLD ARGUMENTS

. . . as a woman I have no country. As a woman I want no country.
As a woman my country is the whole world.

Virginia Woolf

One of the reflexive features of globalization is that the term
'globalization' has now entered academic discourses across the
planet. In the early 1990s the term was, apart from the notable
exceptions of Robertson and Giddens, more or less the property
of business schools. They used it to teach their MBA students
how to market, and often to establish production, beyond the
boundaries of their own nation-state. By the turn of the millennium, however, globalization had become a central topic of
debate across the social science disciplines. Critics had emerged,
most visibly from the progressivist left, whose general thrust was
to assert the continuity of the social structures of modernity,
principally of the main institutions of capitalist society, the
nationally based corporation and the nation-state.

This chapter considers and rebuts three representative forms
of such critiques: that the nationally based corporation, operating

REAL WORLD ARGUMENTS 211

on production principles introduced by the carmaker, Henry Ford, in the early twentieth century, continues to dominate the global economy; that the nation-state remains the principal repository of sovereignty and political power, that it remains the main and necessary actor in the inter-national political system; and that what we perceive as globalization is not a postmodernizing cultural disruption of social structure but merely a process of global homogenization deliberately constructed by American and other Western economic interests.

Of course, such critics need to explain away the issue that many people are impressed by the power of the globalization process and accept it as one of the facts of contemporary life. Some see globalization as offering tremendous opportunities, others regard it with fear and loathing, while a few perhaps see it as offering liberating possibilities. Certainly, academics and journalists routinely insert the term into discourse as if it was unimpeachable. The response of the critics is a familiar one. For them, globalization is one of the big lies of history, to rank alongside the Garden of Eden, the liberating promises of communism, and the white man's burden. For critics, globalization is an ideological construct, a cloak of ideas that disguises the negative consequences of an expanding capitalist system (for collections of critical opinion see Mittelman 1996; Scott 1997). They use such words as 'myth' and 'political rhetoric' to indicate that 'globalization' is a story deliberately told to enhance the neoliberal transformation of the planet. The key ideological elements of that story are:

- that globalization is a progression towards a positive culmination in which all the inhabitants of the planet are affluent, equal and even harmoniously integrated and peaceable;
- that globalization is an inevitable, general and unstoppable process that is pointless to resist;
- that globalization is an impersonal process beyond the control of any individual or group of individuals.

Clearly, if globalization is just a story then this book is a work of fiction, so it takes this last opportunity to discuss some of the criticism in detail.

NOT GLOBALIZATION BUT NEO-FORDISM

Many critiques of the globalization thesis draw on that same progressivist tradition that began with Marx and culminates in the work of Wallerstein. Among them the work of Hirst and Thompson (1996) is highly influential. Hirst and Thompson draw a proper distinction between an inter-national economy and a globalized one, what they call 'Type 1' and 'Type 2' globalization. A brief description can confirm that these correspond with the distinctions drawn throughout this book.

Type 1 is characterized by elaborated migration, trade and investment flows between nations such that there emerges an international division of labour. However, national economies are still the main players and are regulated at that level. Their degree of exposure to international product and capital markets will render them susceptible to impacts that derive from other national economies whether favourable or unfavourable. However, these impacts are always mediated through regulatory systems at the level of the nation-state.

By contrast, in a Type 2 globalized economy these national regulatory processes are subsumed by an autonomous supra-national system of transactions and processes. Markets are difficult to regulate; multi-national companies detach from national origins and become either dispersed or footloose in their operations; organized labour is deeply disempowered by a production system that does not need to be linked to any given local labour supply or skill base; and state political hegemonies become impossible.

This distinction is completely unexceptionable. One might want to question Hirst and Thompson's claim that there is no *process* of globalization without the emergence of the second of these two possibilities, but what is more interesting for present purposes is the evidence they draw on in order to support their view that the world is firmly in the grip of Type 1 and unlikely ever to move into Type 2.

Hirst and Thompson cast moderation to the wind in declaring that globalization is a 'myth', even if a 'necessary' one. In order to demonstrate that globalization is a component of ideology they question the globalization thesis on the grounds that its supporters can only offer evidence of the internationalization of the economy and not its globalization. Perhaps the most surprising of their interpretations of the evidence is the one that asserts that financial and capital markets have not escaped the constraints of international intervention and regulation or, more precisely, that they have not done so for the first time.

However, the analysis that forms the empirical centrepiece to Hirst and Thompson's book is that which shows that multinational corporations remain predominantly fully grounded in the national economies from which they originate, conducting most of their activities there and repatriating profits. On this argument, Unilever and Shell are really still Dutch companies, GM and AT&T are American, Toyota and Sony are Japanese, and the nationalities of Elf-Acquitaine, BP, ABB and BHP can equally be in little doubt. For Hirst and Thompson there are few true trans-national companies (TNCs) and the predominant form is the multi-national corporation (MNC) pattern that characterizes an inter-national economy, as described in Chapter 2 of this book.

Although Gordon (1988), *contra* Hirst and Thompson, regards all large corporations as (globalized) TNCs, it is nevertheless clear that he is in fundamental agreement with them about the incapacity of large corporations to construct a supra-national global order. For him, the cogent phenomenon is competition between TNCs, the consequence of which has been a diminution of their profits. Competition between TNCs is predominantly inter-national competition between corporations that represent the hegemons of serial phases of accumulation. Thus, the British TNCs that dominated the global economy until the Second

World War have been displaced by American ones. They, in turn, now face competition from European and Japanese TNCs. About a third of foreign direct investment is now sourced outside the US and Britain.

Gordon paints a picture of a de-globalizing planetary economy. TNCs collaborate with their home governments to compete with each other in the 'developed' sector of international production. Outside that sector they seek to lock in and control specific spheres of influence so that the capital investment system, far from being liquid and mobile, is much less marketized than previously. This picture of a fixed distribution of production allows him, in a stunning contradiction, to deny both the globalization of production and the emergence of a new international division of labour.

These arguments are also approximately consistent with the views of Liepitz (1982), who also insists that we are not witnessing a globalization of Fordist accumulation practices. However, Liepitz offers a more conventional expression of the NIDL thesis than either Hirst and Thompson or Gordon. If Fordism involves mechanized and Taylorist production of standardized products for delivery to mass markets, peripheral economies cannot, he argues, be globalized because they incorporate only Taylorist production. The products are exported back to the mass markets of the core economies and, by implication, the core exploits the periphery by consuming its surplus value.

To confront these arguments we can turn to Jessop's analysis of the components of Fordism and post-Fordism (1994). His analysis proceeds in terms of four points of reference:

- the labour process,
- the regime of accumulation,
- the mode of economic regulation (organizational formations),
- the mode of societalization (general social cohesion).

On these points of reference, Fordism has the following characteristics:

- it mass produces consumer durables, typically on moving assembly lines tended by concentrated masses of semi- or unskilled labour;
- capital accumulates in a virtuous circle of rising production, productivity, wages, consumption and profits in which mass consumption is a key driver;
- it relies on large-scale, powerful steering systems, to regulate economic activity, including monopolistic, Sloanist corporations, mass trade unions and bureaucratized state systems; and
- society is itself standardized and massified with a consistent emphasis on family nucleation, monocultural nationalism and bureaucratization.

By contrast, post-Fordism emphasises the following characteristics:

- production of consumer disposables by means of flexible specialization based increasingly on human and intellectual as opposed to material capital (Bell 1976);
- diversification of products for differentiated, polyvalent markets maximizing profligacy, instantaneity and consumptional display;
- differentiated, de-regulated and flexible labour markets, individual and enterprise contractualization, smaller, quasi-collegial organizations, rapidly circulating credit and capital; and
- hyperdifferentiated emphasis on difference, individuation and the reflexive construction of taste.

We can now reconstruct the distinction made by Hirst and Thompson between internationalization and globalization but reconstruct the latter in a form that is more consistent with Robertson, Giddens or the analysis in this book than, say, with Amin, Wallerstein or Sklair. Once again we can organize this in terms of Jessop's four reference points but concentrating on what Hirst and Thompson call Type 2 globalization.

In a globalized economy:

- production is geographically mobile and therefore local or regional rather than national in character (see e.g. Sabel 1994);
- consumption is also locality-free, especially in so far as consumers become geographically mobile (through tourism), access to product distributors becomes electronic and an increasing proportion of consumption items is informatic or imagic;
- capital and credit flow freely through electronically mediated transaction systems (Harvey 1989); and
- humanity and the individual become the societalization axis (Robertson 1992; Beck 1992).

Such a globalized economy is radically inconsistent with Fordism but consistent with post-Fordism. Indeed, the terms 'post-Fordism' and 'economic globalization' are alternative descriptors for a single, general set of social processes of change in the economy. Figure 8.1 confirms this argument by completing the scheme for an international economy and demonstrating its particular consistency with Fordism.

It follows from the above that if one seeks to find evidence for globalization in the development of a global capitalist class or a global steering system based on a concert of nations, or a hegemon, or a cabal of TNCs, or in the globalized production of mass consumption items, or even in a division of labour between states in the production of those items, then one will not find it. Such an investigation relies on Fordist assumptions about the form that production will take, that affluent or developed societies are impossible without Fordist dinosaur corporations.

Even MNCs are not immune to the forces of globalization. However, the impact will be greatest where the products are mobile and fluid and lowest where the products are concrete and material. So we would expect globalization, the detachment of the MNC from any particular economy, to be greatest in the mass media, in telecommunications, in finance and in transportation.

	Phase 1		Phase 2	
	Fordism	Internationalization	Post-Fordism	Globalization
Production	Assembly line	MNCs	Flexible specialization	Localization/ regionalization
Accumulation	Mass consumption	NIDL	Instantaneity/ niche marketing	Time–space compression
Regulation	Sloanism/ corporatism	Economic IGOs	Open factor markets	Electronic financial systems
Societalization	Standardized nuclear family	Population & development programmes	Hyper-individuation	Economic human rights

Figure 8.1 Analysis of the fit between post-Fordism and globalization

Nor is the traditional Sloanist divisionalized structure necessarily the vehicle for this development. For example, developing alliances in the airline and telecommunications industries do not amount to the formation of TNCs but they do indicate a supra-national level of regulation that would not be revealed by company-level data.

As a consequence, true TNCs are emerging as globalization impacts on the internationalized system. One would be hard put to decide whether Unilever and Shell were Dutch or British, whether News Corporation was Australian, British or American, whether ABB was Swedish or Swiss, whether Airbus was British, French, German or Spanish, whether BP-Amoco was British or American, whether HSBC (i.e. Hong Kong and Shanghai Banking Corporation) was Chinese or British, whether Vodafone-Airtouch-Mannesmann was British, American or German, or whether DaimlerChrysler was German or American. While Hirst and Thompson, Gordon, and Liepitz can find little evidence of the emergence of Fordist TNCs we are probably witnessing the beginning of post-Fordist ones.

NOT THE POWERLESS STATE BUT THE ELABORATING STATE

The issue of the future of the nation-state is possibly an even more crucial test of globalization theory than is the issue of the future of the Fordist corporation. After all, the nation-state insists on the relevance of geography by mapping imaginary dotted lines across itself and installing real checkpoints that regulate trade, migration and tourism where it imagines those checkpoints should be. In many instances it erects real barbed-wire fences, ditches, minefields or military emplacements in order to defend its territory from invasion or to encapture its own population. It also insists that any denizen of the territory that it includes is subject to its authority and to no higher authority.

As is mentioned *passim* in Chapters 4 and 5, critics of the globalization thesis argue that the nation-state is a long way from maturity, much less from senile decline. It has a great deal of power, much more than is available at any other political level. It still has formal sovereignty over its subjects and its territory, and while interference and invasions of various kinds are always possible, their legitimacy is by no means uncontested even when conducted under the aegis of such supranational organizations as the UN. For individuals there is no more constraining or empowering level of political organization than that of the nation-state. Meaningful politics, that which holds the attention of the average citizen, is national politics and not global politics. If democratization is a global trend then its impact lies at the level of the nation-state, enabling citizens increasingly to elect national political leaders rather than supranational ones.

Mann (1993), for example, a leading authority on the state, assesses the impact of the European Union on the sovereignty of its member states. He chooses the EU because the argument is often raised (as it is in this book) that Western Europe is at the leading edge of developments that disempower the nation-state. EU institutions prescribe three developments that are germane to this argument: the laws of member states must conform with EU law and must often be changed to establish consistency; states must not erect trade or other barriers that prevent the EU operating as a borderless 'single market'; and most of the members are adopting a single currency and therefore surrendering fiscal sovereignty to a European Monetary Institute (EMI), a kind of European central bank that manages the money supply and interest rates. But, argues Mann, the EU has only the weakest of common social policy, it has no defence force and no common foreign policy. It includes both members of NATO and 'neutrals', and it has no singular diplomatic representation or international membership. Mann is able to conclude that: 'Europe is not moving toward a single state or even a federal state' (1993: 127). Yet throughout his article he freely discusses the ways in which the EU cuts into members' sovereignty and their capacity to control their own borders. In a seeming confirmation of postmodernization arguments, and a contradiction of his own, he assesses that: 'Overall sovereignty is now divided and messy' (1993: 127).

Mann extends this dualistic view of state development beyond Europe, where he finds a bewildering diversity: a resolute nation-state in the USA, feeding on its own predominance; an incomplete state in Japan, unable to control its own defence and foreign policy, but certainly a coherent nation; and a kaleidoscope of often weak and even collapsing, occasionally militaristic and isolate states elswhere. For Mann this indicates a range of diverging possible futures for nation-states. Globalization theory equally would not predict consistent development across all instances but would insist precisely that this kind of postmodernized diversity is what might be expected.

Although explicitly an anti-'globalization' theorist, Weiss (1998) offers a persuasive argument about the continuing capacity of states to govern their own economies. Like Hirst and Thompson, and drawing on arguments similar to those offered by Mann, she insists that the global economy and its political governance system remain firmly in what we have, in this book, called the internationalization phase (with the exception of some aspects of the global money market). Such global economic integration as we are experiencing is the consequence not of detached, impersonal, postmodernizing forces but of the actions of strong states seeking to expand their markets and sources of supply. Under this interpretation, the EU is but an extension of German economic power and the apparently reduced capacity of the Japanese state to maintain industrial expansion through the 1990s is an intentional policy designed to reduce trade barriers that operate against Japan's interests. Weiss forsees a differentiation of state capacities to adapt to global developments and widespread economic unevenness. On this view, the prospect of a consistently capitalistic, market-driven, neoliberal world order can be denied.

There are two specific arguments that one might offer against Weiss, one theoretical, the other substantive. Speaking theoretically, and in so far as no globalization theorist would make the claim that states are powerless, the operation of states in the global field is itself an expression of globalization. On the argument of this book, such actions are unavoidable. Withdrawal from the global field, as in such instances as Cuba or North Korea, will lead to regime unsustainability, crisis, collapse and eventual global reintegration. The substantive issue is perhaps more compelling. All the evidence on state development in the 1990s points not towards the diversification of state cultures and their powers but to an emerging consistency. States have become more and more democratized, marketized, human-rights oriented, ethnically homogeneous and prepared both to participate in and accept international economic and military intervention. They have surrendered sovereignty in environmental conventions and economic treaties. Perhaps on many or even most occasions such developments have been the consequence of state-driven policies. But voluntary surrender of powers is still a surrender of powers, and while states are by no means powerless, they are rather less powerful than once they were.

Holton (1998) is possibly more sympathetic to globalization than either Mann or Weiss. He gives two main sets of grounds for the persistence of the nation-state. The first is a functionalist, Marxist claim that global capital cannot operate without state regulation and state capacities for social reproduction. Corporations remain subject to state regulation and protection and rely on states to provide them with infrastructures and labour with varying degrees of skill. The second set of grounds is the robustness and even the revival of ethnic identity and its association with nationality, as discussed in Chapter 6 of this book, although he does go on to admit that the re-emergence of ethnicity might be interpreted as a globalizing process.

In response to these arguments, we can return to some of the points made in Chapters 4 and 5. Globalization theory does not imply that the state is dying or disappearing. Rather, its sovereignty and its potency are being diluted. There is every indication that nation-states will not only continue but proliferate. It seems to be an ideal form of political organization for relatively large, culturally homogeneous populations, but is quite clearly problematic under conditions of an ethnic mosaic. The state is not, under contemporary conditions, powerless, much less imaginary, but its powers are changing. It can no longer negotiate which aspects of the external economic, political and cultural environment will impact upon it (as it could in the internationalization phase), so it is much less sovereign than it used to be. Moreover, it is becoming an element in a hierarchy of political organization stretching from local, community and civic initiatives through to supranational ones. As in the case of many critical analyses of globalization theory we need to be careful to remember that globalization is theorized as a process and not as a static endpoint. Globalization theory does not assert that the state is disappearing or that it is absolutely powerless, but rather that its pre-eminence is becoming problematic and that some of its powers are detaching from and locating in other political units.

NOT POSTMODERNIZATION BUT AMERICANIZATION

In a celebrated piece of popular journalism (*Atlantic* 3/92) Benjamin R. Barber projected that the world appeared simultaneously to be heading down two contradictory paths. The first is the path of Jihad, of holy war between retribalized sections of the planet along the lines found in the contemporary Balkans. The second is towards McWorld, a dull and homogenized place that is:

> . . . being borne upon us by the onrush of economic and ecological forces that demand integration and uniformity and that mesmerize the world with fast music, fast computers, and fast food – with MTV, Macintosh, and McDonald's, pressing nations into one commercially homogeneous global network: one McWorld tied together by technology, ecology, communications, and commerce.
>
> (*Atlantic* 3/92: 53)

Ultimately, Barber thinks that McWorld can win out over jihad: 'My guess is that globalization will eventually vanquish retribalization. The ethos of material civilization has not yet encountered an obstacle it has been unable to thrust aside' (*Atlantic* 3/92: 64). Barber's guess is confirmed, with rather more academic conviction, by George Ritzer (1993) in his claim that contemporary society is afflicted by McDonaldization (see Chapter 7). Ritzer is alarmed by the homogenizing effect:

> [T]he spread of American and indigenous fast-food throughout much of the world means that there is less and less diversity from one setting to another. The human craving for new and diverse experiences is being limited, if not progressively destroyed, by the national and international fast-food restaurants. The craving for diversity is being supplanted by the desire for uniformity and predictability.
>
> (1993: 138–9)

Indeed, this is the nub of the connection between McDonald-ization and globalization, that McDonaldization turns the world into one place by homogenizing it, by reducing all tastes to a single pattern. By implication, because McDonaldization originates in the USA its spread to other parts of the world constitutes Americanization. The term 'globalization' is therefore simply an ideological mask for Americanization or Westernization.

Both of these approaches to the link between McDonaldization and globalization focus primarily on the globalizing flows that fan out from economically advanced sectors to penetrate previously encapsulated cultures. However, McDonaldization can also be seen to have globalizing consequences for metropolitan centres themselves. The main shift in patterns of occupational stratification in advanced societies over the past quarter of a century has been the decline of manufacturing employment and the growth of highly rewarded professional and technical employ-ment. This, in turn, has provided a surplus of manual labour (hence relatively high rates of unemployment) combined with a newly affluent, often dual-income, and 'busy' post-industrial middle class. McDonald's[1] fits neatly into this configuration not only because it can service families with busy parents but because it can tap into pools of low-paid unskilled labour. While those odious 'McJobs' are often performed by students, women and other locals with low bargaining power in the labour market, they are also often performed by immigrant and 'guest' workers who flow in from economically disadvantaged sectors of the planet. This is particularly true in such 'global' cities as Los Angeles, New York, London and Frankfurt that can be called global not merely because of their planetary influence but because they contain within their populations a global mix of the third world and the first.

US Bureau of Labor projections indicate that 'McJobs' is the fastest-growing sector of the American labour force. Between the mid-1980s and 2000 the Bureau projects the creation of some 400,000 new jobs in white-collar and technical labour but of 2.5 million new jobs in restaurants, bars and fast food (Lash and Urry

1994: 162). Incoming migrants flock to the global cities to take advantage of these 'opportunities'. In the early 1980s about 25 per cent of the population of Los Angeles and 14 per cent of the population of New York was made up of immigrants who had arrived in the period 1965–80 (Lash and Urry 1994: 173). Similar patterns can be witnessed in the occupational and spatial distribution of Afro-Caribbean and Asian migrants to Britain and of Mediterranean and East European *Gastarbeiter* in Germany.

On the face of it then, Ritzer offers a persuasive case that McDonaldization is an influential globalizing flow. The imperatives of the rationalization of consumption appear to drive McDonald's and like enterprises into every corner of the globe, so that all localities are assimilated to its American origination. The imperatives of such rationalization are expressed neatly by O'Neill:

> [C]onsumption is work, it takes time and it competes with itself since choosing, hauling, maintaining and repairing the things we buy is so time-consuming that we are forced to save time on eating, drinking, sex, dressing, sleeping, exercising and relaxing. The result is that Americans have taught us to eat standing, walking, running and driving – and, above all, never to finish a meal in favour of the endless snack . . . we can now pizza, burger, fry and coffee ourselves as quickly as we can gas our autos.
>
> (1994: 136; italics deleted)

For O'Neill the globalization of 'McTopia', a paradise of effortless and instantaneous consumption, is also underpinned by its democratizing effect. It democratizes by deskilling, not merely by deskilling McWorkers but also by deskilling family domestic labour. The kitchen is invaded by frozen food and microwaves so that domestic cooks, usually adult women, can provide McDonaldized fare at home. In the process 'non-cooks', usually men and children, can share the cooking. Meals can become 'defamilized' (i.e. dedifferentiated) in so far as all members can cook, purchase and consume the same fatty, starchy, sugary foods. Consequently, while 'America is the only country in the world where the rich eat as badly as the poor' the appeal of such 'gastronomic levelling' can serve as a magnet for others elsewhere (1994: 137).

However, we can put in perspective the alarmist implication in both Sklair's neo-Marxian and Ritzer's neo-Weberian suggestions that globalization will lead to a homogenized common culture of consumption if we expose them to the full gamut of globalization theory. Globalization theory predicts the de-territorialization of social life so that one cannot predict social arrangements by location. Under a globalized cultural regime Islam would not be linked to particular territorially based communities in the middle East, North Africa and Asia but would be universally available across the planet and with varying degrees of 'orthodoxy'. Similarly, in the sphere of political ideology, the apparently opposed political values of private property and power sharing might be combined to establish new ideologies of economic enterprise. In the sphere of consumption, cardboard hamburgers would be available not only in Pasadena but anywhere in the world, just as classical French cuisine would be available not only in Escoffier's in Paris but anywhere. A globalized culture thus admits a continuous flow of ideas, information, commitment, values and tastes mediated through mobile individuals, symbolic tokens and electronic simulations. Its key feature is to suggest that the world is one place, not because it is homogenized but because it accepts only social differentiation and not spatial or geographical differentiation. Ritzer's argument is that every locality becomes the same because they are all characterized by the same consumption patterns. However, this need not imply that in each locality McDonaldized consumption is all that is available.

McDonaldization infiltrates several globalizing flows including ethnoscapes, technoscapes, finanscapes and ideoscapes. However, its effects are by no means universally homogenizing. The dynamics that are at work centre on processes of relativization, reflexivity and localization that operate against the assumed capacity of McDonaldization to regiment consumer behaviour into uniform patterns. The return of agency that many authors have identified (see especially Beck, Giddens and Lash 1994) is not simply a series of isolated and individualized coping reactions of the type advocated by Ritzer (1993: chapter 9) but a generalized feature of contemporary society that arises from the intersection of these globalizing flows. Indeed, such developments might be called the dysfunctions of McDonaldization in much the same way that post-Weberian organizational theorists wrote of the the dysfunctions of bureaucracy.

We can now discuss the implications of these terms. The term 'relativization' was introduced by Robertson. It implies that globalizing flows do not simply swamp local differences. Rather, it implies that the inhabitants of local contexts must now make sense of their lifeworlds not only by reference to embedded traditions and practices but by reference to events occurring in distant places. McDonaldization is such an intrusive, neonistic development that it implies decisions about whether to accept its modernizing and rationalizing potential or to reject it in favour of a reassertion of local products and traditions. In some instances this may involve a reorganization of local practices to meet the challenge. If we remain at the mundane level of hamburgers to find our examples, Sklair (1991: 152–3) tells a story about the introduction of McDonald's in the Phillipines that can illustrate the point: 'Originally, Filipino hamburger chains marketed their product on the basis of its "Americanness." However, when McDonald's entered the field and, as it were, monopolized the symbols of "Americanness," the indigenous chains began to market their product on the basis of local taste.' The relativization effect of McDonaldization goes much further than this of course because it involves the global diffusion not only of particular products but of icons of American capitalist culture. Relativizing reactions can therefore encompass highly generalized responses to that culture, whether positive or negative.

As people increasingly become implicated in global cultural flows they also become more reflexive. Participation in a global system means that one's lifeworld is determined by impersonal flows of money and expertise that are beyond one's personal or even organizational control. If European governments cannot even control the values of their currencies against speculation then individual lifeworlds must indeed be highly vulnerable. Aware of such risk, people constantly watch, seek information about, and consider the value of money and the validity of expertise. In previous eras people learned practical skills and knowledge from parents and older relatives by imitation and word of mouth. In the modern era this function was taken over by schools. But self-transformation now extends beyond skills to possibilities for re-making the entire personality. Such projects are undertaken by oneself but the self is informed by a torrent of self-help advice received through the mass media and the internet. McDonaldization is implicated in this process precisely because it challenges the validity of habit and tradition by introducing expertly rationalized systems, especially in so far as its capacity to commercialize and to commodify has never been in doubt.

The concept of localization is connected with the notions of relativization and reflexivity. The activist middle classes who mobilize civic initiatives and heritage preservation associations often stand in direct opposition to the expansion of McDonald-ized outlets and hark back to an often merely imagined prior Golden Age. And, if we can return to hamburgerish examples of localization, two have recently found their way into the press. The first is a story about an announcement by the mayor of Moscow, Yuri Luzhkov.

> The Western food invasion, he declared, has gone too far. In retaliation, the city would sponsor a chain of fast-food outlets selling traditional fare. A generation reared on Big Macs and French fries would again be able to enjoy such old favourites as *bliny* and *salo* – lumps of pork fat to munch with vodka.
>
> (*European* 24/3/95)

The second is the announcement that McDonald's would open its first restaurant in Jerusalem. This provoked a widespread localizing reaction because the outlet was not going to keep Kosher. The company subsequently announced that it had plans for three new restaurants that would be Kosher.

Returning to more abstract issues, a globalized world is not a McWorld. It is a world with the potential for the displacement of local homogeneity not by global homogeneity but by global diversity. Three developments can confirm this hopeful prognosis.

First, one of the features of Fordist mass production-consumption systems, of which McDonaldization might be the ultimate example, is that they sought to standardize at both the levels of production and consumption. Ultimately, they failed not only because they refused to recognize that responsible and committed workers would produce more in quanitity and quality than controlled and alienated ones, but because markets for standardized products became saturated. The succeeding paradigm of 'flexible specialization' involved flexibly contracted workers using multiple skills and computerized machinery to dovetail products to rapidly shifting market demand. So consumer products took on a new form and function (see Harvey 1989). Taste became the only determinant of their utility, so it became ephemeral and subject to whim. Product demand is determined by fashion, and unfashionable products are disposable. Moreover, taste and fashion became linked to social standing as production-based classes disappeared as central features of social organization.

The outcome has been a restless search by producers for niche-marketing strategies in which they can multiply product variation in order to match market demand. In many instances this has forced a downscaling of enterprises that can maximize market sensitivity. Correspondingly, affluent consumers engage in a restless search for authenticity. The intersection of these trends implies a multiplication of products and production styles. The world is becoming an enormous bazaar as much as a consumption factory. One of the most impressive examples of consumer and producer resistance to rationalization is the French bread industry, which is as non-McDonaldized as can be. Clegg (1990: 108–20) shows how consumers and producers struggled collectively and successfully against invasions by industrialized bakers, the former to preserve the authenticity of their food, the latter to maintain independent enterprises. Bread-baking is an artesanal form of production that reproduces peasant domestic traditions. As a measure of their success about 80 per cent of baking (Ritzer's croissanteries notwithstanding) is still done in small firms. The product, of course, is the envy of global, middle-class consumers.

Such diversification is accelerated by an aestheticization of production (Lash and Urry 1994). As is well known, the history of modern society involves an increasing production of mass-cultural items. For most of this century this production has been Fordist in character, an obvious example being broadcasting by large-scale private or state TV networks to closed markets. Three key features in the current period are: the deregulation of markets by the introduction of direct satellite and broadband fibre-optic technology; the vertical disintegration of aesthetic production to produce 'a transaction-rich nexus of of markets linking small firms, often of one self-employed person' (Lash and Urry 1994: 114); and the tending dedifferentiation of producer and consumer within emerging multimedia technologies associated with the internet and interactive television. The implication is that a very rapidly increasing proportion of consumption is aesthetic in character, that aesthetic production is taking place within an increasingly perfectionalized market (Waters 1995), and that these aesthetic products are decreasingly susceptible to McDonaldization. An enormous range of individualized, unpredictable, inefficient and irrational products can be inspected simply by surfing the Internet.

Ritzer (1993: 18–34) is about right when he suggests that McDonaldization is an extension, perhaps the ultimate extension, of Fordism. However, the implication is that just as one now has a better chance of finding a Fordist factory in Russia or India than in Detroit, it should not surprise us to find that, while McDonaldization is penetrating the furthest corners of the globe, there is some indication, that as far as the restaurant goes, there is stagnation if not yet decline in the homeland. McDonald-ization faces post-Fordist limits and part of the crisis that these limits imply involves a transformation to a chaotic, taste- and value-driven, irrational and possibly threatening global society. It will not be harmonious, but the price of harmony would be to accept the predominance of Christendom, or communism, or Fordism, or McDonaldism.

We can take issue, then, with the position taken by Ritzer, and such sympathisers as Sklair and Barber, on two grounds. First, the Jihad and McWorld tendencies are not contradictions but aspects of a single globalization-localization process in which local sensibilities are aroused and exacerbated in fundamentalist forms by such modernizing flows as McDonaldization. Even in the fast food realm, McDonaldization promotes demands for authenticity, occasionally expressed as fundamentalistic vegetarianism. Second, the emerging global culture is likely to exhibit a rich level of diversity that arises out of this intersection. Globalization exposes each locality to numerous global flows so that any such locality can accommodate, to use food examples once again, not only burgers but a kaleidoscope of ethnically diverse possibilities hierarchically ordered by price and thus by the extent to which the meal has been crafted as opposed to manufactured. Thus, while it is not possible to escape the ubiquity of McDonald's in one sense, because the golden arches are indeed everywhere, in another it certainly is. One can simply pass by and either buy finger-food from a market stall or haute-cuisine at a high-priced restaurant. Ritzer is not wrong, then, to argue that McDonaldization is a significant component of globalization. Rather, he is mistaken in assuming first that globalization must be understood as homogen-ization and second that McDonaldization only has homogenizing effects.

CONCLUSION

One of the curious features of such criticism is the implication that globalization is the property of the wealthy (of the upper class or of the elite). Surely a more convincing analysis would suggest that globalization disrupts and puts under threat precisely those institutions that confer advantage on a plutocracy, the nationally based corporation and the state. If there is no state to capture then it will be difficult for any supposed upper class to control it. Equally, it is not uncommon for progressivist, protest and outsider social movements to adopt a globalizing rhetoric. Marx's declaration that the workers have no country, the environmentalist adoption of Leavitt's marketing slogan ('Think global. Act local'), and Woolf's feminist opinion cited at the beginning of this chapter, are some examples.

It would be quite absurd to suggest that globalization and its collaborating process, postmodernization, imply the wholesale decomposition of large and powerful corporations or even that the state is immediately withering away. Such an implication would indeed be a big lie. However, globalization does have some potential to dilute power and to open up fields of action to previously excluded groups. The following are some of its more obvious as well as less obvious impacts in this regard:

- The state might not have disappeared but it is certainly losing much of its sovereign capacity to control its population. Those populations are now much less regulated and controlled than they once were. Indeed, if one were a true believer in the capacity of the state to reproduce capitalism, then one might view this as a positive development.
- The fact that global corporations are now obliged to operate in much more open markets reduces their capacity to monopolize and monopsonize those markets.
- The institutions that are being disrupted by globalization are precisely those that are implicated in the main inequalities of power characteristic of modern societies. The

management–worker division is being rendered problematic in metropolitan societies as routine and arduous jobs are exported elsewhere. More importantly, the state and the corporate firm are, overwhelmingly, the key institutions of the public sphere. They are arenas dominated by men and relatively exclusive of women. Such globalized political phenomena as NGOs and social movements are characterized by high levels of participation by women. Their loose structures make them open to penetration by disadvantaged groups.

- The key process of time–space compression also opens up possibilities for the disadvantaged. It allows political coalitions to link up across the planet and provides a world theatre for symbolic iconographies, for manifestations, for terrorist acts and for rhetoric that can impact back upon national arenas. The Internet provides an obvious site for exchanges of commitments and information, but the fact that the mass media can nearly instantaneously transmit images of political action across the planet enhances the impact that any political event can make. Monopolies of power operate best in secret, and globalization increases transparency.

The last message of this book is, then, that the complexity of globalization extends beyond its multi-dimensionality to poly-valence. From the outset the book has argued that globalization represents an expansion of capitalist production, market-based consumption and Western culture. But we should not forget that it also involves at least opportunities for expansions of collective responsibility for the mitigation of inequality, of human rights, of environmental values and of feminism.

NOTE

1   I use the name McDonald's throughout not only to imply that particular restaurant chain but all other enterprises that work on similar principles.

REFERENCES

Albrow, M. (1990) 'Introduction' in M. Albrow and E. King (eds) *Globalization, Knowledge and Society*, London: Sage.

Althusser, L. (1977) *For Marx*, London: New Left.

Amin, S. (1980) *Class and Nation*, New York: Monthly Review.

Anderson, B. (1983) *Imagined Communities*, London: Verso.

Anderson, M. (1984) *Madison Avenue in Asia*, Cranbury: Associated University Press.

Anderson, P. (1979) *Lineages of the Absolutist State*, London: Verso.

Appadurai, A. (1990) 'Disjuncture and Difference in the Global Cultural Economy' in M. Featherstone (ed.) *Global Culture*, London: Sage: 295–310.

Archer, C. (1983) *International Organizations*, London: Allen & Unwin.

Archer, M. (1990) 'Theory, Culture and Post-Industrial Society' in M. Featherstone (ed.) *Global Culture*, London: Sage: 97–120.

Archer, M. (1991) 'Sociology for One World: Unity and Diversity', *International Sociology* 6(2): 131–47.

Arnason, J. (1990) 'Nationalism, Globalization and Modernity' in M. Featherstone (ed.) *Global Culture*, London: Sage: 207–36.

Barbalet, J. (1988) *Citizenship*, Milton Keynes: Open University Press.

Barker, E. (1991) 'The Whole World in His Hand?' in R. Robertson and W. Garrett (eds) *Religion and Global Order*, New York: Paragon: 201–20.

Barraclough, G. (ed.) (1978) *The Times Atlas of World History*, London: Times.

Baudrillard, J. (1988) *Selected Writings*, Stanford: Stanford University Press.

Beck, U. (1992) *Risk Society*, London: Sage.

Beck, U., A. Giddens and S. Lash (1994) *Reflexive Modernization*, Cambridge: Polity.

Bell, D. (1976) *The Coming of Post-Industrial Society*, New York: Basic Books.

Bell, D. (1979) *The Cultural Contradictions of Capitalism* (2nd edn), London: Heinemann.

Bell, D. (1987) 'The World and the United States in 2013', *Daedalus* 116(3): 1–30.

Bell, D. (1991) *The Winding Passage*, New Brunswick, NJ: Transaction.

Beyer, P. (1990) 'Privatization and the Public Influence of Religion in Global Society' in M. Featherstone (ed.) *Global Culture*, London: Sage: 373–96.

Brubaker, R. (1984) *The Limits of Rationality*, London: Allen & Unwin.

Bull, H. (1977) *The Anarchical Society*, New York: Columbia University Press.

Burton, J. (1972) *World Society*, Cambridge: Cambridge University Press.

Carpenter, E. and M. McLuhan (eds) (1970 [1960]) *Explorations in Communication*, London: Cape.

Cassese, A. (1990) *Human Rights in a ChangingWorld*, Cambridge: Polity.

Cassese, A. (1991) 'Violence, War and the Rule of Law' in D. Held (ed.) *Political Theory Today*, Cambridge: Polity: 255–75.

Champagne, D. (1992) 'Transocietal [sic] Cultural Exchange within the World Economic and Political System' in P. Colomy (ed.) *The Dynamics of Social Systems*, London: Sage: 120–53.

Clegg, S. (1990) *Modern Organizations*, London: Sage.

Cockroft, J., A. Frank and D. Johnson (1972) *Dependence and Underdevelopment*, Garden City, NY: Anchor.

Cohen, R. (1987) *The New Helots*, Aldershot: Avebury.

Crook, S., J. Pakulski and M. Waters (1992) *Postmodernization*, London: Sage.

Dicken, P. (1998) *Global Shift* (3rd edn), London: Chapman.

Dickenson, D. (1997) 'Counting Women In' in A. McGrew (ed.) *The Transformation of Democracy?*, Cambridge: Polity: 97–120.

Dohse, K, U. Jürgens and T. Malsch (1985) 'From "Fordism" to "Toyotism"? The Social Organization of the Japanese Automobile Industry', *Politics & Society* 14(2): 115–46.

Dore, R. (1989) 'Where Are We Going Now?', *Work, Employment and Society*, 14(2): 425–46.

Duke, J. and B. Johnson (1989) 'Religious Transformation and Social Conditions' in W. Swatos (ed.) *Religious Politics in Global Perspective*, New York: Greenwood: 75–110.

Dunning, J. (1993) *Multinational Enterprises in a Global Economy*, Wokingham: Addison-Wesley.

Emmott, B. (1993) 'Everybody's Favourite Monsters', *The Economist* 27/3 (supplement).

Featherstone, M. (ed.) (1990) *Global Culture*, London: Sage.

Featherstone, M. (1991) *Consumer Culture and Postmodernism*, London: Sage.

Foster, R. (1991) 'Making National Cultures in the Global Ecumene', *Annual Review of Anthropology* 20: 235–60.

Frank, A. (1971) *Capitalism and Underdevelopment in Latin America* (rev. edn), Harmondsworth: Penguin.

Friedman, J. (1990) 'Being in the World: Globalization and Localization' in M. Featherstone (ed.) *Global Culture*, London: Sage: 311–28.

Fröbel, F., J. Heinrichs and O. Kreye (1980) *The New International Division of Labour*, Cambridge: Cambridge University Press.

Fukuyama, F. (1992) *The End of History and the Last Man*, London: Hamish Hamilton.

Garfinkel, H. (1967) *Studies in Ethnomethodology*, Englewood Cliffs, NJ: Prentice-Hall.

Germain, R. (1997) *The International Organization of Credit*, Cambridge: Cambridge University Press.

Giddens, A. (1981) *A Contemporary Critique of Historical Materialism*, London: Macmillan.

Giddens, A. (1985) *The Nation-State and Violence*, Cambridge: Polity.

Giddens, A. (1990) *The Consequences of Modernity*, Cambridge: Polity.

Giddens, A. (1991) *Modernity and Self-identity*, Cambridge: Polity.

Gill, S. and D. Law (1988) *The Global Political Economy*, Baltimore: Johns Hopkins University Press.

Gilpin, R. (1987) *The Political Economy of International Relations*, Princeton, NJ: Princeton University Press.

Gleich, J. (1987) *Chaos*, London: Cardinal.

Goldblatt, D. (1997) 'Liberal Democracy and the Globalization of Environmental Risks' in A. McGrew (ed.) *The Transformation of Democracy?*, Cambridge: Polity: 73–96.

Gordon, D. (1988) 'The Global Economy: New Edifice or Crumbling Foundation?', *New Left Review* 168: 24–64.

Greene, O. (1997) 'Environmental Issues' in J. Bayliss and S. Smith (eds) *The Globalization of World Politics*, Oxford: Oxford University Press: 313–37.

Habermas, J. (1987) *The Theory of Communicative Action, Vol. 2: The Critique of Functionalist Reason*, Cambridge: Polity.

Haddon, J. (1991) 'The Globalization of American Televangelism' in R. Robertson and W. Garrett (eds) *Religion and Global Order*, New York: Paragon: 221–44.

Hall, N. (ed.) (1992) *The New Scientist Guide to Chaos*, Harmondsworth: Penguin.

Hall, S. (1992) 'The Question of Cultural Identity' in S. Hall, D. Held and T. McGrew (eds) *Modernity and its Futures*, Cambridge: Polity: 274–316.

Hardin, G. (1968) 'The Tragedy of the Commons', *Science* 162: 1243–8.

Harvey, D. (1989) *The Condition of Postmodernity*, Oxford: Blackwell.

Held, D (1991) 'Democracy and the Global System' in D. Held (ed.) *Political Theory Today*, Cambridge: Polity: 197–235.

Hirst, P. and G. Thompson (1996) *Globalization in Question*, Cambridge: Polity.

Hobsbawm, E. (1992) *Nations and Nationalism since 1780* (2nd edn), Cambridge: Cambridge University Press.

Holton, R. (1998) *Globalization and the Nation-state*, Basingstoke and New York: Macmillan and St Martin's.

Hook, G. and M. Weiner (1992) *The Internationalization of Japan*, London: Routledge.

Hopkins, T. and I. Wallerstein (eds) (1980) *Processes of the World-system*, Beverly Hills, CA: Sage.

Hopkins, T. and I. Wallerstein (eds) (1982) *World-systems Analysis*, Beverly Hills, CA: Sage.

Hoskins, C. and R. Mirus (1988) 'Reasons for the US Dominance of the International Trade in Television Programs', *Media, Culture and Society* 10: 499–515.

Huntington, S. (1991) *The Third Wave*, Norman: Oklahoma University Press.

Huntington, S. (1993) 'The Clash of Civilizations?', *Foreign Affairs* 72(3): 22–50.

Inglehart, R (1990) *Culture Shift in Advanced Industrial Society*, Princeton, NJ: Princeton University Press.

Jackson, R. (1997) 'The Evolution of International Society' in J. Bayliss and S. Smith (eds) *The Globalization of World Politics*, Oxford: Oxford University Press: 33–48.

Jessop, B. (1994) 'Post-Fordism and the State' in A. Amin (ed.) *Post-Fordism*, Oxford: Blackwell: 251–79.

Kanter, R. (1995) *World Class*, New York: Simon & Schuster.

Kavolis, V. (1988) 'Contemporary Moral Cultures and "the Return of the Sacred"', *Sociological Analysis* 49(3): 203–16.

Keohane, R. and J. Nye (eds) (1973) *Transnational Relations and World Politics*, Cambridge: Harvard University Press.

Kerr, C., J. Dunlop, F. Harbison and C. Myers (1973[1960]) *Industrialism and Industrial Man*, Harmondsworth: Penguin.

King, A. (1990a) 'Architecture, Capital and the Globalization of Culture' in M. Featherstone (ed.) *Global Culture*, London: Sage: 397–411.

King, A. (1990b) *Global Cities*, London: Routledge.

Kosselleck, R. (1988 [1959]) *Critique and Crisis*, Oxford: Berg.

Krol, E. (1992) *The Whole Internet*, Sebastapol: O'Reilly.

Kuttner, R. (1991) *The End of Laissez-faire*, New York: Knopf.

Lash, S. and J. Urry (1987) *The End of Organized Capitalism*, Cambridge: Polity.

Lash, S. and J. Urry (1994) *Economies of Signs and Space*, London: Sage.

Lechner, F. (1989) 'Cultural Aspects of the Modern World-System' in W. Swatos (ed.) *Religious Politics in Global and Comparative Perspective*, New York: Greenwood: 11–28.

Lechner, F. (1990) 'Fundamentalism Revisited' in T. Robbins and D. Anthony *In Gods We Trust*, New Brunswick, NJ: Transaction Books.

Lechner, F. (1991) 'Religion, Law and Global Order' in R. Robertson and W. Garrett (eds) *Religion and Global Order*, New York: Paragon: 263–80.

Lechner, F. (1992) 'Against Modernity: Antimodernism in Global Perspective' in P. Colomy (ed.) *The Dynamics of Social Systems*, London: Sage: 72–92.

Lenin, V. (1939) *Imperialism*, New York: International.

Levitt, T. (1983) 'The Globalization of Markets', *Harvard Business Review* 83(3): 92–102.

Levy, M. (1966) *Modernization and the Structure of Societies*, Princeton, NJ: Princeton University Press.

Liepitz, A. (1982) 'Towards Global Fordism', *New Left Review* 132: 33–47.

Long, T. (1991) 'Old Testament Universalism' in R. Robertson and W. Garrett (eds) *Religion and Global Order*, New York: Paragon: 19–34.

Lovelock, J. (1987) *Gaia*, Oxford: OUP.

Luard, E. (1990) *International Society*, Basingstoke: Macmillan.

Lyotard, J-F. (1984) *The Postmodern Condition*, Manchester: Manchester University Press.

McEvedy, C. and R. Jones (1978) *Atlas of World Population History*, Harmondsworth: Penguin.

McGrew, A. (1992a) 'A Global Society?' in S. Hall, D. Held and T. McGrew (eds) *Modernity and its Futures*, Cambridge: Polity: 62–113.

McGrew, A. (1992b) 'Conceptualizing Global Politics' in A. McGrew, P. Lewis et al. *Global Politics*, Cambridge: Polity: 1–29.

McLuhan, M. (1964) *Understanding Media*, London: Routledge.

McLuhan, M. and Q. Fiore (1967) *The Medium is the Massage*, London: Allen Lane.

McLuhan, M. and Q. Fiore (1968) *War and Peace in the Global Village*, New York: Bantam.

Mann, M. (1986) *The Sources of Social Power Vol. 1.*, Cambridge: Cambridge University Press.

Mann, M. (1993) 'Nation-States in Europe and Other Continents: Diversifying, Developing, Not Dying', *Daedalus* 122(3): 115–40.

Marceau, J. (ed.) (1992) *Reworking the World*, Berlin: de Gruyter.

Marshall, T. (1973 [1949]) *Class, Citizenship and Social Development*, Westport, CN: Greenwood.

Marx, K. (1977) *Selected Writings*, Oxford: Oxford University Press.

Mathews, J. (1989) *Tools of Change*, Sydney: Pluto.

Meadows, D., D. Meadows, J. Randers and W. Behrens (1976) *The Limits to Growth*, Scarborough: Signet.

Mittelman, J. (ed.) (1996) *Globalization: Critical Reflections*, Boulder, CO: Rienner.

Moore, W. (1966) 'Global Sociology: The World as a Singular System', *American Journal of Sociology* 71(5): 475–82.

Mowlana, H. (1985) *International Flow of Information: A Global Report and Analysis*, Paris: UNESCO.

Muldoon, J. (1991) 'The Conquest of the Americas: The Spanish Search for Global Order' in R. Robertson and W. Garrett (eds) *Religion and Global Order*, New York: Paragon: 65–86.

Nettl, J. and R. Robertson (1968) *International Systems and the Modernization of Societies*, London: Faber.

OECD [Organization for Economic Co-operation and Development] (1987) *Interdependence and Co-operation in Tomorrow's World*, Paris: OECD.

OECD (1992) *Globalisation of Industrial Activities*, Paris: OECD.

O'Neill, J. (1990) 'AIDS as a Globalizing Panic' in M. Featherstone (ed.) *Global Culture*, London: Sage: 329–42.

O'Neill, J. (1994) 'McTopia: *Eating Time*' in K. Kumar and S. Bann (eds) *Utopias and the Millennium*, London: Reaktion: 129–37.

Parsons, T. (1964) 'Evolutionary Universals in Society', *American Sociological Review* 29: 339–57.

Parsons, T. (1966) *Societies*, Englewood Cliffs, NJ: Prentice-Hall.

Parsons, T. (1977) *The Evolution of Societies*, Englewood Cliffs, NJ: Prentice-Hall.

Parsons, T. and N. Smelser (1968) *Economy and Society*, London: Routledge.

Ritzer, G. (1993) *The McDonaldization of Society*, Thousand Oaks, CA: Pine Forge.

Robertson, R. (1983) 'Interpreting Globality' in his *World Realities and International Studies*, Glenside: Pennsylvania Council on International Education.

Robertson, R. (1985) 'The Relativization of Societies: Modern Religion and Globalization' in T. Robbins, W. Shepherd and J. McBride (eds) *Cults, Culture and the Law*, Chico: Scholars.

Robertson, R. (1992) *Globalization*, London: Sage.

Robertson, R. and W. Garrett (eds) (1991) *Religion and Global Order*, New York: Paragon.

Roche, M. (1992) *Rethinking Citizenship*, Cambridge: Polity.

Rosenau, J. (1980) *The Study of Global Interdependence*, New York: Nichols.

Rosenau, J. (1990) *Turbulence in World Politics*, Princeton, NJ: Princeton University Press.

Sabel, C. (1994) 'Flexible Specialisation and the Re-emergence of Regional Economics' in A. Amin (ed.) *Post-Fordism: A Reader*, Oxford: Blackwell.

Scholte, J. (1997) 'The Globalization of World Politics' in J. Bayliss and S. Smith (eds) *The Globalization of World Politics*, Oxford: Oxford University Press: 13–30.

Scott, A. (ed.) (1997) *The Limits of Globalization*, London: Routledge.

Shields, R. (1991) *Places on the Margin*, London: Routledge.

Shupe, A. (1991) 'Globalization versus Religious Nativism: Japan's Soka Gakkai in the World Arena' in R. Robertson and W. Garrett (eds) *Religion and Global Order*, New York: Paragon: 183–200.

Sklair, L. (1991) *Sociology of the Global System*, Hemel Hempstead: Harvester Wheatsheaf.

Smart, B. (1993) *Postmodernity*, London: Routledge.

Strange, J. (1991) 'Two Aspects of the Development of Universalism in Christianity' in R. Robertson and W. Garrett (eds) *Religion and Global Order*, New York: Paragon: 35–46.

Swyngedouw, E. (1987) 'Social Innovation, Product Organization and Spatial Development: the Case of Japanese Manufacturing', *Revue d'Economie Régionale et Urbaine* 3: 487–510.

Thomas, C. (1997) 'Poverty, Development and Hunger' in J. Bayliss and S. Smith (eds) *The Globalization of World Politics*, Oxford: Oxford University Press: 449–68.

Thompson, P. and D. McHugh (1990) *Work Organisations*, Basingstoke: Macmillan.

Turner, B. (1990) 'The Two Faces of Sociology: Global or National?' in M. Featherstone (ed.) *Global Culture*, London: Sage: 343–58.

Turner, B. (1991) 'Politics and Culture in Islamic Globalism' in R. Robertson and W. Garrett (eds) *Religion and Global Order*, New York: Paragon: 161–82.

Turner, L. and J. Ash (1975) *The Golden Hordes*, London: Constable.

UIA [Union of International Associations] (1992) *Yearbook of International Organizations 1992/3*, Munich: Saur.

United Nations, Department of Economic and Social Affairs (1973) *Multinational Corporations in World Development*, New York: United Nations.

Urry, J. (1990) *The Tourist Gaze*, London: Sage.

van der Pijl, K. (1989) 'The International Level' in T. Bottomore and R. Brym *The Capitalist Class*, Hemel Hempstead: Harvester Wheatsheaf: 237–66.

Vogler, J. (1992) 'Regimes and the Global Commons' in A. McGrew, P. Lewis et al. *Global Politics*, Cambridge: Polity: 118–37.

Wallerstein, I. (1974) *The Modern World-System*, New York: Academic.

Wallerstein, I. (1980) *The Modern World-System II*, New York: Academic.

Wallerstein, I. (1990) 'Culture as the Ideological Battleground of the Modern World-System' in M. Featherstone (ed.) *Global Culture*, London: Sage: 31–56.

Walters, R. and D. Blake (1992) *The Politics of Global Economic Relations*, Englewood Cliffs, NJ: Prentice-Hall.

Waters, M. (1989) 'Citizenship and the Constitution of Structured Social Inequality', *International Journal of Comparative Sociology* 30(3–4): 159–80.

Waters, M. (1994) *Modern Sociological Theory*, London: Sage.

Waters, M. (1995) 'The Thesis of the Loss of the Perfect Market', *British Journal of Sociology* 46(3): 409–28.

Weber, M. (1978) *Economy and Society*, Berkeley: California University Press.

Weiss, L. (1998) *The Myth of the Powerless State*, Cambridge: Polity.

Weissbrodt, D. (1988) 'Human Rights: An Historical Perspective' in P. Davies (ed.) *Human Rights*, London: Routledge.

Wilkinson, B., J. Morris and N. Oliver (1992) 'Japanizing the World: the Case of Toyota' in J. Marceau (ed.) *Reworking the World*, Berlin: de Gruyter: 133–50.

INDEX